Adventures of a Pirate Girl

Adventures of a Pirate Girl Hitchhiking the High Seas

by
Davina Menduno

Lafayette, CO

Adventures of a Pirate Girl: Hitchhiking the High Seas

Copyright © 2021 Davina Menduno. All rights reserved. No part of this book may be reproduced, stored in a retrieval system or transmitted in any form or by any means without the prior permission of the copyright owner, except for the use of brief quotations in a book review.

Cover design by Davina Menduno. Original cover photograph by Amy Goodman.

Maps and drawings by Davina Menduno

ISBN 978-1-7371327-0-7 (trade paperback)

ISBN 978-1-7371327-1-4 (eBook)

Library of Congress Control Number: 2021909002

Printed and bound by IngramSpark

Table of Contents

Chapter 1	Dreams	11
Chapter 2	Getting on the Boat	19
Chapter 3	At Sea	29
Chapter 4	Sint Maarten	36
Chapter 5	Shayela	64
Chapter 6	Between Boats	107
Chapter 7	Dominican Republic	116
Chapter 8	Cariño	128
Chapter 9	French Polynesia	163
Chapter 10	Mistress	190
Chapter 11	Free in Fiji	225
Chapter 12	Hakura	236
Chapter 13	No More Boats	246
Chapter 14	Finally, Home	262
Epilogue		277

I dedicate this book to my mom,
who, despite any fears she may have secretly harbored,
has always cheered me on.
This book could not have happened without you.

I am a pirate of the new age
I sail a pirate ship
I am a free agent
a citizen of the world
I am not owned by government or state
I am not controlled by corporate powers
or influenced by public opinion
I navigate by an internal compass
I am a high seas revolutionary
I do not rape, pillage and plunder
The power I possess I do not count in gold
for I know the strength of true power
Source power
of which we all have access
I capture the imagination of women
and the hearts of men
but not by force
for it is always more powerful
to seduce
than to conquer
I know where the treasure is buried
Our fortune is universal
the same X marks the spot
for us all

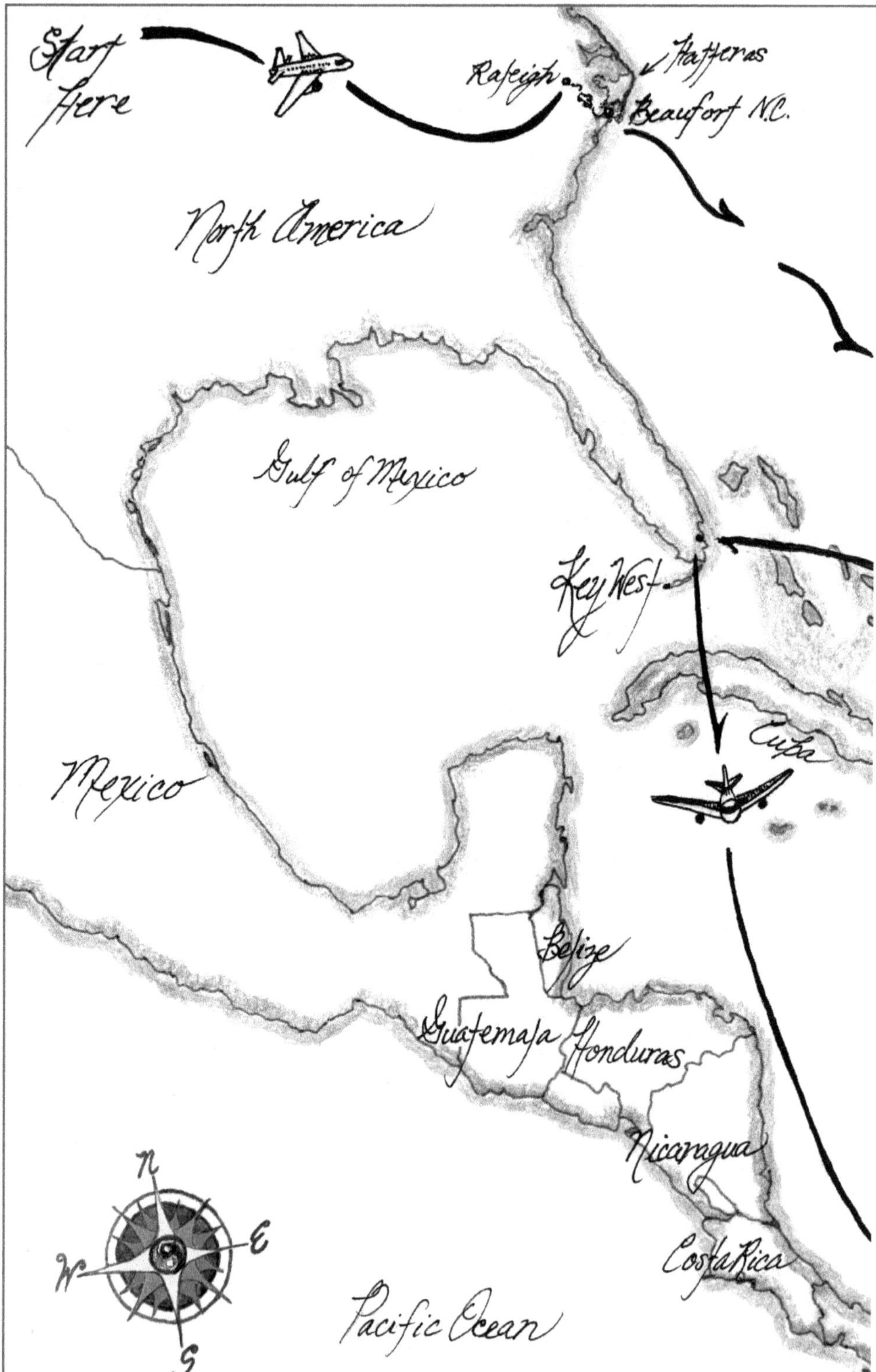

Start Here
Raleigh
Hatteras
Beaufort N.C.
North America
Gulf of Mexico
Key West
Cuba
Mexico
Belize
Guatemala
Honduras
Nicaragua
Costa Rica
Pacific Ocean
N
E
W
S

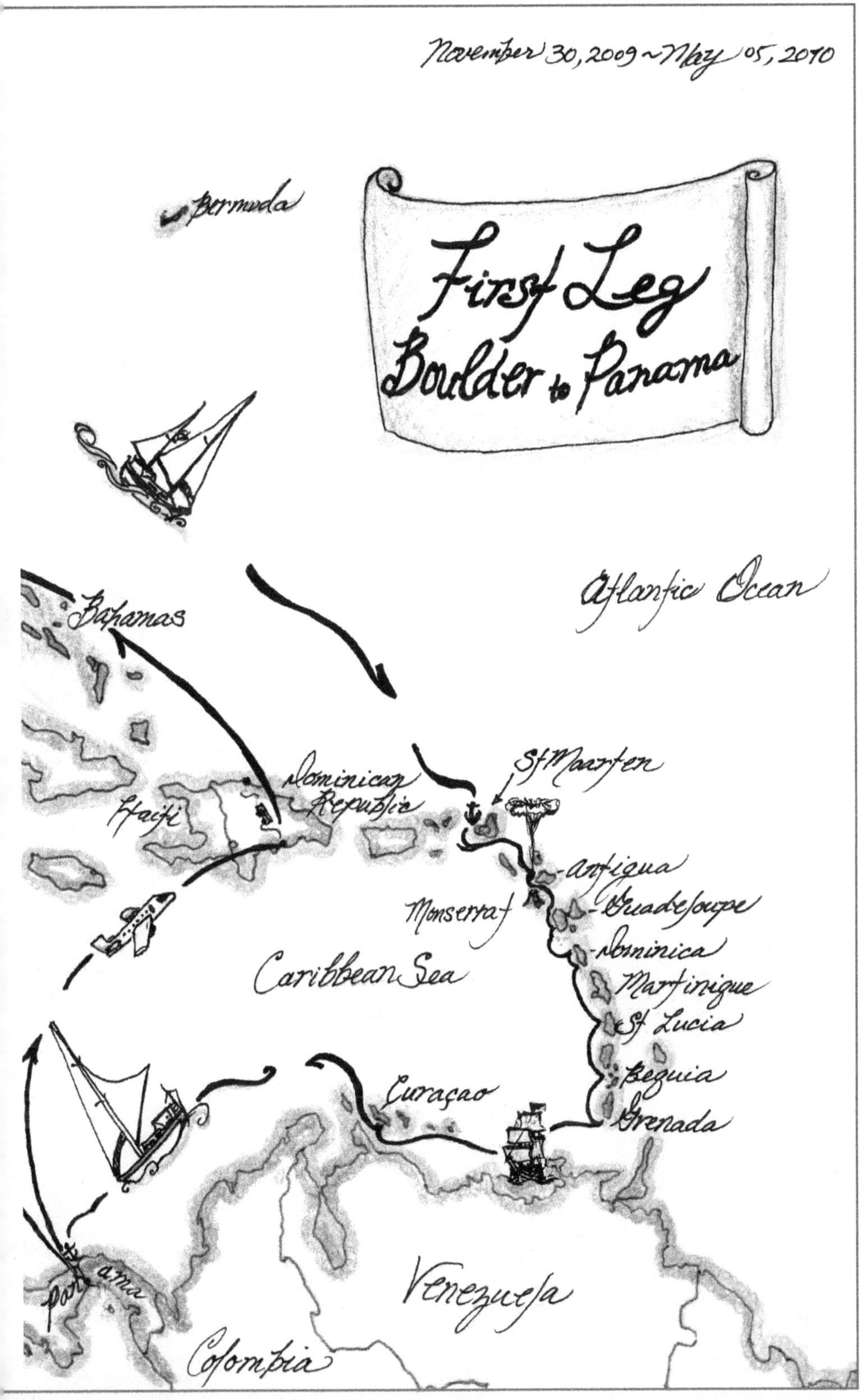
November 30, 2009 ~ May 05, 2010
First Leg
Boulder to Panama
Bermuda
Bahamas
Atlantic Ocean
Dominican Republic
Haiti
St Maarten
Antigua
Monserrat
Guadeloupe
Dominica
Caribbean Sea
Martinique
St Lucia
Bequia
Curaçao
Grenada
Panama
Venezuela
Colombia

CHAPTER 1

Dreams

Boulder, Colorado
2009

    This was going to be harder than I thought. Not the traveling around the world part—no, I imagine that would come pretty easy. The hard part was going to be not getting caught up by a man. My body was not to be trusted. I was 34 and my biological clock was ticking... loudly. I'd always planned on having a family. I'd been married... twice. But I was never ready for kids; I was always too busy working on the dream.

    My dream was to sail the world and have an amazing man. These two things were always woven together in my imagination and in my heart—I didn't want one without the other. Together, my guy and I would cruise the world ever so slowly: poking in and out of bays, crossing oceans and hanging out on islands, taking our time. Occasionally we would set up home for a while when a place grabbed us. We'd explore this amazing planet, following our fancy along with the wind and tides.

    During the journey, after we'd mastered the lifestyle, we'd add a few kids to the mix. Their education would be a family affair. Continuing our adventure, we'd taste, touch and smell the richness and texture that all life had to offer. Our kids would learn math through navigation and money exchange, history through the major museums and historical ports of the world, languages and stories through the world's people. They'd learn all about our mother earth, the environment, the ocean and weather, the mechanical aspects of a boat—not to mention politics and the unbalanced distribution of wealth. They'd learn what matters in life: the universality of human kindness and the spiritual connection we all share with each other and this living planet. I still can't think of a more vibrant or interesting way to live a life and get an education.

I said *was* when referring to this dream because by now, 13 years after I'd first committed to making it happen, all that remained was a tattered scrap of white cloth waving limply in the breeze. Love and sailing, it turned out, hadn't woven together smoothly as I'd envisioned. And so I teased the two strands apart, reducing that richly embroidered tapestry to just me hitchhiking my way around the world on other people's boats: a last-ditch effort.

When I finally sold my boat and moved to Colorado to be with family, I'd dropped the sailing thread altogether, or so I thought. By then, my biological clock was no longer just ticking; the alarm was blaring at top volume. And so, with the complication of sailing out of the way, I began working exclusively with the love strand of this dream. I set my intention on finding a partner, letting the Universe know I was serious by signing up for an online dating service, inspired by the very romantic success story of a girlfriend. It had to be easier now that my future beloved and I wouldn't have to live in a tiny, rocking tub surrounded by water with only one way to shore.

I did meet someone in Colorado who seemed like a possibility: he meditated regularly, looked very attractive in his selfie showing off the dragon tattooed across his muscular shoulders, didn't drink or do drugs, seemed self-aware and intelligent, and once had a threesome with his long-time girlfriend and another guy. If his online profile was the label on a bottle of wine, it might say: Deep and serious, with hints of a wild side; sexy with a spiritual finish. And in my cart it would go.

We were both excited to find each other but it quickly became clear that my pesky sailing dream was still messing up the love one. Already a father, he was not willing to travel great distances. Once the remnants of my not-dead-yet dream slipped out in conversation, he pointed out how uncompromising and single-minded I sounded. Not like someone who really wanted a partner (someone with whom one should consult and compromise with), but a free and independent, "ain't no one gonna hold me back" type of girl. He had a point.

So I stopped the online dating thing and pressed snooze on that incessantly buzzing biological clock. With that shut off, I returned to the sailing thread. If it wasn't going to let me go, I'd have to just get it out of the way.

Dreams

I had already done plenty of solo sailing and was well aware that the reality of setting off on my own would result in loneliness and the unanchored feeling of not having a routine. The constant state of watching my own back would wear me out. On the other hand, if I was sailing on other peoples' boats the tension of not having my own space and the strain of not being in charge would be hard. But what could I do?

I settled on a plan to save lots of money by working for a year so I could be financially prepared. I would go about accomplishing the remnants of my dream like a mature adult.

And so, determined with my new plan, I began spinning the exciting tale of my future adventures to all my adoring customers at the Walnut Café in Boulder where I was waitressing, building my mystique with stories. But the Universe, apparently onboard with the sailing dream and totally opposed to safety nets, had other plans: Mya called. She and Brian, her husband, knew this guy and he was sailing to the Caribbean and paying for the food. They were going and I should too.

"Nope, sorry," I said, solid as a rock. "I'm saving money all winter, plus I have to finish my book. And I don't want to island hop anyway. I'll get bored with the daily happy hour of retirees in the Caribbean. I want to sail the Pacific and have a safety net when things don't work out and I find myself stranded in some faraway place," I declared, so utterly sure of myself. I was too, for a couple of days. Until it hit me: if I am going to do this thing, then I should just do it. Fuck trying to control the details. And fuck money; I'd never traveled with any before and deep down it seemed too safe anyway. Not having money always makes for a better story. The opportunity had arisen; the Universe had spoken, with the added benefit of beginning the journey with one of my best friends.

"Okay, Universe, I'll take it!"

Apparently Mya was biding her time, knowing I'd come around.

A few weeks later, I went to research backpacks. It had been a long time since I'd owned a good, travel-worthy pack. I had bought one at 18 to take to Europe. I carried that sucker for years—through Europe, across the States and into Mexico—until it got stolen on what I'd assumed was a deserted beach in Tulum. One of the major motivations to buy a boat (for someone who knew nothing about boats or sailing, back when I was 22) was that I would no longer have to lug a pack around—the pack could carry me! But now, after many years, I was returning to having everything I owned on my back, like a turtle: loaded down, but free.

I began my research at the Army Surplus store to see what was available and how much it would cost. I don't particularly like shopping, but the salesman was good. I left the store with the very last Kelty—woman specific, baby blue, 4500 cubic inch—with a zipper up the front so I wouldn't have to dig down blind to find my bikini by feel—pack. I immediately phoned Mya while driving home from the store, to fan the flames and keep my fire stoked.

"Bad news," she informed me, "Brian just got promoted, so we can't go."

Hmmmm, good one, Universe. You got me. I've got the pack. It's on.

The Universe's Humor

And what did the Universe do, in all its boundless humor, a month before I was to leave? It sent me a man, of course!

I met him at a rooftop bar, around a few tables pulled together for happy hour beers and an eclectic group of people wanting to practice their Spanish. I'd gone alone and was happily involved in various levels of conversation. There was the older gentleman from Spain who challenged my abilities with his smooth linguistics and quick wit, leaving me not quite sure if he was making a joke *with* me or *about* me. A wild-haired Brazilian woman whose warm personality and Portuguese twists made talking with her a genuinely interesting exchange. There were also, of course, a few less fluent students who were stuttering through dialog. The warm summer darkness and cold beers helped to ease the flow and the young waitress with a very short skirt, who, every time she leaned over a crowded table, flashed us her bare ass, assured an easy topic of conversation.

I was well lubricated and chatting away with the last remaining few in our group; the Brazilian lady had left and no one else sparked my interest beyond *hablando español*. I was about to head out when he came over and pulled up a stool. I didn't think much of it. He was my age, broad shouldered and fairly fluent. Somehow we got talking about paragliding, which I'd always wanted to try. He'd just gotten into it and was stoked. This led to other adventures, the conversation picking up speed like a river flowing downhill. Soon we were expressing ourselves in Spanglish, the conversation tumbling on any way it

Dreams

could. We discovered a shared interest in languages and, when I got up to leave, he asked for my email, saying he'd send me info about a similar group who met to speak French.

We met for that, though my French wasn't nearly as easy as my Spanish. Next it was rock climbing one evening in the gym. As we took turns mounting the wall, balancing precariously on an awkward foot while lunging to reach the next handhold, the easy flow of dialogue continued. But this time we talked about our ex-partners, relationships, family. Standing on the blue mat, below an overhanging wall dotted with colorful plastic grips, encouraging him to make it past the place where he'd fallen before, laughing together in easy rivalry when I made it farther than he did, I started to realize that he looked good, his strong dark jaw and prominent brow, his stout arms straining, even his shiny shaved head. We didn't have instant sexual chemistry, but he was smart and interesting, social and engaged with life.

We continued to get together, often with his Costa Rican roommate Enrique, who was equally engaging and cool. There was salsa dancing, Mexican food and a spontaneous movie. After about a month of this I wanted to know where we stood. We obviously liked each other but it didn't seem to be progressing. So after a movie in a planetarium about the navigators of the South Pacific, me in a dreamlike state, my mind romanticizing about my pending sailing adventure while my body eased itself as close to him as it could possibly get, I finally worked up the courage. Once he'd parked his customized white truck and turned toward me to say goodnight, I started,

"PJ, I want to talk to you about something."

He waited expectantly.

"I, uh, I find you really attractive and I, uh…"

"I just want to be friends," he jumped in. "I mean, I like you, I like hanging out with you. I'm just not feeling like that. Here, give me a hug."

Slightly stunned, I hugged him and hobbled out into the night.

"That's okay," I told myself. "That's good." From the first night I met him, he talked about traveling and made little comments about being stagnant in Boulder. He'd mentioned the possibility of going to the Caribbean, of learning to sail. I'd developed this whole fantasy that he'd join me. I'd started to whittle down my around-the-world intentions to just sailing for the winter with hopes

15

that he'd come too. Apparently, the Universe was helping me stay on track with the sailing dream this time. Fine.

But then, at my going-away party, he stayed right till the end. His roommate was about to leave and he was, too, when I blocked him in the stairwell.

"Stay, PJ. Just stay."

"Enrique really likes you, Davina. He's had a crush on you this whole time. I would feel bad."

"I don't care. I like you PJ. I'm about to leave. Just stay. Please."

He did. And finally, after a few months of hanging out, he leaned in to kiss me. There weren't any lightning bolts, but I didn't care.

Since moving to Colorado, my once-active sex life had fizzled to nil. Maybe it was because my standards had changed. That my type—the tall, blond, ocean-going, hunter gatherer who tended to be emotionally immature, not intellectually stimulating or spiritually focused—just wasn't enough. I wanted an equal partner. Someone I could have a really good conversation with. It had been good to have a break from my serial monogamous relationships, but after a few years I was just frickin' horny. And PJ *was* smart and interesting.

This was a job for Pirate Girl.

"Come on," I grabbed his arm and forcefully lead him upstairs. By this point everyone had either left or found a place to crash and, sure enough, there was a dark sleeping mass on the floor of my room. I lifted the blanket. It was my cousin's friend Sasha, so I started to shake her, knowing she'd understand. "Come on Sasha, you gotta move."

"Davina, I feel bad. Just let her sleep," PJ protested.

"No, she would do the same to me. I have never had a guy in this room and I am not going to let Sasha ruin my chances, damn it." I said to him, then to her, "Come on Sasha, move."

Bleary eyed and stumbling, she left.

We got in bed, he stripped off his shirt and cuddled up with me. I untied my bikini top (it'd been a tropical themed party), because it was digging into my neck.

"Hey," he protested, "you shoulda let me do that." Problem was, he probably wouldn't have. We kissed some, but mostly talked. The fact that there was no burning passion didn't bother me; it was refreshing to have a guy who could communicate. We'd lost the vibe, and I blamed it on the Sasha incident. He got up to leave—but we made a date for the Wednesday before my flight.

Weeks before this I had lined up my ex-boyfriend to pick me up at the airport in Raleigh, North Carolina, and drive me the four hours to Beaufort, where I'd get on the boat. Sex was not only implied, it was texted about and masturbated to. Now that things were unfolding in Colorado, this presented a slight moral dilemma.

So I called my ex, trying to figure out how I could word this gently. He beat me to it:

"Ah, Davina, listen. My truck is pretty feeble. I'm not sure if it's up for doing the drive, and actually I don't think it would be healthy emotionally for me."

Wow, he'd never mentioned emotional health before!

Off the hook, I could follow the desires that had been growing with my nutrient-rich imagination. This was a great distraction from my pending epic journey. Never mind that I was leaving indefinitely the following Saturday. Never mind that I had a million-and-one other things to think about. Not one of them was as intriguing as a big, muscular body hard up against mine.

We had an enjoyable evening in the privacy of his roommate-less apartment, a rare thing as we always seemed to be chaperoned by Enrique. We had stimulating conversation over beers and a little smoke and watched a death-defying documentary about paragliding. He even got out his parachute and held up the harness for me so I could sit in it and get a feel for the rig. Then we watched a movie in Portuguese about a poet. Listening to this romance language while reading the English subtitles with prose like "she had my member in her mouth" and "a vagina wet and inviting like a cave" didn't strike him as sexual, and he was surprised to find that it turned me on.

After telling me that he liked to find the topic that made someone squirm and then prod them with it, I used the same tactic, attempting to reveal his true feelings about me. He changed the subject. He kissed and cuddled me, but without desire. He even asked me to stay, kissing me till I relented and got in bed with him. But then he didn't want to have sex. The communication was great though.

"The fact that I'm just not feeling any desire seems spiritual," he said. "It's like a gift of freedom."

I could see that. I would have loved to have the same gift, but I was burning up.

"I'm sorry." I said. "I can respect your feelings. I can just be friends, but not pressed up against you under the covers." I left.

Whatever it was, the only thing I could think was that the Universe, although taunting me a little, was behind this sailing-around-the-world thing. I guess it was helping me stay on course—damn it.

CHAPTER 2

Getting on the Boat

Crossroads

Beaufort, North Carolina
November 30, 2009

After the three-hour flight to Raleigh, I rented a car to drive the four hours to Beaufort, where I'd get on my first boat.

Beaufort sat at the very southern end of the Outer Banks on the east coast of the United States: a long strip of barrier islands forming a pencil-thin line of land in a triangular shape, protecting the inshore waters of the Pamlico Sound. Back in the 1700s, this was Blackbeard's stomping grounds.

Beaufort was an old signpost marking a major crossroads in my life. Back in 2000, after three years of owning and rebuilding my boat, I sailed my little purple ketch—*Azurlite*—up the East Coast from Key West, Florida, and into this harbor. Once I navigated the inlet with its shifting sandbars, multitude of waterways and various barrier islands, I'd followed the marked channel to where a hundred or so boats were anchored: local "live-aboards," big motor yachts in slips, native charter boats, fishing boats and cruisers. Beaufort was an international port of call, so yachts from all over the world could be found sheltered within its waterway.

Having logged some sea time and garnered some technical know-how to maintain and repair my boat on the way, I had finally felt like a real sailor. But I was also lonely and felt ripe and ready for a partner. It had just seemed like the time: I had my boat and my dream, I just needed the man. He'd be waiting around the next corner, and I was keeping my eyes peeled.

Adventures of a Pirate Girl

It had been raining for weeks, and I was going stir crazy inside my bare boat. I had yet to tackle the projects that would make her more comfy so living aboard still resembled camping. These were the days before I had a cell phone or computer, and I burrowed deeper and deeper into my hermit world, awkward around people when I occasionally went to shore.

Finally the skies cleared and I took the opportunity to put myself out there, sitting cocked back in a white plastic chair on the patio of the Dock House Bar, overlooking the water, talking to my mom on a pay phone. Some old salt started buying me beers, and then young Sarah Joe walked in—a girl who'd just bought her own boat and spun tales of a life that seemed twice as long as the one she'd actually lived—trailing six commercial fishermen, proving that not *all* of her stories were tall ones. I joined their long table, accepting the beer that was put in front of me. The guys were shark fishermen from Hatteras, a couple islands up the Outer Banks. I made an impression on them when "Pete Pete Repeat" didn't heed my warning to back off. He was loud and drunk and way too close to my face. Bam, I did what I warned him I'd do and clocked him one in his runaway mouth. He went over backward in his chair and I won the hearts of those burly men.

Matthew was one of the younger ones in the group with blond hair, gold-rimmed glasses and, after a few weeks at sea, the beginnings of a soft golden beard. He had an honest face. And, he didn't get defensive when I challenged the guys by asking, "So is it true? Are you commercial fisherman really killing all the fish and raping the oceans?"

He responded with thought and intelligence, and we sat together for the rest of the evening. Later he walked me back to my dinghy and, before I could step in, he pressed against me, his big strapping physique slightly soft over solid muscle, cuddly like a teddy bear. He planted a sloppy goodnight kiss on my lips.

The next day the guys returned to sea and, though I didn't have any way to stay in contact, I never questioned Matthew's feelings. I liked him and he liked me and I knew he was coming back. But after a few weeks, I got restless and was about to sail the few days up to Hatteras to find him.

I was on my boat, which was prominently anchored in front of the Dock House Bar. You couldn't miss it. Bikini-clad and lathered up for a bucket shower in my cockpit, I happened to see him pacing the shore. I knew he was looking for me, but I didn't want to make it easy for him so I feigned ignorance of his dilemma and ducked into the cabin where I could secretly watch him through the porthole.

To my delight, he disappeared and then reappeared sans shirt and shoes and dove right in. Tickled by his can-do attitude, I popped back out on deck, beaming a smile like a lighthouse, waiting for him to get close enough. Then in I went, headfirst, meeting him underwater. We surfaced in a kiss.

At that moment I chose a direction, I followed the sign that pointed to Hatteras, where I ended up spending five years finishing the major rebuild of *Azurlite* and building a house with Matthew. In 2004, Matthew and I got married.

The path from Beaufort to Hatteras didn't lead to living my dream—sailing around the world with the love of my life—as I thought it would. It turned out the relationship side of things wasn't as easy as rebuilding a boat—I couldn't just cut, glue and bolt a man into being "the One." I broke up with Matthew. After another few years on the island, I started to realize that island boys tend to be small town boys, not world travelers. And Hatteras was not where I wanted to be: I found it isolating and I was often depressed there.

That's when I sold *Azurlite*. It all happened fast. I went to bed stuck and depressed, had an epiphany in my sleep and the following week sold her for peanuts and moved to Colorado.

In hindsight I can see that by holding on to my vision so tightly, I'd strangled it. I couldn't let go enough to let the natural flow of creation help me out. But I've learned a thing or two about the law of attraction since then. Like creating a piece of art, you start off with an idea, but once you begin, the work takes on a life of its own. You have to let go and allow it to evolve naturally in order to generate something inspired. So here I was again, back at the same crossroads. This time I was following the other sign: the one that led directly out to sea.

Meeting Troy
Beaufort, North Carolina
November 29, 2009

When you stop moving, objects collect like dust, or like leaves on a forest floor. It had only been two years previous that I'd sold my boat and crammed everything I owned into my Ford Taurus to drive from Hatteras to Colorado. But in those two years my stuff had greatly expanded and I was having a hard

Adventures of a Pirate Girl

time deciding what to take and what to leave behind: dancing shoes? climbing gear? jewelry-making supplies? dive gear? But at least I wasn't carrying the emotional weight of a new love affair. PJ had made sure of that.

There I was again with everything I owned in a car. I left my excessive baggage in the rental and strolled up the dock to meet the man with whom I would be spending the next month. An acquaintance of my friend Mya, we'd made all of our plans for this trip via email, so I'd never actually talked to him. He was on deck adjusting the rigging of *LoneSilver*. In his early 50s, he was on the shorter side, solid and fit, with dark hair dusted gray and a mustache that curved around his friendly smile. He was in worn jeans, a faded tee shirt and brand new white Velcro sneakers that added a decade to his look.

We shook hands and I told him not to laugh about how much stuff I'd brought. I had warned him in an email that I was having a hard time narrowing it down and he'd sent a picture of himself in his early 20s on his way to Colombia with just a tiny, over-the-shoulder bag. He had written a mindful paragraph about how traveling light is a spiritual practice. How you develop a trust in the Universe and get a direct experience of manifesting your life. These were sentiments I totally agreed with; after all, I had hitchhiked penniless around Mexico. But hot damn! That was when I was 19!

When I fetched my load from the car, he was relieved to see that it wasn't as bad as I'd made it out to be... but it was still way too much.

Troy's boat was a 42-foot ketch-rigged Pearson. Her decks and cabin top were shipshape and well equipped without the shiny teak and brass of some yachts. Those were just made to sit at the dock and look pretty like bikini-clad women in full make-up and heels. You ever try to walk down the beach in heels? We wouldn't have to deal with that kind of high maintenance on this boat. Her sail covers were minty green, and the only woodwork was the silvered grab rails and trim around the companionway. Troy immediately started showing me around his baby, getting caught up in the story of each of his refits like a proud father. As a single-hander I could totally relate. I had spent thousands of hours and dollars rebuilding *Azurlite* and knew it's mostly only yourself who appreciates just how ingenious you truly are. It's gratifying when someone else can appreciate it too.

Not everybody would be open to this kind of instant intimacy. I'd never even met this guy, and here I was moving into his small and personal space. A little like that movie *Being John Malkovich* and sitting inside someone else's head. Troy had spent the past three years outfitting this boat and not only was every piece of it him, but as the Captain he had a million things to think about for this voyage. Over the next few days we did the provisioning and all manner of boat chores, and I could see his gears spinning. Understanding how overwhelming it could be, I was trying to be supportive and helpful, not questioning the small illogical glitches. But my at-your-service, eager-to-please crew member shell was beginning to morph into the totally-competent, speak-her-mind Pirate Girl. While Troy's shell—the world-traveling Captain with a long story that trumped mine on every topic—was wearing away.

The way he'd been open to my dietary influence and my culinary skills, the way he noticed my ability with knots and gave me the job of lashing down everything on deck, the diplomatic way he handled himself with the owner of the dock, his voiced appreciation for all of my help, and especially the way he quietly arranged my space in the v-berth while I was out, so that when I returned at night with a good buzz on I didn't have to clear a place to lie down. All of these little details painted the picture of a thoughtful person, confident enough in his abilities, but humble enough to accept the abilities of others. At least that's what I hoped.

The Going-Away Party

With all the chores done, the food and supplies purchased and packed away, and everything strapped down on deck, we were just waiting on weather.

LoneSilver was at a dock way down the creek, past the main township of Beaufort with its bulkheads and wooden docks, waterfront bars, restaurants and shops. Here the water washed naturally into marshy grass with an occasional personal dock jutting out over the wetland from a house built back off the water. Troy was out doing some of the last-minute chores and I was just stepping onto the boat, when I saw a funny-looking vessel passing the T-pier almost right below our bow. It was a tiny tub crowded with two women and a preteen boy; the whole vessel tipped precariously forward, one of the girls leaning over the side, paddling with her hands. They were all howling with laughter, having way too much fun in their struggle to make it across the creek.

I watched for a minute, giggling. Finally, close enough to the water's edge, the boy spluttered over the side, knee deep, and pulled them to the grassy shore.

"Hi," I called out.

They all looked up, still laughing, and called out, "Hi!" in unison, which only evoked more laughter.

Then the girl with black ringlet curls and creamy skin dotted with freckles, said, "Hey, are you Davina by any chance?"

"Uhhh, yeah," a curious smile turned up my lips, "Yeah, I'm Davina."

"Hey, I'm Kris, a friend of Hope's. She told me you might be in town."

I'd left a message with Hope earlier in the week. She was a single-handing sailor girl I'd met up in Ocracoke a year or so before when I'd flown out for Mya's pirate-themed wedding. I'd Captained one of the three boats that rafted up for the ceremony, and Hope ran another one.

"Hey, it's cool to finally meet you. We've run in the same circle for years. You have a purple boat, right? We're friends with Jonah. He told a lot of stories that you featured in."

"Ah, my old friend Jonah, yep. He and I were close way back when I first bought *Azurlite*."

"I remember hearing about you," piped in the kid, who looked about 12 and had the same curly black hair. He pulled their little round craft up into the grass. "Jonah called you a Pirate Girl," he said with a sly smile. "My name's Jonah, too."

"He's mine," added Kris, nodding toward the boy.

"I can see that."

"So what are you doing?" she asked.

"About to sail down to Sint Maarten and then on around the world, is the plan."

"Awesome! But what about in, like, an hour? We've just got to get out of these wet clothes. Then we're meeting Hope at the pub. Do you want to join us?"

"I'd love to!"

Cleaned up and ready for a night out, I first stopped by another friend's boat. Earlier that day while jogging, I'd run across Jay, someone I knew from Hatteras. Stocky and tan, with a mess of curly brown hair, we'd made a plan to meet later for a toke. I called out, "Hey Jay," and waited for permission to come aboard from a scruffy little mutt who was barking to protect her territory. Jay emerged from inside his 30-foot sloop.

"Perfect timing. I was just about ready to stop working. Do you want to pass me that skill saw, and I'll just put this stuff away." Once we had everything stowed beneath seats and under bunks, we climbed down below and sat across from each other on the settee.

Once the small cabin twirled and twisted with curls of marijuana smoke and we'd talked boats and projects and my big sailing plans, Jay turned the conversation to our shared history.

"Remember that party?" he asked, while passing me the joint.

"I'll never forget it." It had been a pirate party at Springer's Point on Ocracoke Island, right where Blackbeard and his crew would have congregated in the 1700s.

One of my first purchases after buying my boat had been a bustier and ruffly white shirt at a Renaissance fair—my pirate outfit. But this party, many years later, was the first time that the indomitable Pirate Girl spirit had completely filled me, almost as if I was possessed. Some small aspect of my personality, which normally stayed tucked away within the whole, swelled and expanded until it took over all the other parts of me and I was filled with this wily, raucous and aggressive force, as if I was channeling her from a different lifetime. She swaggered through that night, accosting innocent partygoers and making a piratical scene to the merriment of her crew. What a swashbuckling night it had been!

After both of us took turns recounting the details, Jay and I were tearing up with laughter. By then it was time to head to the bar, so we climbed out of the boat and into the clear winter air. The red brick building was only a few blocks away but I'd worn flip flops. The cold of early December was especially nippy while I peered in through the round porthole in the heavy wooden door of the pub. Inside there were warm tones of varnished wood, the dancing light of the fire and the glowing cheeks of merry revelers. We pushed in to a roar of welcome.

Kris was at the small bar near the entrance with Hope, a blond with a direct, almost masculine air. Looking in further I saw a dear friend and his new girlfriend, who'd welcomed me and put me up the night I'd arrived. I was a little awestruck, just standing there, when someone swooped me up in a hug.

Adventures of a Pirate Girl

It turned out to be another old friend. The last time I'd seen her she was married to her one-time nemesis, but they were no longer together, she reported. She now had her own boat.

"You inspired me!" she added, before swooping away to serve beers and clear tables.

On the eve of thrusting myself into the unknown with this stranger, Troy, I tried to fully soak up the warm embrace of these old salty friends while laughing and telling stories in front of the fire. I was, of course, high and therefore extremely animated, and all the love had me extra charged up. Kris's son, Jonah, would pop up into the middle of the action every so often and fight to keep in on the conversation.

They filled me in on what mutual friends were up to, which devolved into talking shit about other people we'd known. I tried to hold course on the positive.

Later Kris leaned in close and elaborated on how she'd heard of me over the years. How when her son was a baby and she was faced with the colossal undertaking of singlehanded parenting, she had sometimes called on that image of the Pirate Girl resurrecting her sunken boat, now wild and free, Captain of her own destiny. With her arm around my shoulder, she pulled me in closer and locked eyes with me:

"You gave me strength," she said, both of us smiling through shiny tears.

Then, abruptly, Captain Hope announced, "That's it ladies. Drink up, we're outta here!" Kris and I took turns downing the beer Jay had just bought me. He sat there with big eyes, sad in the face of the inevitable, as the girls, with waves and hugs all around, whooshed me out the door.

We stomped through the bracing night to Kris's place to fix us some supper. While Kris and I were prepping, Jonah and Hope were engaged in an impromptu wrestling match: She was trying, by force, to put him outside, and he was giving her hell, both of them laughing. But, seeing she wasn't getting anywhere, she relented. Jonah started whooping and jumping up and down, yelling, "I won! I won!"

"Yeah, you won, little boy," she conceded.

Then he turned to me, "You'd better be anticipating how I'm going to kick your ass next."

"I'm not going to anticipate anything," I said, feigning disinterest while cracking eggs. "I choose to live in the moment. Anticipation sometimes diminishes the actual event."

But he wouldn't let it go, so I wiped my hands. "Okay, you're on. Where we doin' this?"

He led me into his bedroom, and my eyebrows went up as he closed the door behind him. But the sexual undertones were so innocent I didn't say anything. The bed filled most of the room so I stood up on it, crouched in a wrestling stance, while he turned on "Rage Against the Machine." Once he was facing me, I threw him down and pinned him. "One, two, three, I won," I declared, popping off the bed.

"I'm never going to admit I lost!" he shouted, so I pinned him again, but he still wasn't going to admit it.

"Are you an honorable man or what?" I asked.

"What do you mean?"

"I mean, in a few years you will be able to beat me every time, no problem. Well, maybe a little problem. But still. You'll be able to beat me. But to be an honorable person, someone who people can look up to and respect, you have to be able to admit when you're wrong or when you lose. It shows character. And it takes way more strength and courage to admit defeat than being all cocky and not admitting it when you lose fair and square."

He took to this immediately, practicing under his breath with swagger as we left the room, "Yeah, she beat me."

"Hey," I turned back to him before we reached the kitchen where the girls were. "It's been a long time since a boy wanted to wrestle with me. It was fun," I winked.

Once we had some food in us, we settled down a little. Kris was clearing up the little kitchen and Hope was in the other room, leaving Jonah and me alone at the round dining room table. Still chewing, and in a contemplative mood, he said, "I hate my name."

"What?" I looked up.

"I hate my name. I want to change it."

"You're still figuring yourself out," I said. "When I was your age, I had a really hard time. I was depressed, actually. But you know what? Looking back I can see I was like a caterpillar, and the depression was my cocoon. I came out a butterfly. With awesome, colorful, powerful wings, just like you're going to have. And if you change your name now, before you even know what color your wings are gonna be… how're you gonna find the right name?" I ruffled his head. At that, their little black dog yapped from under the table as if in agreement.

Intended Landfall

Our other crew member, Jen, arrived the next night. She was exactly one day older than I, tall, buxom and blond, with a tiny endearing gap between her front teeth, which showed itself in her ever-ready smile. I was totally impressed before I had even met her because she was a pilot for Continental Airlines, which qualified her as a badass in my book. But it was her talking about running her father's boat, how she had trained a girlfriend to be her "number-one boat bitch" and her assertion that "good-looking guys are for decorating the bow" that won my heart.

Our first intended landfall was Sint Maarten—1500 nautical miles east/southeast of Beaufort—about a 10-to 14-day crossing. We wanted to leave as soon as we had all our provisioning done, but Mother Nature had different plans. Troy had been downloading the colorful pictures of weather and we'd been watching the powerful winds as they pushed our departure date further away. Saturday had seemed like the day to go but a deep red bloom on the computer screen, indicating 45 to 50 knots, appeared right in our intended path.

The Gulf Stream hugs the east coast of North America and runs like a great river, 50 miles wide, taking its warm waters up to the cold north and around toward Europe. The winds were forecast to be 20 to 30 knots from the northeast which, when they rubbed up against the current of the Gulf Stream, would kick up the seas like petting a salty dog's fur the wrong way, making for a rough 50 miles. But, like I told Troy, I'd rather have eight hours of terror than two weeks of boredom. It was already late in the season to leave; the longer we waited, the greater the chance of winter storms. It was decided: We'd leave the next day.

CHAPTER 3

At Sea

Beaufort to Sint Maarten
December 6, 2009

    The morning started out glassy calm. We motored up the waterway in the wee hours, the glowing white moon reflecting off the silvery purple surface, disturbed only by the wake that trailed out behind us. As we fueled up, our very last chore, the sky brightened to a clear blue. It was a bitingly cold day. Jen and I were bundled up in our red foul-weather gear jackets and jeans, woolen beanies low over our ears. We'd packed for the tropics and didn't have any warm clothes to spare. The infamous Gulf Stream was out ahead of us and we didn't know what to expect; potentially it could be very rough, but it would get warmer the further south we sailed. Once we passed the last sea buoy we began the routine of keeping watch: Troy took noon to 3:00, then me 3:00 to 6:00, then Jennifer 6:00 to 9:00, and so on.

    As land shrank behind us and finally disappeared into the horizon, the seas became confused and sloppy. Even Troy, who had logged more than 125,000 miles offshore, started to feel the effects. The dip and sway of the moving vessel had us all unsettled. I couldn't stop yawning, like a fish out of water trying to extract more oxygen from the air. None of us threw up, though after watching video footage of the rocking cockpit *in* the rocking cockpit, I nearly did. Bracing against the random pitching movement so as not to be slammed into a bulkhead, just moving inside to my bunk in the main salon was a chore, My whole body ached; I felt weak and had a hard knot at the top of my stomach.

    Jen and I were bunking on the settees on either side of the main salon. I felt okay while lying down, snuggled in my sleeping bag, held safely in place by a lee cloth. I had a few hours till my first night watch from midnight to 3:00, and began to contemplate eating. Sustenance would do me good. I decided I could handle it, got up, then quickly lay back down. It took me several tries but, figuring I had a few hours to digest in the horizontal position, I finally managed to crawl off the bunk and stay up just long enough to heat some black beans I had made from scratch the night before. Tortillas were out of the question. I have never eaten a meal so slowly: lying on my side, hugging my bowl, chewing every bite and resting in between. I knew I didn't have it in me to put the leftovers away so I worked at it until I'd accomplished eating the whole bowl. Then I lay back, relieved to have completed the job.

There was a small diesel stove mounted on the bulkhead at the foot of my bunk with a glass front so you could see the little fire inside. It kept us toasty warm and feeling cozy. During the last half hour before my bitter cold watch in my ill state, I stupidly rested my feet on the glass. I snatched them away when I smelt something burning—leaving a melted nylon footprint on the heater and clouds of feathers puffing out of my down sleeping bag... Oops! After I cleaned it up as best I could and even more wretched, I crawled into the cockpit to relieve Troy. I was determined to stand my watch come puke or death by exhaustion, but Troy gave me a little red pill, and that was the end of my seasickness for the rest of the journey. Troy and Jennifer took a little longer but we all recovered, which is a good thing because the weather didn't.

For seven days the seas remained sloshy—causing the boat to move like a sloppy drunk lurching and swerving down the street—and the winds remained strong, between 25 and 35 knots. The swells were never big enough to deserve bragging rights (Jennifer guesstimated 15 feet), but were enough to make life severely uncomfortable. I felt like a pinball while moving around the boat, buffeted from side to side. There was no rhythm to it. It would buck and sway and occasionally the boat would launch off a wave, providing a second of free-falling, stomach-in-the-throat sensation before slamming violently down with the sound of a cannon firing. Anything that wasn't secured shot across the cabin and commenced to roll around. The V-berth up front was mayhem, stuffed with all the miscellaneous gear that didn't have a home: the dish drainer, the big white fenders, a fishing net, a box fan, and Jen's and my stuff crammed in front of that. When we were on a starboard tack, her bag would topple onto the floor; when we were heeled the other way, it was my stuff spilling over. Eventually we left it all where it lay. Troy had plastic containers with little slide-out trays full

At Sea

of nuts and bolts. The slamming caused these to work their way out and join the other flotsam on the floor. Thank Goddess that each tray had a sealed lid!

All of this movement caused an orchestra of sound, an audio assault to the ears. From deep under the floorboards came a weary groan. From within the metal mast came the rubbing tap of wires. Every pot, pan, cup and plate made gentle ticking and clinking sounds. Above Jen's bunk the chain plates complained of their load, sounding like an old man snoring. Under the companionway ladder, the wooden cabinet made high-pitched clicks like a pissed-off dolphin.

One night, I was awakened from a deep sleep by a crash and what sounded like BBs rolling and bouncing back and forth across the cabin floor. I jumped out of bed to clear up the mess. Jen and Troy both watched me dumbfounded, wondering what the hell I was doing. Apparently we had been listening to that particular noise for days. The sound of the ocean rushing by was almost drowned out by this cacophony, but the howl of the wind was a constant, accentuated by the cymbal clash of a wave slapping the hull.

Collision Course

The main job of steering *LoneSilver* was delegated to the autopilot. I never had one on my boat, and though I could sometimes balance her under sail, I usually spent all of my time while underway alone at the helm, with only quick dashes below to pee or grab food. Having one would have made all the difference. An autopilot is to a single-handed sailor what a vibrator is to a single girl—essential equipment if you don't want to wear yourself out or rely on others to get you to where you want to go. On this boat there were two.

With steering covered, our main duty on watch was to keep a keen eye out for ships. It can take as little as 10 minutes for a ship to steam from a dot on the horizon to a mammoth beast towering above you. Even though, as a vessel under sail, we have the right-of-way, these ships are plowing through the sea fast and potentially blind. With their autopilots, GPS and radar all working in unison, I could just imagine the man on watch going down three flights of stairs to grab a cup of joe and getting caught up in a conversation with the cook. We didn't see many of these merchant ships—but it only takes one to run you down.

The third night out, when the toll of our uncomfortable voyage had leeched the positive attitude out of Troy and Jen, and was starting to deplete mine, we had a memorable evening starting with one such close call. I was on the 6 to 9 pm watch, and Troy was trying to catch up on much-needed sleep. We had four to six feet of confused seas. I sat there—five minutes, 10 minutes—fixated on a tiny speck as it grew into a bright star on the horizon. I could tell we were on a collision course, because it was fixed between the mizzen stay and the cabin side. I took a compass bearing and it remained at 210 degrees and got bigger. It morphed into the higher white stern light and lower white bow light of a ship under steam, and I could start to make out a hint of red, indicating that I was seeing the port side. At this point I had been watching it for 40 minutes. I woke up the Captain. The green light came into view looking like a bull with multi-colored eyes and in-line horns, inches of darkness in between them, coming dead on. Troy came on deck and picked up the VHF radio, "East-bound ship, east-bound ship, sailing vessel *LoneSilver*. We are the vessel directly in front of you." His call spurred the pilot into action and we watched as the red light disappeared and the green and white ones swept to one side, highlighting the invisible black hulk as it made a clear and obvious course change. That was the closest collision course I've ever experienced.

After Troy went back to his bunk I decided to sit below and just pop my head up for a visual sweep every five minutes. Troy had said this was perfectly acceptable. I found Jennifer awake and declared my intention: "I'm on watch, but I'm gonna sit down here." I couldn't help feeling slightly guilty, as if I was shirking my responsibilities.

Just as I expressed this, CRACK WHACK, something hit the deck. We stared at each other, wide eyed, listening as a heavy vibration started to quake the cockpit. I popped my head back out and found a black plastic blade lying exactly where I would have been sitting on watch. I looked up and saw the wind generator, now with only two blades, rotating lopsided and making the whole mizzenmast shimmy. Wind generators spin at an extremely fast rate. I'd heard of a guy who got hit by a blade while under sail. It broke his arm in five places and he had to be helicoptered out. The one and only time I had felt like doing my watch down below and I had narrowly avoided this disaster.

Poor Troy! I hesitated to wake him up, but we couldn't find the off switch and the whole mast was vibrating like an eggbeater. We'd been relying on the wind generator to charge our batteries. The refrigerator sucked them dry. Luckily he had a replacement blade; but to climb the mast in these messy conditions was out of the question, so he decided to run the generator to charge the batteries, then went back to bed.

At Sea

Nine o'clock rolled around and Jennifer got suited up. We were both in full foul weather gear, the reflective bits glaring in the shine of our headlamps. We were flying the mainsail and the stays'l. Since the weather had been so nasty and we'd done everything *but* go over how *LoneSilver* was rigged before leaving the dock, Troy insisted on doing all of the sail changes, clipping his harness into the jack line so as not to be tossed overboard while leaving the protection of the cockpit. He hadn't slept in days.

The shrill of the wind was increasing, and *LoneSilver* was dipping farther over with each gust. Troy came out like a bear awakened early from his winter hibernation: groggy and potentially dangerous. In his cotton sweatsuit, he donned his harness and went forward to drop the stays'l—and was instantly slapped by a wave with a sense of humor. Sail down, he came back to the cockpit soaked to the bone and cussing. Then he decided that we'd better reduce the mainsail too. His motto, he often told us, was "reef early." Once that was done, our speed dropped to less than three knots and the boat really began to roll. He changed into another all-cotton outfit and came up again, thinking the stays'l would help us maintain forward motion and dampen the roll.

Just to be clear, we identified the correct sheet together so I would be sure to pull in the right line once he got the sail up. Again he went forward and again got drenched. He hoisted the sail and I pulled on the sheet to stop it from whipping around. But the stays'l sheet shared the winch with the Genoa sheet and they looked exactly the same. The agreed-upon rope was not the correct one and nothing happened. He was up there, wet and exhausted and screaming to be heard over the wind and the flogging sail, "Get the right FUCKING line!!!"

Reacting off his energy and trying to work fast, I undid a line that was using the cleat I needed, mumbling an expletive to myself about the clusterfuck as I let it go. Instantly what sounded like rapid gunfire exploded as the Genoa rolled out and began to beat in the wind.

"Roll that FUCKING thing in!!!" he bellowed, while trying to avoid being whipped by it and bucked overboard. The stress was infectious. Jen and I rushed to heave in the line. We had the deck lights on, and their glaring radiance darkened the night around us and made it feel ominous and evil. Our bubble of light was fragile indeed.

Once Troy got back to the cockpit, I apologized profusely and, in his more characteristic way, he assured me that it was okay, we all make mistakes.

"Even I fuck up," he admitted, "though you girls probably don't notice because it's usually up on the bow." We were barely able to contain ourselves until he turned away before busting out in huge, knowing grins and stifled laughter. Yeah, we never noticed.

We tried every sail combination possible: hoisted the mizzen to dampen the roll, dropped the main, dropped the mizzen and raised the main. Jen and I were trying to move quickly, sorry that we couldn't help more. Troy assured us, "It's okay now, we're safe and you can just chill and work at a calmer pace."

Then he decided to heave to, setting the rudder and sails opposite each other, causing the boat to stop forward motion. "It'll be just like sitting at the dock," he assured us. We did this but, with the wind increasing and the messy seas, the motion did not resemble being dockside *at all*.

We'd been trying to get far enough south to avoid a low pressure system, which potentially meant heavier wind and rain. Hoping for a weather report, Troy made a call on the VHF, and from somewhere out in the dark void a fellow sailor responded. Apparently the low was predicted to form right in our path. This news added to the anxiety that buzzed like electricity in the air, but Troy needed to sleep if he was going to be of any use over the next few days. I stepped in as first mate: "Troy, we should stay hove to. You need to get your ass in bed. Sailors get in big trouble when sleep deprived and we're depending on you for tomorrow." It was 2:30 am by this point and I volunteered to keep his watch. I fought sleep till 5:00 and then Jen took over till 8:00. Oh what a night that was.

The Romance

On the seventh day, I crawled out on deck for my midnight watch and was stunned into awe. When I sit for my usual hour of meditation, after my mind finally calms, I occasionally reach a place inside myself that is peaceful and still and all encompassing, like every single thing in the entire cosmos is deeply and completely right. Looking up at the stunningly clear night sky, hundreds of miles away from any human light, that powerful feeling was emanating not only from within me but was mirrored by the sky. There were billions of stars and a meteor shower raining heavenly bodies; everything was deeply and completely right.

The remaining four days of our crossing to Sint Maarten reminded us all why we put ourselves through this. The sunshine's warmth and an eased sea lulled us back into the delight of our love affair with sailing. We sat around the cockpit and shared a few beautiful meals together, painstakingly prepared while strapped into the galley in a forward lunge position, all the food items and utensils set where they wouldn't fall, either on the floor or in the sink, as the boat heeled. This made eating that much more enjoyable, in easy camaraderie, poking fun at each other, especially at Troy: "Yeah, sure you only yell to be heard over the wind," while sailing over the bluest blue imaginable.

We read, slept and wrote in our journals. I did my daily half-hour French lesson on my iPod and managed to sit for an hour of meditation now and then. Mostly, offshore sailing is the practice of being present and relaxed.

We finally let out the trolling line to fish, and caught a shimmering, day-glow yellow mahi-mahi. We gave thanks to the ocean for this precious life before devouring such a delicious gift.

On the last day, we saw dolphins and remembered the whales we had seen on our first day, good omens for sure. After 11 days at sea, we spotted the first cloud-like mirage of land. Jen and I jumped up and down in silence so as not to wake Troy. In his earlier days, his extensive voyaging had been navigated celestially, but with GPS, he told us, there was nothing for him to marvel at and so had asked us not to wake him. For us it was still magical that we had crossed this expanse of open ocean and found the land we had set out to find. We sat and stared, took pictures, chatted and drank a beer, and watched what the chart described as a crumb go from a grayish cloud to a black line and then a hump and then a mountainous green oasis dotted with lights as the night descended. With the aid of radar, we found our anchorage in the dark and dropped the hook amongst megayachts lit up like floating hotels. In the shocking still and quiet, we toasted our arrival with rum and slept a watchless sleep.

The next morning, we motored *LoneSilver* under the bridge and into the huge lagoon. Dazzling in the sun were the bright rainbow colors of the tropics and hundreds of sailboats at anchor and underway. With international flags flapping and people waving, it seemed like a festival and me a rock star up on the bow, even without my purple boat.

Even with all the hardships, sailing is a romance for sure. Oh, my darling, I've been gone for so long! I am a sailor and the wild freedom and simpler, self-sufficient life is the one for me.

CHAPTER 4

Sint Maarten

Arriving

December 17, 2009

A 42-foot boat is not a lot of space for three people on a 12-day cruise. While slipping over the last few hundred miles of sea, Jen and I had made dream plans of our arrival on land. They started out as pure illusion: "As soon as we drop the hook we're hitting the scene," and became more realistic as we made our approach. Of course, by the time we actually inched into the bay, we were exhausted and ready to crash. And the next day, by the time we moved *LoneSilver* through the bridge and into the lagoon, re-anchored, did a major clean and tidy, unlashed and put together the dingy, pumped it up, mounted the engine, and then all piled in and made our way to report to customs, we were pooped. Jen and I could feel the tension mounting with Troy, and it was clear that we all needed some space.

St. Martin or Sint Maarten as it's known in Dutch, is a tiny island divided into a French side and a Dutch side. There's a huge lagoon that boats can anchor in with a bridge that opens on a schedule to allow yachts to come in and out. Someone on the VHF radio cruiser's network was nice enough to inform us that we could avoid the entrance fee charged by the Dutch by checking in on the French side; the French were apparently more relaxed about regulations. The border lies right down the middle of the lagoon, so you can easily pass from one side to the other depending on where you land your dinghy. The Dutch side was more spread out and built up and had more marinas and dockside bars. They spoke English, the streets were dirtier, and it felt a little more third world.

Sint Maarten

The French side had more preserved land, nicer beaches and posher shops, but was more expensive.

In the dinghy we headed to the French town of Marigot and were funneled past a higher and higher density of moored boats until we came to where the water ended and the town wrapped around its little corner of the lagoon as if floating; chic restaurants, high-end gift shops and boat rentals crowded the area. The immigration office was a kiosk on the dock. After Troy agonized over filling out the French document on a computer, we paid the nominal entrance fee and Jen and I set out to explore. We'd make our own way back to the boat later.

We walked through wall-to-wall jewelry shops and expensive clothing boutiques that created a narrow maze crowned with apartments like you'd find in a European city. There were tiny European cars backed up in the clogged arteries of the town and lots of islanders running errands and speaking French. Jen was feeling the effects of her sea legs—rocking and rolling as if she was still on the boat—and we were both feeling exhausted and overwhelmed. Instinctively, we made our way toward the ocean side and wandered onto the cement seawall, gazing out at the open water and sky as if in a trance. We looked over and there was Troy, emerging from the mayhem of the condensed city toward the ocean as if in the same trance, and we quickly agreed that this was all too much and happily returned with him to our haven.

First Night Out

The next day we helped schlep all the boat's laundry to shore along with all of Jennifer's stuff—it was her last day calling in sick to her real life—and we girls went off on our own, well-rested and ready to make the most of it. Being a pilot, Jen had money to spend so we went straight to a big hotel on the Dutch side. After 12 days without a proper wash we were salty and sweaty, and the refrigerated isolation of a sterile hotel room was so refreshing. After a luxurious shower, we enhanced the pleasure by totally pigging out: Jen on chocolate cookies and me on a French baguette and Brie cheese.

Once restored, we ventured out into the intense heat of the tropical sun radiating off concrete and grabbed a bus, which was just like hailing a cab in the U.S. When you saw a white minivan with a hand-painted sign propped in the windshield, you waved.

Adventures of a Pirate Girl

Jen and I ended up at the Soggy Dollar Bar, a little open-air place on a dock overlooking the lagoon, in front of a line-up of megayachts. Sitting at a picnic table, sipping our beers, Jen nodded toward the next table (crowded with guys) and loudly pointed out, "What's wrong with them? Why aren't they talking to us?"

I spoke up, happy to help, "So you boys work on one of these mammoths, do you? This is Jennifer, she's an airline pilot and flies 747s," I added, proud to be associated with such respectable company. They turned out to be a cool group from Australia, England and Brazil. Meanwhile, the bar filled for happy hour and one-dollar beers.

I could feel the eyes of a good-looking guy with mocha skin follow me as I went up to the bar. He made his move swiftly, like a bird of prey; none of the cautious, let-the-girl-make-the-first-move tactics that American guys use. Leaning in close, and with the intense stare of a falcon, he said, "I like your energy gurl. You are strong; I like dat." He was from Jamaica and in the "pharmaceutical business."

After getting me stoned, he laid it out, "I'm tirty-ate, I'm ready starrt a family, gurl. I wann get married and have keeds. You and me gurl, we can be happy together." But when he mentioned his dream of owning a strip club to support the family, I knew for sure that our respective worlds were too far apart.

Jen, who must have gotten annoyed with me for disappearing to get stoned, left the bar without saying goodbye. After searching for her and being told by some random guy, "Your friend, she go," I went to grab a bus back to the hotel. Some cutie 23-year-old local kid told me (along with how much he would love to kiss me) that there were no buses this late and that I should hitchhike: "You'll be safe gurl. It's a happy island."

"Thank you, sweetie," I stuck out my thumb at the long line of slow-moving vehicles and instantly a car squealed over.

"*Bon soir*," a chubby dark-skinned dude greeted me through the open window. He had on oversized faux-diamond earrings and music bumping. I leaned in to negotiate locations, but he looked at me like a deer caught in headlights, confused and innocent. We were stopping traffic, so I went with my first impression and jumped in. Instantly he turned down his music and indulged me in the slow work of communication.

Back at the hotel, I dropped my bag, changed my clothes, then shared the elevator down with two girls. One had on a tiny white dress that fit like plastic

Sint Maarten

wrap over her curvy caramel body, helium boobs and a sculpted nose. The black girl was more of a natural beauty: six feet tall or more in clear plastic stilettos. She had on an itty-bitty white tennis skirt and a white push-up bra top. Her legs were so long and thin that, in those tippy heels, she reminded me of a baby giraffe. They were speaking Spanish, so I asked where they were from.

"Colombia."

"*Ah, Colombiana! Ustedes miran muy sexy esta noche.*"

They took my compliment like unsure teenagers: half surprised, overly self-conscious, but clearly appreciative. I wondered what their stories were, how they found themselves so far from home. They reminded me of the young girls in Cuba who, out of economic desperation, sold their bodies to feed their families. I slowed down in the lobby to watch them teeter out. Walking a little too close to each other, both of them tugging discreetly at their skirts, they glanced nervously around the polished hotel. Everyone was watching.

I marched across the sand toward the Sunset Bar. The airplanes buzzed low over this short stretch of beach to land at the airport right on the other side of the street. I didn't experience it myself but allegedly if you clung to the chain link fence when the huge jets took off, the force from them powering by would lift your feet off the ground. Jen was walking toward me as two cute French men walked past.

"Hey, you guys look like you know where you're going." I piped up.

"Come with us ladies, we're going to a disco over here. We're locals, we can get you in for free."

The disco was swank. Everyone was dressed to the nines: ladies in high heels and strapped into stylish little dresses, their hair done up in the elaborate styles only possible with African tresses. Men were in slacks and button-down shirts. Despite my inadequate attire I strutted in like a peacock in flip flops, my short brown hair spiky, a multitude of shell earrings dangling from my ears, and a small wispy brown skirt showing off my downy-haired legs. People were just standing around the dark edges drinking and smoking cigarettes so, after I bought the boys a beer for getting us in, I kicked off my shoes and proceeded front and center on the empty dance floor and got down to the slamming music. This, of course, inspired the spectators and soon the floor was crowded with people shaking a tail feather. Then I sauntered off toward the bar and slid by Jen who was perched on a stool. "My work here is done," I said, smiling. She followed me out. The heavy cloud of cigarette smoke had been choking me. Everyone seemed to smoke here, despite the very direct warnings on the packs: "Smoking kills," complete with gruesome pictures of dead fetuses and rotten lungs.

We wandered back to the Sunset Bar and then over to another high-end club, Bliss. I was feeling tired and not ready to pay the $13 to get in.

"Are there people here?" we asked the big bouncer.

"Of course there are," he assured me.

"What's the music like? Let me check it out first, I'm just here to dance, man. If the music sucks, I don't wanna pay." The doorman just smiled his slow, bright Caribbean smile that lit up his dark face.

It was a beautiful outdoor club with a pool and big tables surrounded by white, wrap-around couches under their own wooden canopies with white curtains and a crowded, multi-level dance floor. But they were playing techno, not my music of choice. I wandered back to the entrance gate and found the doorman and Jen chatting away.

"Hey what's your name, man?"

"Andres," he informed me.

"Hey thanks, Andres, for letting me in, but that's not my type of music and I'm tired anyway."

"Come with me, I'll pay for you," Jen pleaded.

"I don't want her to pay for me," I confided in Andres, "I don't like her to pay for everything."

"Go on gurls, you're cool." And, just like that, we were in.

I had already reached my preferred altitude with beer and had switched to water, making sure to take the doorman, Andres, a bottle because he'd informed us that it was the only thing he didn't get free on the job.

"Anything you need, gurl," he said with a warm smile, "pass by me."

The dance floor was a little too crowded for my taste so I commandeered a canopy and pushed out the table to have an oasis to dance where no one could touch me. Still, numerous local dudes came by to say hi and acted surprised when I said I didn't have a boyfriend. In general, I found them to be respectful

Sint Maarten

of my space. It wasn't my façade that got these guys' attention; after all, I hadn't put much effort into my no-product, no-makeup, dirty-feet look. It's the way I walked that they liked: cocky like them, looking them right in the eye, shoulders back, head up.

After a while I'd had enough. Jen tried to convince me to stay, she was on a roll, but I was done. I said goodbye and strutted out, declining interested men on the way. Along the road a car passed by, billowing marijuana smoke. I took a deep breath of it and then scored when the dude flicked half a joint onto the road. The roar of the surf, the balmy night air and every single thing felt like a direct gift from heaven. I went to the hotel and with absolute gluttony, took another shower and discovered that a bidet with good water pressure can be used for more than just washing up.

Jen crawled in around 4:30 am and had to leave to fly home at 6:30, so I was left with this clean, light space all to myself. I slept in, meditated, wrote in my journal, and recharged my batteries with solitude, the absolute height of luxury after 12 days on a boat with two other people. Life is so good when you know how to take care of yourself.

Tension with Troy

Once Jen was gone and I was left alone with Troy, I wasn't sure what to expect. Maybe he was ready to be on his own again, but after my one night out with Jen I was surprised by how welcoming his boat felt. Troy was making dinner, and I sat writing in the warm cabin, soft world music playing in the background. It felt like home and I even started to think maybe I could just stay on with Troy.

In the morning I brought up that idea, suggesting since we got along well in general, maybe I could cruise south with him until he found himself a girlfriend. But that turned out to be the problem.

"I feel like our relationship has developed into friendship," he started, "and maybe we could have some friendly sex."

My insides tightened in a cringe, which I hoped didn't show.

"I am really holding out for a partner," I said gently. "I'm not interested in sex if it doesn't come with love." He was as old as my father…eeeeewwww. Of course a lot of women are attracted to older men, but the thought grossed me out. I suspect this had something to do with my dad, who was charismatic,

Adventures of a Pirate Girl

young-looking and attractive. I was 13 when my parents divorced and soon after that my dad took me to a party in Santa Cruz, at the house of his new girlfriend. It was a great shindig with a diverse crowd of hippies, surfers, Rastas and punk rockers. I would have been totally down, except that I couldn't help feeling awkward—his girlfriend was only five years older than me! Too weird.

When I was 20 and lived with my dad in Key West, we went to an aerobics class together. One time, when he didn't join me, the teacher asked, "Isn't your husband coming today?" Like I said, eeeeewwww!

But Troy was intent on finding a girlfriend...

"Wow, and I thought 34-year-olds are in their sexual prime," he said. "I can't bring home a woman if you're onboard, but if I had my sexual needs met, this wouldn't be an issue."

"Don't you know? Having me with you would actually increase your chances of finding a woman," I countered. "You'd seem more trustworthy with me as your crew." It was a mature conversation—only the tiniest bit awkward—and we came to the conclusion that the time had come to part ways.

The next few days were okay, but with the perspective of hindsight I realized how entrapped I felt. I helped him take *LoneSilver* to the fuel dock to fill up our water tanks and spent one morning doing some small projects on the boat, but I was also putting time into writing my blog and making jewelry. Whatever I was doing, I always stopped to listen politely to his endless stories. Being a listener seemed to be my main function as mate. He only went to shore for an hour here and there and wouldn't let me use the dinghy on my own. We never went to any Happy Hours to meet people. We'd go to shore to use the internet and he would sit right beside me so that talking on Skype or being really candid in an email was impossible. Relying on him for a ride and a place to stay was hard. I wasn't used to being so dependent on someone.

Energetically withdrawing from being his crew, I began to direct my intentions toward my next step. By Christmas Day, I was desperate to get off his boat. It wasn't the most logical time to leave, but the pressure had built between us and I just wanted to get away from it. I spent the morning packing but, by the time I was ready to go a steady rain was falling. We were trapped together and Troy said, "I wasn't going to say anything, but here we are stuck together for one more day, and I like you so I'm just going to say it."

Sint Maarten

"Do, please." I encouraged, mentally preparing to receive whatever it was he needed to get off his chest.

"You're a taker more than a giver."

I sat there and attempted to stay open, slowly nodding, letting the words settle in like water over stones, and make their way into all of my crevices without resisting or reacting to them.

"I'm telling you this as someone who is probably one of the more selfish people. I'm not saying that I'm *not* a taker, but if you're going to be on other people's boats... I mean you did a few hours' work the other day and that was great, and you were great in Beaufort and on the trip. But since we've been here..."

I watched as my ego jumped up to defend the work I had done. I watched as it considered bringing up all the tedious hours of listening and being supportive, like a dutiful wife. I watched as it laughed sarcastically, "Ha, typical! Of course women's work is not even counted." But I kept my mouth shut and nodded.

"You will get everything that you ever want," he added, "if you just help other people get what they want."

Finally, the day after Christmas, I freed myself from the confines of Troy's boat and paid for a bed in the Crew House, which was on the Dutch side of the lagoon. The holidays came complete with a whole troop of ready-made international friends who were in between crew jobs on the ridiculously massive private yachts lining the docks. They all had time to kill and were keen to hang out. But $25 a night for a bed in a crowded hostel was expensive. And what cost me even more was the anxiety of wondering what I was going to do, while watching my meager savings shrink.

Next Move

I began fishing around for my next move. I knew that every morning at 7:30 on the VHF, there was a "cruisers net" on channel 14. I listened in on a friend's boat at the dock. The commentator would start it off with the local weather forecast. Then he'd invite new arrivals to announce themselves and for people heading out to share their plans and say goodbye. There was a segment on safety issues for anyone who had something stolen or who had been harassed, though so far that part had been silent. He quickly moved on to anything anyone had

43

to trade, sell, or give away and then general announcements, which was where I jumped in.

"Good morning, what do you have to announce?"

And on I went with my spiel to sell myself: "I am looking to crew on a boat heading for Panama. I am a licensed Captain, I've sailed 6000 nautical miles, I owned my boat for 10 years and single-handed," and so on.

Another possibility was the ARCH boats, a big group of sailors from Europe who were down in St. Lucia (a few islands south from Sint Maarten), due to leave for Panama in seven days, and then sail on around the world. They sailed in a pack and had a tight itinerary. If I got my ass down-island in time I might be able to get on as crew. But that just seemed too fast and too forced.

I worked on an ad to post around town: "To and through the Panama Canal and beyond," listing all my experience with a cute, but not-too-provocative photo of me sailing.

Another idea was to visit an old sailing friend of mine from Beaufort who had bought a restaurant/bar in the Dominican Republic. I figured I could live there for a while, work in his bar, and concentrate on my writing.

With my intention of letting go and going with the flow, who knew where the winds would take me. A rhumb line is a straight line you draw on your chart to represent your intended course from where you are to your destination. But inevitably, with changing winds and currents, your *actual* course weaves back and forth through it. No one ever sails on a ruler straight line directly to where they're going.

The second time I made an announcement on the cruisers net, I wasn't as clear about my next ports of call. The commentator laughed and made some remarks about how my plans kept changing. I assured him, "My rhumb line's the same. There's more than one way to go around the world."

Graham

I was feeling torn about what I should do and was having a hard time being in a state of limbo. That's when the Universe stepped in. I was hanging out with a Kiwi girl named Rosie, one of the six people in my room at the Crew House. Her boyfriend was working on a week-long charter and she didn't want to spend the holiday alone. Everyone else in our room, though super fun, was younger

Sint Maarten

and into partying all night, often crawling into their beds right before I was getting out of mine. So Rosie and I stuck together.

We had already cooked ourselves a nice light supper in the shared kitchen and then wandered down to the Lagoonies Bar and Restaurant for *one* drink. This establishment, a simple covered bar with tables and seating, was downstairs from the Crew House on the wharf. Lagoonies became the hub of my community.

Instantly, Graham approached us. Graham was a tall and tan Aussie bloke, probably in his mid-60s, with white hair that still had the golden patina of his younger years. He was a social butterfly and befriended us with ease in his heavy Australian accent, "G'deye mite!" his smile big and white.

"I've made a big bowl of pasta alfredo," the woman who ran the bar and restaurant announced. "Anyone who wants to eat, put your hand up."

A fellow Crew House friend from Finland invited Rosie and me to eat with him. We tried to decline, but he had a tribal rule about not offending anyone, and wouldn't let us refuse. With 10 takers, Graham and I decided to make it a group affair and started pushing tables together and putting place settings down. Though I'd been trying to keep to a cleaner diet—cream and pasta not being on it—turning down an opportunity like this seemed like the wrong message to send the Universe. It felt like one big happy family, all of us chatting away, passing around the bowl of delicious pasta. I wanted family in my life.

It turned out Graham was heading to Panama, so I mentioned that that was precisely where I wanted to go. He explained that he was reluctant to take on crew due to his recent experience with an ex-girlfriend, who had demanded he pay for her accommodations and flight home to Brazil when they broke up.

"I understand," I assured him, "and I totally respect that. But, just so you know, I am an experienced traveler and am totally responsible for myself. I would never expect someone to pay for me like that. Besides, she was your girlfriend." The conversation flowed, Graham and I were taking a real liking to each other, and before I knew it he said, "Yeah, I wouldn't have offered if I thought you were like that." He *hadn't* offered, but I wasn't bringing that up.

There was a salsa band playing that night at a beach bar on the other side of the lagoon and so, despite Rosie's and my intention to have only one beverage, we loaded into Graham's dinghy and had a late night of dancing and drinking. And Graham, old enough to be most of these kids' grandfather, was still shaking and twisting and beaming his childlike smile into the wee hours with the rest of us.

Adventures of a Pirate Girl

After we made our way back across the dark lagoon and said our goodbyes to Graham, who had dropped us at the Crew House, I asked everyone, "So what do you all think of him?" They all agreed that he was an absolute gem.

Having a plan in motion was like being a train on a track. Even if I wasn't moving, I knew the direction I was heading. This allowed me to relax and enjoy the festivities without being worried about how much money I was spending or where I was going to live in three days when my prepaid week at the Crew House was up.

Moving onto *Reva Nui*
January 3, 2010

I slowly packed my bag—more manageable now that I'd given away a bunch of stuff—and headed to the bar to await my new Captain. The 48-foot catamaran that Graham and his mate had delivered from South Africa for the absentee owner was anchored a stone's throw from the end of the dock at Lagoonies.

"Bad news," Graham said while landing and tying up the dinghy. "We aren't going to Panama. The owner has changed his mind, yet again. You can still move aboard though. You never know, his plans might change back tomorrow."

The night of New Year's Eve I'd had some deep revelations and I was feeling trusting: the Universe had my back and knew exactly where my path lay, so I didn't let this bit of news faze me.

The boat, *Reva Nui*, was practically new and beautiful. The captain and mate's quarters were in one pontoon, and mine was in the other along with the owner's cabin and a desk. There was a spacious area between the pontoons with a sliding glass door that opened all the way so the inside and outside living areas felt seamless, an airy light-filled space like a floating, high-class apartment.

Even though I might not go anywhere on this boat, I decided to put my all into being good crew, which was easy because I liked Graham so much. Each day I dedicated some time to various jobs: cleaning the owner's cabin, scraping the barnacles off the bottom, some dinghy and outboard maintenance. In exchange, I had a free and luxurious place to live, meals onboard, and the occasional drink

Sint Maarten

and dinner out. Graham was relaxed and easygoing, letting me know his plans for the day so I could coordinate my comings and goings with him without having to be glued together. He always made me feel welcome and appreciated.

Through Graham's efforts, we got hooked up with a day charter, so Graham and I spent an enjoyable (and profitable!) time taking a family around the island. We missed the bridge coming back into the harbor, so returned our guests by dinghy. This turned out to be a blessing because, instead of being anchored in the murky water of the lagoon, I could now start my day swimming to shore in the crystal-clear Caribbean water and go for a jog barefoot in my bikini, down the long white beach. Sometimes Graham would join me.

The owner was planning to show up soon, but we didn't know exactly when. Graham had written to him of my attributes and had gotten his blessing for me to stay onboard while in Sint Maarten, but it sounded like his plans with the boat were erratic. I couldn't stand to wait around to find out where they would end up cruising to, and if I could even join them. Sint Maarten had been a blast, but I didn't want to become one of the regular faces at the bar indefinitely.

And so my search continued, but in a different way. My earlier drive had been replaced by an easy, "I'm exactly where I'm supposed to be," peaceful feeling. I was enjoying each day as it came, knowing that the path I was supposed to take would reveal itself when the time was right.

Teaching the Boys

Early January

One night, at Turtle Pier Bar and Marina, on the other side of the lagoon, I met the boys at a cruisers' get together. As the gathering was clearing out, I approached a table of cute young dudes. The three of them had been sitting there all evening, smoking cigarettes, playing cards and drinking beers. They didn't seem clean enough to be local Dutch boys; their golden skin had a slight dirt layer and their black jeans and tee shirts were dusty and faded. They reminded me of boatyard bums.

"So, you boys on a boat?" I asked, leaning my hipbone on their table.

"Yeah, we live on a boat here at the marina."

I couldn't place their accents. Dennis, who was smaller than the others and had sparkling warm eyes, an olive complexion, wispy longish hair, and a little bit of an Italian emphasis to his words, I guessed was French. Jacob and Johan, the tall, blond, broad-shouldered brothers, I guessed were Dutch. Turns out they were all from Sweden, and their English was so good that I forgot that it wasn't their native language.

They were all in their early 20s and had bought a boat without a clue: boys of my own heart. We ended up hanging out that night. I followed them to the casino to watch them blow their money, while I took advantage of the free drinks. Then we went dancing, and just as I had bragged earlier in the evening, they couldn't keep up with me. They made an effort, though; the two young brothers jumping and whooping around me. But all those cigarettes ruined their stamina and kept forcing their retreat.

Jacob, on the prowl that night, tried to come on to me by asking if I'd ever been with a Swedish guy.

"Yeah," I said, my voice going all dreamy. "It was in southern California. I was 19 and newly single. He was a blond surfer. I was walking down to the water and he was coming up from it and our eyes met. I guess he was in the same fun mood as I was and as our paths came together, we spontaneously embraced in a full-on, swing-around hug. When he found out I was sleeping on the beach, he offered to let me have his bed, saying he would sleep in his car.

"'I wouldn't stay in your bed without you in it,' I answered, so we shared it. We were on the bottom bunk in a crowded hostel room making so much noise getting it on that everyone revolted and kicked us out. Then we spent three awesome nights together, sleeping in his car. On the day I was supposed to leave for Mexico, he came in from surfing and took me into the bathroom. He sat on the toilet seat in his wet shorts and gave me a bath, caressing my naked body all over with his big, soapy hands. It was so hot!"

"You see…," Jacob said, clearly wanting to say something clever and provocative, but he ended up stammering, "…that's, ah, I could, ah, yeah, us Swedish guys."

It was around sunset a week later when I went by their boat, but it seemed dark inside. I called out and then pulled the bow in closer to make the big step across when Dennis popped up.

"Hey sweetie!!!" I cried, clamoring aboard.

Sint Maarten

They were in Sint Maarten to live cheap and do something different, but sailing wasn't their dream. Johan and Jacob were carpenters and looked forward to getting back to work and a regular life. Dennis was more of a free spirit, with plans to buy a motorboat and keep it anchored in the Caribbean. I could see the hint of a sailor in him.

After spending months in Sint Maarten, drinking too much, chasing girls, getting beautifully golden tans, swimming and fishing and hanging out, they had grown slow and lazy. I could feel their depression in the stifling heat of their 37-foot sailboat, where they laid about sweaty and listless. But I had blown into their languid world like a steady, off-shore breeze.

It was just a shell of a boat; they had made small efforts to spruce it up but, without a full refit, it didn't have much hope. They believed their boat was worth $12,000, and they livened right up when speaking of their hopeful plans to sell her and return to Sweden. I hate people who tell me I can't do whatever my current hare-brained scheme is, and there was no way I was going to rain on their parade. So I tried to help. They showed me the ad they had made with two good pictures of the boat, but all it said was: "Toilet and stowe—$16,000," misspelling stove.

"You gotta put more than that," I said.

"It doesn't matter." Dennis was sure, "They will just call and we will show them."

I insisted though, giving them a list of details that they should include. Dennis dug me out a cool-ish Coors Light from the styrofoam cooler and sat in the cockpit with me, smoking his cigarette and listening attentively to my story about meeting Graham, moving aboard the catamaran and how I was trying to stay at peace while in total limbo.

I read them my pirate manifesto and they loved it.

"Read us more," they quipped, reminding me of the times my mom would take away our TV for the summer and read us books: *The Lion, the Witch and the Wardrobe* series and *The Hobbit* series, among others. My three siblings and I would gather around, scratching her back, hungry for the next chapter. I read another piece to them but hesitated after that, not wanting to bore them.

"Read more," Jacob called from the darkness of the v-berth. "It's giving me a hard-on." A great compliment, for sure!

Adventures of a Pirate Girl

"I love this, you guys. If I had a dinghy with an engine, I would come every night and read you bedtime stories. You're like my little Lost Boys."

I'd intended to stay up and be social with Dennis and his friend Ramone, who was meant to come around, but was feeling tired so I crawled up in the v-berth between Jacob and Johan and fell asleep, happily cuddled between these gorgeous young guys.

～

In the morning I snuck out and went up to the restaurant to have a coffee and write. Dennis came up and invited me back to the boat to smoke some pot. He told me of their plan to go fishing with Ramone, who was supposed to come back with his car. But, in the meantime, Dennis was getting hungry.

Jacob said, "Well, I guess we'll have to catch some fish because we can't afford to eat at the restaurant." They'd bought a whole set of new pans so they could stop eating out, but they were sick of ramen noodles and didn't know how to cook anything else.

"Okay, you guys, I'll make some food. You catch some fish to go with it. Where's the closest store?"

"It's too far. We should just wait for Ramone."

"I'm gonna go, you guys set up the plan with Ramone."

"Get me some raisin bread and Philadelphia cream cheese," Dennis requested, digging into his wallet and handing me $10.

"No, I'm gonna do the food."

"Yeah, don't get him that," the quietly stoic Johan jumped in. "He eats that every day."

"I just eat meat. I don't like salad," Dennis was getting nervous.

"Well, I guess you'll have to catch some fish, then." I said, emptying my pack for the 15-minute walk to the store. After the brisk exercise, the cool shop was refreshing as I looked around for what was cheap and colorful. I like to represent the rainbow with what I cook. I made sure to buy enough to fill four hungry boys and me, which all came to $19; the taxi back was $1. Perfect.

Ramone hadn't called and we couldn't go fishing without him because not only was he the ride, but he had all the gear.

Sint Maarten

"Well, I'm not making food in here," I declared. It was oppressively hot inside the cabin of their boat. "If you guys want to eat, you have to get off the boat."

I grabbed a knife and a brand new pot to mix stuff in and set up shop on the abandoned plywood bar on the dock.

There was a family I'd met before who lived on a 60-foot racing sailboat at the T-end of that same pier. I walked down and explained to Doreen that the boys, who she also mothered from time to time, didn't know how to eat cheap.

"Yeah, all they eat is bread," remarked Alan, who was sitting in the cockpit sorting out rigging hardware.

"So I'm giving them a cooking lesson."

Doreen lent us dishes and silverware and we began. I put Jacob to work opening cans while Dennis was marveling at all the things I'd bought: avocados, four cans of butterbeans, two cans of stewed tomatoes with balsamic flavor, black olives, garlic, onion, some limes and a few French baguettes, wondering how on earth it was all going to go together.

"How are you gonna cook it?" the teenage kid whose parents owned the marina wondered.

"We're not," I answered.

Johan began rinsing off dishes, and I set Dennis to work chopping.

Doreen came out with her camera and started snapping pictures, laughing at Davina's cooking class. Jacob and Johan were getting excited, amazed at how much food I had bought for $20, while Dennis was still unsure. I mixed it all together, explaining to my pupils about the importance of a good range of colors and how salt and lime and garlic make everything good.

Then we sat in a circle in the shade on the dock, the big bowl in the middle, and dug in.

"This is how we used to always eat while traveling," I remembered happily. "If you're going to travel, you've got to learn to eat cheap. Restaurants will kill ya."

They were stoked, eating with the gusto of starving boys, moaning and making luscious sexual sounds. It *was* fucking good. The kid, who Dennis warned me was a little crazy, was sitting up on the dirty bar watching us, so I handed him a bowl. They all had seconds and ate almost half a loaf of bread each, then laid back in the sun to relax. I took the rest of the pot, which still had a lot left, to Doreen to feed her crew, happy to get a chance to repay her for an earlier kindness.

They were just boys. Somebody had to teach them.

Giver

One Sunday morning, I showed up at the Lagoonies dock empty-handed after a night on shore; my money and computer were on *Reva Nui* and I had no way back. I met another three guys. They were Norwegian, in their early 30s and had bought a boat with the intention of sailing around the Caribbean for one year before sailing back to Norway to sell her. I told them of my predicament, so they invited me along for a trip in their dinghy. We spent a lovely day on the beach and later, back at their boat, we all cooked a colorful meal and shared it sitting around the table in the cockpit, all of us expressing our gratitude for such a wonderful day and such great company.

Christian was a beautiful, tall blond with a deep, caramel tan and an enticing smile. He was a psychologist back at home: intelligent, with a calm, laid-back energy that I found super attractive. While we talked, I could feel myself inching in closer, wanting to press up against him. Bjornar had brown hair, a compact, muscular body, and a sharp mind. And Karl, blond with a dark goatee and a chubby belly, had building and electrical skills and had been doing most of the work to their boat before they set off. He had a strong Nordic accent and a hilarious sense of humor. One day I invited the three of them to dance the following night. Karl said, "Oh, I can't tomorrow, I have to work."

I said, "I'm not talking about dancing during the day, we'll dance at night."

He said, "Why can't we dance in the day? What's wrong with that?"

I said, "We can't dance during the day because you have to work."

He said, "If you want to dance in the day, I'll quit my job."

There was a live salsa band at La Bamba bar on the beach on Tuesday night. We all went together along with Elle, the wonderful Italian/Egyptian woman with a head full of corkscrew curls, who ran the Lagoonies bar. I took turns dancing with each of the guys who I'd assumed, being from the icy north, would be stiff and uncoordinated. But I was thrilled to discover that every one of them was hot-blooded on the dance floor.

Sint Maarten

Later they were all hanging out on lawn chairs on the beach beside the stage, and I was over by the bar looking for someone to dance with who could help me show off my salsa moves. Someone prodded me and said, "Dance with him, he's a great dancer," pointing to a middle-aged black guy. I could tell he had been good looking, with a tall, straight back, wide shoulders and thin hips; but life had been hard and he bore the evidence in the lines pulling down the corners of his full lips and across his dark brow. He had made an effort to look nice in a suit jacket, button-up shirt and slacks, but they were made of cheap, wrinkled polyester, and his shirt was yellowed around the collar. He held out his big, rough hands for me and, even though he was wearing worn-out work boots, he led me around the dance floor with the rhythm and pizzazz of a true dancer. I felt classy and proud and was thankful for the dance.

He came over to the lawn chairs to chat afterward, explaining to Karl that it was his 52nd birthday, and he hadn't been with a woman—or even kissed one—in 10 years.

"Ten years?!!" I asked, "And it's your birthday?!!" I saw in his eyes an honest, hardworking man.

"I'll give you a kiss for your birthday," I said and took his hands. I leaned in and softly pressed my lips to his big, warm ones. I let myself sink into him for a few seconds and then pulled away, giving him another peck to end it.

He was mesmerized and said something about how he had to go to work, but he wanted to take me with him.

"That's not gonna happen, honey," I said with just enough force, and sat down on the lawn chair at the feet of Bjornar and Elle to emphasize that I was with my friends.

I asked him about not having been with a woman for so long, and he said, "I love too hard. It hurts too much."

"I know. I do too. But love is what there is. You have to do it anyway, even if it's going to hurt."

He told me about his daughters and his heartache and how he loved to sing. He took out a piece of paper and read the lyrics to a song he had written. I looked around to get the others to listen but realized they were engaged in other conversations and this was our moment. So I leaned in and focused on listening. It was interesting, but after a while my attention waned. When he got up, I gave him a hug goodbye, "It was really nice meeting you," I said. And, "Take care of yourself," while nudging him in the right direction.

Christian ran off to find us a joint and returned with his prize. The band had finished and Elle brought back a tray of drinks, more than one for each of us, before the bar closed.

"Oh Elle, you shouldn't have," I protested, thinking of the cost. I was always conscious of who paid for what. Growing up, most of my childhood friends lived in bigger houses and had more toys and better clothes than I did. This often left me feeling that I didn't contribute enough or I wasn't equal. Christian pointed out that I worried too much about these things.

All of the other people had left. Bjornar and Elle were wrapped up in each other on their chair, and I sat between Christian and Karl.

I had been thinking about what Troy had said about the giver and the taker. It had been on my mind but I had never mentioned any of this to these guys.

Now Karl said, "I have a gift for you Davina," getting my attention. "I have an important gift for you," taking my hand in his. I could tell this was big and I was feeling close, so I grabbed Christian's hand, too. "This thing I'm going to tell you, it is a very important gift… It is very important for you." I squeezed both of their hands, feeling like I was touching two hot wires, the electricity coursing through me.

"You are a giver, Davina. You are a giver."

Christian nodded in agreement, "I see you, Davina."

News Bulletin

January 12, 2010

EHHHHHHHH EHHHHHHHH EHHHHHHH

"We're interrupting your current story for an important announcement. A catastrophic earthquake, 7.0 magnitude, has just hit Port-au-Prince, Haiti. Deaths are estimated upward of 300,000 people."

Haiti was only a little way up the island chain from where I was, in the same part of the world as Sint Maarten. Earlier that day I'd heard the news, so when my taxi driver turned out to be Haitian, I asked him about his family and as soon as I did, his story poured out: He was terrified for his people, he couldn't get through by phone to find out if they were okay, he had no idea if they were even alive. Hearing the pain and fear in his voice, I wanted to say: "I can go there, I can find them for you." But, given how uncertain my path was, all I could do was put my hand on his shoulder, listen deeply and tell him how sorry I was.

And again, in September of 2017, while I was writing this book, the Caribbean was smashed by a string of hurricanes. Sint Maarten and Dominica, two places where I had spent time, were particularly hard hit.

We humans are putting increasing pressure on our Mother Earth and she is rightfully getting annoyed. True, more and more of us are becoming painfully aware of the environmental crisis and its pending doom. And those of us who have the luxury of living above survival mode are doing our best to change our ways: buying organic food, recycling, carrying reusable drink bottles, riding our bikes, buying electric vehicles. But, alas, the gigantic world-eating machine grinds on, decimating precious forests and seabeds and dumping toxic waste into our food systems, waterways and our bodies as if there were no tomorrow. It's polluting our airwaves, fracking our mountains, drilling our oceans, as if money was more important that life. And we're supposed to stop using plastic straws, write to our legislators, sign some petitions and hope for the best!?

We're fucked.

Or so it seems.

This is where pirates step in.

Now, you may think of pirates as vicious and violent thieves; the traditional narrative paints them that way. And, of course, there were psychopaths among them. But in some ways the golden age of piracy was a social justice movement, disrupting the economic system that held poor people down. This is the same system that has us marching toward our doom as we speak.

The early 1700s were a dangerous time. Kings and queens held absolute power and the slave trade was the backbone of the European economy. Pirates used violent means to disrupt the economy by robbing merchant ships, including slave ships. Approximately one-third of pirates during that era were Africans. Upon seizing a slaver, some pirates offered these traumatized people a choice: join us as free individuals or take your chances on land.

We've come a long way since those days because we've fought hard for our rights. But the underlying story hasn't changed. The structure of society is still stacked against us. It's a pyramid, with most of us and our planet on the bottom. Up at the top is big money controlled by the 1% of humans who manipulate the world's governments, media, money systems and our natural resources.

We are still indentured servants to a money system that demands constant growth in order to cover the interest it's based upon. A money system that rewards the rich and forces the rest of us—through fear—to run like rats on the incessantly spinning wheels of consumerism. Out of desperation, most of us choose to work in jobs we don't love so we can earn a living instead of protecting the environment.

Meanwhile we're fed this narrative about free markets: that it is up to us consumers to put our money where our beliefs are and change the world through our buying power. This despite the fact that some of our most destructive industries (fossil fuels, industrial agriculture, commercial fishing) are federally subsidized. New, innovative solutions are often shut down by those who control these industries because their profits are threatened. If that weren't true, Nikola Tesla's free energy would be powering our houses and we'd be driving cars that run on water by now. We have the ability to solve all of our environmental problems, but how do we make that happen when there's no financial incentive for the 1%?

The 1% are not the bad guys; our money system is. As long as we have to pay the Federal Reserve or the central banks to create money out of nothing, then pay interest to borrow that money, our economic system has to continually grow to cover those costs and we will continue to convert our natural world, along with our cultural and social commons, into money. This is undermining the health of our planet. Our Mother. Our home.

We need a new money system where all of the unseen ecological and social costs are included in the price of things, so the more a product or service causes harm, the more expensive it is. We need a money system that discourages hoarding, that enables us to connect and cooperate, that uplifts everyone while holding the natural world sacred.

Earth can't handle our lifestyle anymore and our lifestyle doesn't make us happy anyway. Just as children stop physically growing when they reach adolescence, it is time to stop the economic growth paradigm and step into our adulthood as a species. We need to move from our childish relationship with

Mother Earth—one of only taking—to a co-creative adult relationship where we also give back.

No wonder she's upset.

I'm not calling for a return of the violence of the historical pirates who sabotaged merchant ships. I'm calling for the new pirates: rebels, revolutionaries and rogues who stand up for what is right, even when that means breaking the law or going against mainstream culture, tradition or the prevailing narrative. The people who, despite the fear we are constantly bombarded with, manage to keep their own minds free.

Drained Battery

End of January

Most cruising boats have both solar panels and wind generators to produce electricity, which is stored in big batteries. But nowadays, with computers to charge, the fridge to run, water to make, and a water heater for hot showers, the charging system often can't keep up with the load. That's exactly what was happening to me.

I was draining my batteries in Sint Maarten. My flirtatious ways, drinking and staying out late, were too much of a load and my charging system wasn't keeping up. My lack of a steady routine or any private space made it hard to maintain the exercise, meditation and healthy eating I needed to stay happy. My batteries weren't getting a full charge and I began to rely more and more on the attention from guys, along with alcohol and caffeine for fuel.

The Lagoonies bar had become my living room. I'd sit there with my computer and try to write, but it was getting harder and harder to accomplish anything with all the distractions. In fact, I'd started to feel like that about the island in general. It was time to go, and I reinvigorated my search for a boat.

I'd posted my info on two crew-finder sites, though I had stopped putting much effort into keeping up with them because the flood of responses from 60-year-old men looking for girlfriends made me feel like I had joined a dating site for seniors.

One day, when I strolled into Lagoonies, Elle (the manager, who was acting as my secretary), gave me a message, "JP says he'll meet you here at 2:00."

I had just engaged a girl at the bar to help me clean out my computer. She was sitting with her young shipmates and a much older guy, Anthony, who was obviously the Captain. We were busy with this task when JP showed up. I was pleasantly surprised to see that he was young, probably around 30, of smallish stature with olive skin, an unshaven face, shoulder-length brown hair, and a tidy white polo shirt. He was French, though I wouldn't have guessed it by his accent. Turned out he was born of German parents in Sierra Leone and grew up in Costa Rica.

"I don't usually take crew," he told me, "because I don't trust people with my boat. They will say that they have so much experience, but it usually turns out they don't know what they're doing, and they end up being totally useless on the boat." He came off as cocky, especially since he'd only been sailing for six months.

But I could be cocky too: "I'm not going to try and prove myself to you. I've been sailing for 10 years and have plenty of experience," I informed him with a quick smile. I gave him a half-interested run-down of my skills and accomplishments while simultaneously learning how to clean up unwanted files on my computer. Then I played him the slide show of rebuilding my boat on my MySpace page.

He, in turn, impressed me with his own adventures. He may not have been a sailor for long, but he was a world traveler. He had driven a Land Rover all over Africa and Australia and was planning to sail around the world. It was appealing that he was so young. Also he told me he wasn't a heavy drinker. He admitted to only an occasional beer or wine, not typical of most sailors.

We ended up going to a party together—put on for all the out-of-work kids looking for crew jobs—for the free food. JP left early but said he'd be around for two weeks, so we had time to discuss it further.

When I showed up at the bar the next day, Elle handed me two slips of paper with boat names and emails of people looking for me. One of them, who had answered my ad on a crew website, came up to me at the bar. He was an American with white hair and a beard and immediately rubbed me wrong. "You said you were the cream of the crop," he smiled, eyeing me up and down as if he hadn't eaten for awhile and I was a tenderloin. "I wanted to know what that looked like."

Sint Maarten

"Yeah, well, I had to write something to catch people's eyes," I said coolly. He asked if I wanted a drink, and then complained that my red wine was more expensive than a beer.

"I'll get it," I answered, "I can't keep my figure…," I said, as I swept my hand past my tanned midriff, "if I drink too much beer." This he understood and paid for my drink.

He sat there dumbly for a bit, then asked bluntly, "Are you really serious about going sailing?"

"Yes, I am," I said, turning toward him, "but not with you." I smiled sweetly with a tilt of my head and a shrug of my shoulders. He sat there baffled for a second, but I turned back to my computer and he drifted away. One thing I'd learned while traveling in the precarious way I did, was that you always follow your gut.

Happy hour was just getting started, and the Norwegian guys bought a red wine for me and sat at my bench. I saw Elle directing a guy toward me and knew this must be the other guy who'd answered my ad. Donald was a big, middle-aged American with shorn gray hair and sweaty, tanned skin. He wore dainty reading glasses and bright orange Crocs. He came up to me, and I stood to shake his hand.

"You heading for Panama?" he asked. "I have very little experience. I wouldn't even consider taking on crew because I wouldn't want to be responsible for anyone's life, but because you are so experienced, I think I could learn a lot from you." I appreciated his humility and upfront attitude, though after a few stories the "I haven't talked to anyone in ages" vibe leaked through and I got itchy to mingle. I called Graham over and introduced them, then bounced away to flirt with my friend who ran the marina.

By the time I came back and made a slow migration around the crowded bar, Graham was still with Donald, who, again, was in the middle of a monologue. When Graham and I piled into our dinghy later, I apologized for leaving him, "I figured you would get away." But Graham had spent the time singing my praises.

Donald had suggested that I could come out to his boat the next day to help him with some projects as a way of our getting to know each other.

"I will compensate you, of course," he assured me. "Just come up with a price for a day's work and email it to me."

"Deal."

It was 4 am when I crawled into my luxurious bed on the catamaran that night, and 9 am when I awoke and called Donald. Graham dropped me off at the bar, and I apologized for being slightly hung over and sleep deprived. But the work Donald had in mind for me wasn't demanding and started with a leisurely breakfast. Then, after a lengthy dinghy ride over to the French side of the island (which I had barely seen since we'd first checked in), we shopped for lunch.

Donald had escaped his life. His beloved father and mother had died, and he had been there to nurse them and ease their passing: his dad first, and his mom a year later. Then he had packed all his worldly possessions into his 45-foot Morgan, *Annah Foster* (named after both his parents), and untied the dock lines. Without much knowledge or experience, he had headed offshore for 10 days. He had been tested in every way: bad weather, a lost rudder, and at one point he'd completely let go and surrendered to the Creator. Facing himself and the unknown took real courage, and I admired him for that.

When I saw his boat, the story came to life. It was as if he had taken his house full of possessions, tipped it on its side and dumped it directly into *Annah Foster*. There wasn't even room to sit down.

We took the davits off the stern and mounted the 15-horsepower outboard on the inflatable to take it to a mechanic. But mostly we swam and lunched, and I listened. Over the next few days, I helped him clean and organize, though he wasn't willing to get rid of as much as I suggested; I stopped being so hard on his packrat ways once I realized that my main job was to be good company. He even joked one day about how this was the lowest level of prostitution: me being paid as a companion.

"Maybe the highest," I said with a wink and a smile.

I had no interest in crewing if my main job was to listen to someone's endless commentary. Plus there was literally no room for me; the guest cabin was still packed full of stuff. But Donald was a sweet guy, and working for him was a blessing. For one I was making an easy $70 a day, the amount I had suggested by email, and for two it was a welcome distraction from the crazy week I had had, my flirtations finally coming to a head.

The night before my first day of "work" was salsa night at La Bamba Beach Bar, and my Norwegian friends joined me. It was a late night, which ended with me kissing Christian, stripping down on the beach and following his lead into

Sint Maarten

the water. He was someone I could really fall for, but he made it clear that he wasn't interested in being anything more than friends. I had also let it slip that I would love to go sailing with him and his friends. I knew it wasn't logical or possible but still, rejection always stings.

Knowing that I didn't want to show up at Christian's boat again, after work the next night I had Donald take me to the Turtle Pier where my little Swedish Lost Boys kept their boat. I figured they'd help get my mind off Christian. It turned out to be their last night in town. They had invited me to their going-away party online, but I hadn't been checking email.

We all knew which way that night was heading since we'd been flirting around the possibility for weeks. The build-up was exciting. My little boys were chasing a high and it was their party, so I had a tequila shot, drank some beers and even did a line of coke, which I hadn't done in years. I made sure to balance the alcohol with water and urged them to do the same, but they were going hard like 20-year-olds are wont to do. I shared with them the fantasy I was developing: me whipping them and their boat into shape and all of us cruising the Caribbean, bare-bones and fancy-free.

"I don't know about you being the Captain," Dennis worried out loud.

"Of course she would be," said Jacob.

By the time we made it back to the boat, Dennis was puking in the bushes; he and Johan were both wasted. But Jacob and I had been full-on flirting all night, and I couldn't let it go; I was hot and bothered.

"Come on, Jacob, you said you could keep up with me," I whispered, holding his arm back from climbing into his bunk. Jacob obliged out of the kindness of his heart and the hardness of his cock. He was surprisingly skilled for such a young guy, someone had taught him well. In the morning he offered to buy me breakfast at the restaurant—though in all fairness it should have been *me* buying *him* breakfast—then gave me a big, warm, heartfelt hug goodbye.

After sleeping the whole next day, I felt like death. Going fast was addictive, and I got stuck in a cycle of fueling up on social stimulation, drink and caffeine, which left me more drained. I needed solitude to recharge my battery. I wanted to lean on someone, to let their love heal me. Jacob, after our night together, came to mind, but that wasn't love. In my journal, I wrote, "I keep looking for love and attention on shore, but what I really need is love and attention from myself."

The next morning, I had Graham drop me off on JP's boat, the young French Captain who potentially might take me on as crew, an hour before I was to meet Donald for work.

"Morning," I called to JP, as Graham slowed the engine and we drifted toward his vessel. He popped his head up and invited me onboard. He was just in the middle of adjusting his battery charger. We had gotten a chance to talk more in the past few days and the prospect of sailing with him was becoming more attractive, especially when I saw his immaculate boat. It was a classic monohull built in Taiwan, just like mine had been. It was raining so he ushered me below and asked me to help him with a chore. He obviously cared for his boat with the precision of a surgeon: The brightwork of the warm, wooden interior was flawless and not a thing was out of place, even though my visit was unexpected.

JP was in the middle of sorting out an electrical fault with the float switch in his bilge, his tools all lined up neatly on a cloth as if for an operation. This was my chance to convince him of how invaluable I could be—after all, I *had* wired my whole boat, twice—but my solid skill set and winning attributes were all gummed up by the slow gooey mess of my brain after a night of partying. It was a relief when Donald came by to pick me up for our casual day of work.

That night I was stranded at Lagoonies with no boat to go home to. Graham and his mate had taken the catamaran to Phillipsburg, and it was too late to take a bus to meet them there. The last place I wanted to be was at the bar, but people kept handing me glasses of wine and I proceeded to get trashed and then to cry. I ended up sharing a bed with a friend from the Crew House, and though it was totally unnecessary, pointless and unsatisfying, I had sex with him in the shared room of the hostel. Another late, exhausting night. The next day I wanted to hide from the world. What was I doing? Self-destructing, apparently. Time to leave.

As I was slinking out of the Dock House (not proud of my performance the night before), I bumped into the girl who had helped me clean out my computer, who was lugging her bag up the steps.

"I've cleared off the boat I've been on," she informed me. By then I had chatted with Anthony, the Captain, at the bar a few times. He seemed like a reasonable guy. So I asked her what he was like, and with a disdainful look she said, "I'm sick of traveling with old guys. I feel like he was always watching me, and the boat was a mess." Her words weighed me down like lead; I was utterly depleted.

Sint Maarten

That evening after working with Donald, I had him drop me off at JP's boat. He told me his dad was visiting for two weeks, and he wasn't sure he wanted to take me on anyway. Fuck.

Even though it was raining the next day, I was determined to find a boat. I checked with a guy I'd met on the internet, but he was down-island somewhere and wanted to charge per day. There was only one option left. I ran down the dock to Anthony's boat: my last card. I laid it out on the table. "When are you planning on leaving, and where are you going?" I asked, as Anthony made me a coffee.

He laid out his hand, "I'm leaving this Thursday, and I'm headed down-island and then across to Panama." Bingo!

"Anthony, take me away!"

CHAPTER 5
Shayela

Sint Maarten to Antigua
January 29, 2010

Imagine winning the trip of a lifetime: a cruise down a tropical island chain, complete with warm breezes, hot sun, and clear radiant water. The catch: It's just you and someone 30-plus-years your senior, in whom you have no romantic interest. Your 60-day trip includes staying at lush mountainous isles laced with rivers and waterfalls and visits to quaint fishing villages. Every night you share a private dinner complete with wine. The relationship might not be sexual, but it is a partnership in every other way, and enjoying each other's company is crucial.

Anthony and I had three days to get to know each other before we set sail. While buying beans and avocados, we made a commitment to travel together until Panama: a trip of two months and 1200 nautical miles. It was a decision I made based on intuition and faith. The Universe had put me in front of his door and the key fit.

Between wheeling loads of cans from the grocery store and practicing planing on his brand new dinghy with the 9.8 horsepower outboard motor, we sat over coffee and talked. He wasn't desperate for company or seeping with endless stories. He was easygoing, intelligent and genuinely interested in what I had to say. We agreed on our need to escape the incessant party of Sint Maarten; we'd both had enough. But the wind had other plans, with gusts up to 35 knots and a huge north swell. The day after our going-away party we stayed put. I had been saying goodbye for a week by then and I didn't want to show my face in Lagoonies Bar again, so Anthony and I had coffee on the French side and spent the rest of the day on the boat.

Shayela

The day we left the winds were still strong and the swell had not subsided, but enough was enough. Anthony secured the anchor while I steered *Shayela* to the bridge, threaded us through the narrow passage between megayachts, and we were free. Instantly the water turned from mucky brown to the clear azure of every Caribbean postcard you've ever seen. As Sint Maarten shrank behind us, we rejoiced in the sun. The stress we'd accumulated on land like caked-on grime was swept away in the ocean breeze and we lay back to enjoy our escape.

Shayela had a mainsail that rolled up inside the mast, though this particular model of roller furling turned out to be more trouble than it was worth. We could get it to unroll and roll in only on a port tack so we had to change directions to set sail. *Shayela* also had a cutter rig that required us to roll up the Genoa when we tacked to get it in and around the inner forward stay. If you don't know what I'm talking about, trust me when I say the rig was a pain in the ass.

The wind was from the east but with some south in it, the direction we were heading, and still blowing 20+ knots. The swell was right on our nose. Our rejoicing quickly deteriorated into annoyance as the heavy *Shayela* struggled to plow into the wind, stopping dead with each swell. We had 90 miles to go. I sat my four-hour night watch in darkness because I had forgotten to buy a headlamp so I could read. She was bucking like a see saw and making only 2.5 knots (frickin slow!). It took us 32 hours, but we finally, cautiously motored into Antigua's Falmouth Harbor in the dark and dropped anchor. We were on our way.

Antigua was commandeered by England in the early 1700s because of its two secure and easily defensible harbors: English and Falmouth. The ruins of the stone dockyard and fort were restored in 1947 and maintained by the park service, which helped to make Antigua one of the big yachting capitals and tourist destinations of the Caribbean. They host a variety of sail races and, like Sint Maarten, attract opulent private motor yachts and 200-foot sailboats, the kind with towering masts lit up like carnival rides and crew scurrying like ants over the decks, polishing the already blinding shine of teak and stainless steel.

Anthony had already been to Antiqua and the plan was to keep moving south. But one of the major lessons in sailing is that we can't control everything; the weather or other unforeseen circumstances always have the final say. After the whirlwind of Sint Maarten, the Universe seemed to deliberately put the brakes on.

A bug bite on the crease where my butt met my thigh did the trick. The day after arriving in Antigua it developed into a bulging red button that made sitting uncomfortable. By the following day I was miserable: The bite was throbbing and I hadn't slept most of the night.

It's not any man who I would let crouch down behind me and mess with my bum; this emergency was a test of our compatibility. Thank Goddess I felt comfortable with him, because it was time to pop this thing and Anthony was the man to do it.

While I lay on my belly, Anthony—with hands washed and reading glasses perched on his nose—squatted down behind me and poked it half an inch deep with a needle. Squeezing it was torture and didn't bring out much of the pus. Then we had the brilliant idea of using the wine bottle sealer to suck it out. The moment he pulled the handle that applied the suction, I cried out in agony; it became clear that suction wasn't the answer. Anthony went to shore that night and came back with good news: There was a doctor who made visits to a nearby beauty salon and she would be there in the morning.

Dr. Petra Nanton got right to work poking and prodding. She was efficient and friendly, and prescribed antibiotics. I had meant to ask how much this was going to cost before she did anything, but decided that whatever the cost, it was gonna be worth it. When she was done, she remarked that she liked my earrings and I said, "Oh, good! I make them and I'll bring you a pair."

"Did you make your necklace, too?" I was wearing my favorite: a purple cowry shell flanked by two shark's teeth. She suggested that, if I made one for her nephew, the next visit would be free. That's my kind of doctor!

Anthony wanted to get to Panama by late March to have plenty of time to enjoy the typhoon-free season in the Pacific. He took me out to a lovely dinner on shore (me sitting cockeyed on the bench) and we talked about the trip.

"I won't leave you," he said, "however long this thing takes to heal."

I protested that he couldn't miss his window of opportunity in the Pacific, but his chivalrous declaration was comforting. When I suggested that I would go back to the States if the awful boil didn't go away, he asked, "Well, what good would that do you? It's not like you have free medical care in the States." He was already planning on returning home to Jersey, a small island between England and France, for 10 days to see his first grandchild.

"If this doesn't go away," he continued, "I'll just bring you home with me and they'll treat you for free."

Shayela

But I knew it would heal. This was my body's protest for the wild life I had been living, but now the Universe had stepped in and forced me to curb my drinking because of the antibiotics. This became easier when Anthony announced that, for the past 20 years, February had been his annual dry month. I settled into this quieter life: I did a bunch of writing, realized my need for space and had a day ashore alone, went on a five-mile run, hiked up to Shirley Heights (an old English fort overlooking the harbor), and generally took better care of myself. I padded my meager funds by selling some of my jewelry at a local craft store. Anthony and I even saw an acrobatic show put on by a French couple, who gracefully climbed and twirled in their sailboat's rigging, collecting tips to fund their own trip around the world.

Anthony had shown himself to be a gentleman. He took care of me when I needed him to and respected my need for space. We took turns cooking and washing up. He appreciated my sailing skills and let me know it. If this was a test, we had passed. The bite healed and off we went, south to Guadeloupe.

The Good Life

Guadeloupe
February 10, 2010

Our first Guadeloupe anchorage, Deshaies (pronounced DeHays), was a quaint town transplanted from the French countryside, nestled within a bay, with no megayachts or even a marina. A small white steeple was its highest point. An industrious, bleary-eyed blond guy immediately approached and wanted to take our order for bread that he would deliver in the morning. I put in our order: a *pan au chocolat* for Anthony and a baguette for me, but after that my budding French quickly wilted and died. Ah... fresh French bread: something I could live for.

We walked around the town once, checked in with the authorities, and went to the ATM; then it was back to the boat. The nine days of antibiotics were almost over, and red wine was just what I needed to wash down all that bread and the growing sense of boredom.

The next anchorage in Guadeloupe was windy and unprotected, not somewhere safe to leave the boat, so we had a full day to stare at the shore. I ate a whole bag of popcorn and then, while Anthony was asleep, I quietly stuffed in two bowls of cereal covered in sugar. Then I pretended I was hungry for dinner and had a huge bowl of buttery, cheesy pasta.

Les Saintes was next: tiny islands with the sweetest little town. If it hadn't been for the turquoise water, I would have thought we were in the middle of France. The first day there I gave up any semblance of health or self-care. I had a beer with Anthony—whose dry month hadn't lasted a month—at midday and just kept 'em coming. I was bored, and I made a real effort to drown that feeling with alcohol and food. They might not bring lasting happiness, but momentary happiness seemed better than nothing.

I'd been listening to CDs to learn French, but I found myself shy onshore. I went off on my own to try to sell my jewelry to shops but, just as I began my mission, they began to close for the three-hour break during the heat of the day. They all seemed filled with cheap African imports anyway. My shoulders sagged and my head bowed, I wandered around for about the time it would have taken me to actually talk to a few shop owners. Then I met Anthony for another beer.

Next morning I got myself up, dressed and to shore by 7:30 for a run. That was the best I'd felt for a while, body moving, heart pumping, checking out the island at a clip. But for the first time in years, my thighs rubbed a painful red raspberry where they touched. Fuck. I walked out onto the long floating dock after my jog at the same time as two blond guys I'd seen on a boat in the past few anchorages. We chatted a bit and they told me they were also crewing for the owner.

"Have fun!" I said, as I untied the dinghy.

One of them replied, in a sarcastic voice, "Yeah, like drinking too much and not having anything to do is a lot of frickin' fun."

That made me laugh. We were moving down the Caribbean chain from anchorage to anchorage so fast now, there was little opportunity to connect with anyone or do any exploring, and it was reassuring to know I wasn't the only one struggling to stay happy while cruising in paradise.

That afternoon, as Anthony and I had a drink in the cockpit, a bright yellow steel boat, rough with rusty patches staining the crevices, motored close behind us, searching for a place to drop their hook. Those days it seemed like every cruising boat was a minimum of 40 feet long, with gadgets and technical contrivances galore, shiny paint, extensive canvas awnings and sailors in their later years.

This simple little, brightly colored boat being run by half-naked young people grabbed my attention instantly.

Anthony went below to have a "kip" and I contemplated grabbing my boredom by the back of its neck and forcibly holding its head in a glass of wine until its legs stopped kicking. It was either that or go say hello to the couple on the yellow boat.

It was the first time I'd taken the dinghy without discussing it with Anthony, but I was desperate and he was sleeping, so I left a note. They were in their cockpit when I motored over, circling around their stern. I maneuvered up to the side and immediately began talking, out of practice with my social skills, and then realized: "Oh, do you speak English?"

"Yes," they both laughed. "We're from England," and they invited me aboard for a beer. Maybe in their late 20s, they'd been working in England and flying back to the Caribbean to sail, but were now on their way to Sint Maarten to look for work and try to make a living without having to fly home. I was so eager to talk to people I could relate to, I forgot to give them any useful information about clearing in or anchoring in Sint Maarten.

The good life was killing me.

Dominica

Portsmouth, Dominica
February 12, 2010

We had both been looking forward to Dominica. Anthony was planning on staying a few days to check out some of the affordable properties that were advertised in a *Caribbean Homes* magazine. And Carnival was happening!

Sailors may travel the world but, it was starting to occur to me, they tended to be more homebodies than travelers. They'd drop hook in a new port, go to shore to dump trash, buy groceries and check the internet, perhaps have a beer on land before retiring to their private floating abode.

I was a sailor. But before I bought my boat I was a traveler. And now that I no longer had the burden of my own vessel, I was back to my traveling ways. Dominica was my big chance!

A sovereign island nation, Dominica missed the tourist boom and was now attempting to develop ecotourism. With 365 rivers and high lush mountains covered in rainforest, it was an undiscovered paradise. We were still a few miles away from Portsmouth when a guy approached us in a bright yellow, wooden skiff with a pointy bow. He introduced himself as Alexis, a professional river guide, and easily convinced us to go on a tour with him.

The main feature in the wide bay where we anchored was a mammoth, abandoned cargo ship that had apparently run aground years before; it acted as a breakwater at the mouth of the river. We brought our dinghy in around it, as instructed, and tied up to the little dock where all the colorful, wooden, river tour boats were tied. Immediately the guys hanging around started trying to sell us a tour, but our guide hurried us into his boat.

The green, jungly river was protected from outboards and fishing, so Alexis rowed us, pointing out the useful plants, some birds and an iguana along the way. He led us into his brother's plantation and demonstrated Dominica's fertile abundance by plucking fruits right off the trees. We sampled the sweetest grapefruit I'd ever had. Passion fruit vines hanging with shiny round orbs, not yet ripe and wrinkled, were growing everywhere. I found a banana that hadn't been ravished by the birds like the rest of its bunch. We sipped the refreshing milk of a coconut, sucked the sweet white goo off cacao seeds, munched on some sugar cane, ate a sweet and crisp star fruit, and smelled the bark of a cinnamon tree. All that—and there was plenty more growing. Alexis was a professional: He left us both wanting to see more, but the trip didn't satisfy the kind of social connection I was looking for.

Back at our anchored boat, a few other guys came out: One sold us juicy ripe mangos and passion fruit. I'd never tasted passion fruit before; the tangy sweet gelatin-like fruit was so delicious I was hooked!

Another guy was smart and brought out a courtesy Dominican flag for sale. In each new country, sailors must fly a yellow, quarantine flag in the rigging, announcing that they haven't checked in with immigration. Once cleared, it's customary to fly a small courtesy flag of the country in the starboard spreader. Having cleared immigration first thing, we bought a Dominican flag and put it up.

When we came out on deck the next morning the sky was a hazy white, with the sun a feeble lamp shining through. The entire boat was covered in a fine dust. It took us a minute to figure out this must be ash. The volcano on Montserrat—an island northwest of Dominica—had erupted in 1995 after being dormant for 300 years; the volcanic activity continued still.

Shayela

After we'd done our best to wash the falling ash off the topsides, we sailed down the coast and pulled into Roseau, turning down the assistance of the first boat boy who zoomed up. The second guy, Desmond, was smart. When we told him, "No, we don't want a mooring, we'll just anchor," he said, "Ok, I chill out. If you change your mind, I be here."

We circled around, too near to shore to feel comfortable with the swell, but we were still in 60 feet of water, which was too deep to anchor. A mooring is like a permanent anchor that's secured to the bottom, with a rope attached to a floating ball, so it's easy to just tie on. It didn't take us long.

"Okay, we'll take a mooring."

We made it to the market the next morning. This was where the fresh food was; it sure wasn't in the little shops we had passed. Here were hundreds of tables lushly piled with colorful, local produce. The sparkle in the eyes of some of the old lady vendors, after I'd plied them with many questions and my big smile, gave me a hint about the true heart of these people.

We returned to the boat and to problems. The mooring we had rented was too close to the next one. The catamaran that was now tied up there was dancing around its mooring ball like ring-around-the-rosy and no one was home. We sat and watched all day as it threatened our boat and actually hit us twice, while Anthony tried for hours, in vain, to rustle up some assistance on the VHF. Finally, in the late afternoon, we got a response. Sea Cat, the owner of the mooring we had rented, had another mooring at the north end of the bay near the cruise ship dock and a guy came out to lead us there. But once we made our way over, he got sidetracked towing someone else. We drifted idly, waiting while he finished, then watched in confusion as he sped away. Again Anthony got on the radio. Finally, 50 minutes after we let go of the first mooring, Sea Cat himself came out in a small inflatable, a little annoyed with us, and pointed out which mooring to take.

Once we were safely tied on, we sat inside to enjoy a snack, figuring that aside from the swell, this might be a better spot since we were so close to town. I happened to look out the portal—Oh no! We were side-to and approaching the beach, fast! I jumped up, alerted Anthony, and started the engine. But instead of helping me take care of the situation, he got back on the radio. This pissed me off. I was sick of dealing with Sea Cat and first things first; if he didn't want his boat washed onto the beach, he'd better jump to it. I rapped on the cabin top and demanded his assistance to get clear of the rocky shore.

That's when Desmond showed up. We were so glad to see his familiar, smiling face. He had us head south again and then went to check out the mooring we'd just left. He piled the ball into his skiff, along with the thick, slimy line, which kept coming and coming until the severed end, which was supposed to be secured to the bottom, plopped onto the pile.

While we were following Desmond to another buoy, Anthony declared his need for a drink. I replied, "Alcohol might be your drug of choice, but marijuana is mine. I want to smoke: I'm gonna ask Desmond."

He immediately tensed. "Don't ask the boat boy. That's not his job."

"Of course it is." I assured him. Anthony had absolutely no experience with weed.

"Well, just don't ask him from the boat. What you do on shore is your business."

"Okay," I agreed.

Once Desmond got us safely situated and the Captain was distracted messing with the mooring lines on the bow, I held my thumb and pointer finger together like I was holding a teacup. Putting this to my lips, I sucked. Then I put my palms up and nodded with my chin.

Captain said not to ask, and I hadn't say a word. For goodness' sake, the guy had a joint behind his ear! Desmond didn't have a chance to answer before Anthony, done with his task, asked him where he hung out on shore while he was working. I paid attention, hoping to make it there before the day was done.

Desmond was really open to listening to my complaints about how his boss had treated us, and was so genuine about wanting to make sure we were happy and the boat was secure, that the Captain gave him a good tip, and I felt like I had made a friend.

We went to shore that evening, motoring to the massive cruise ship-sized docks near town. While the dinghy rose and fell in the surge, we had to scurry onto the rubber tire and climb up the eight-foot cement quay, which for Anthony, who liked things to be civilized, was a "real bugger." Me, I was just starting to have fun. A little excitement is just what I needed.

Shayela

I appeased Anthony's dark mood by having dinner out with him, something I normally couldn't afford to do. He ordered a bottle of wine and a starter on top of our meals. The service was horrible, and Anthony was stuck on how uncouth everything was; every word out of his mouth was negative. So when the starter he wanted wasn't available, I quickly picked another before he could say anything rude to the waitress, then ran down to check on the dinghy because he was worried about it, and generally tried to smooth things over. When the bill came, because my fast action had saved his boat earlier, I figured he would cover it. But he insisted we split it. I took out my meager cash, while disappointedly shaking my head. I would have been much happier eating on the boat and smoking some pot.

Desmond and the Carnival

Roseau, Dominica
February 15, 2010

The following morning, I was desperate for some space. Cruising with Anthony was feeling like a stale pseudo-marriage—and I was definitely a single girl. We made a plan to meet later, and I struck out to explore some of this breathtaking tropical island. I figured I'd go by bus. The receptionist at the Anchorage Hotel set me straight on my plans.

"It's Carnival! Der's no bus today!" But I learned a new phrase: When I got excited about the carnival, asking her if there was dancing involved, she asked, "So you like to jump up?"

"Oh yes, I was born to jump up!"

Traveling is all about going with the flow, and I walked away happy to have had such a nice conversation and curious about what the day would present. Strolling down the street, I could hear voices below the house where Desmond had said he hung out. I peeked around the side, calling out "Hello," and slowly descended the steps toward the waterfront. A shirtless guy greeted me.

"I'm looking for Desmond," I said, which provoked some whistles from the other guys hanging out. The house was built on a slope that created an outdoor area underneath, which they called "The Counsel." There was a table and some rickety wooden chairs, an overturned bucket, a few half-broken lounge chairs, and a rough wooden bench that created the bar, with an open bottle of rum

Adventures of a Pirate Girl

and some cut-up grapefruit. Desmond smiled sheepishly and passed me his half-smoked spliff.

"I wanted to explore the island by bus today, see some natural beauty," I explained.

"You need company, gurl?" another guy butted in. "I go wit chu, no problem, gurl, I show you around."

"Thanks, but no thanks," I replied, which set the rest of the guys laughing and teasing their friend. Letting go of my original plan, I asked for a drink—what the hell. Desmond got busy organizing a clean plastic cup for me and someone else gave up his seat.

I recognized a tawny white guy who had paddled in on a kayak, obviously a fellow sailor, and nodded my chin up at him.

"What boat are you on?" I asked.

He responded, "I don't speak English," in the strongest French accent he could muster, apparently he wasn't impressed by my presence. Dominica is an English-speaking country.

"*Ah bon, je peux pratique mon Français,*" I replied. After a few sentences from me in French, his English improved dramatically. I wasn't your average tourist, which evidently became clear. I guess I had passed his test because he bought a bit of marijuana wrapped in a rolling paper and argued for a piece of locally-grown tobacco. Using a hollowed-out gourd to mix the two, he rolled a joint just for me. Everyone was smoking but apparently the "pass it around" tradition, standard courtesy in the States, didn't apply in these parts.

The next morning was *J'ouvert* (pronounced jew-veh), the official start of Carnival. Some of the guys were working on their prop for this, which had a political message. On a trash bin they had plastered a candidate's photo and above that was another party's bumper sticker. Being a foreigner and with the guys' heavy accents accentuated by alcohol, I thought the guy in the big color poster was someone they were *promoting* and didn't catch the reference to the trash bin.

Once I figured it out, I declared, "That's not the way people's minds work! You've got this big poster and I thought you were advertising *for* him." The little bi-color bumper sticker for the United Workers' Party seemed secondary.

Shayela

I could get fired up when I smoked (especially since it had been awhile) and, with their permission, I took over their trash bin and showed them what I meant. I quickly collected some rubbish—easy, because it was strewn everywhere—and tore off the offending candidate's picture, which at first shocked all the dudes watching me. But when the owner of the bin saw what I was about, placing the poster, crumpled but still visible, *in* the bin, he had to laugh. After this performance, they all seemed to warm to me a bit more. Apparently I'd gained some respect.

After an hour or so of hanging out, I started to get restless. Desmond, who had been a quiet observer, noticed this. He motioned me aside onto the beach, which was covered in round bread-sized rocks, some of them wobbly. He asked me in an intimate voice if I wanted his company for the day, assuring me he meant as friends, not as a tour guide. Suddenly my knees got rubbery, and I struggled to keep my balance with each foot on a separate rock. I claimed it was my sea legs but I understood his flirtatious invitation and I wasn't altogether sure it was unwelcome.

"Take your time," he said, leading me to a wrecked skiff to sit on. "I'm already the one welcoming you," he pointed out.

"That's true," I conceded, I *had* come to see him. I really did like his sincere smile and felt very comfortable with the relaxed way he behaved. Present, but not glued to me. "You want to go on a hike?"

"Anything you want," he said.

I watched him as we headed up the street away from the city. He was young: I guessed 22 but he assured me he was 26. Long and lanky, his feet kicked, shuffling out in front of him. His skin was a rich chocolatey brown and he had short twisted dreads to his shoulders and one blood-shot eye.

Just down the road, we turned toward the mountains and hiked up a stream through an overgrown rainforest. Desmond led the way: through the brush and over rocks through the streambed.

"Normally I would have a machete with me," he commented, which would have helped; we were definitely off the beaten track. We found a trickling waterfall where sunshine pierced through the dense green foliage, and we both got to work cleaning up the palm fronds and other fallen debris around the small pool, before finding comfortable places to sit in the clearing. Using a banana

Adventures of a Pirate Girl

leaf as a tray, Desmond crumbed marijuana and rolled us a few joints, and we smoked them as we talked.

"How you get so strong, gurl?" he asked me in his rhythmic island accent. "You don't need a man?"

"Hmmm," I smiled, while taking a long slow inhale off the joint, considering his question.

"I wouldn't say I *need* a man," I began, the swirl of thoughts and ideas his inquiry conjured filling my awareness.

"I come from a long line of strong women. My great-grandmother was a real feminist in her own way. She came to the States on a ship from Slovenia, in Europe, when she 18. The story goes that she was so poor she didn't have any shoes."

Desmond nodded, listening thoughtfully, so I continued.

"Her brothers had already immigrated to America so she followed them. She'd grown up Catholic but denounced the Church because she thought it took advantage of poor people and because birth control was a sin. She didn't like the way the church ostracized women who got pregnant out of wedlock, but didn't do anything to the men who'd gotten them pregnant. She had five children but, when she was pregnant with the last one—my grandmother—her husband died suddenly. She married twice after that but divorced both men, which was unheard of; most women in that situation kept their mouths shut and accepted their lot in life. But both those guys were drunks and didn't treat her well. She wasn't going to accept her fate and put up with a useless man. She bootlegged whiskey out of a bogus candy shop to support her kids, and moved them to the country during the Depression so she could grow her own food. She sold eggs, raised her own beef, had a cow for milk and butter. She was one of the first women in her Slovenian community who learned to speak English. She owned a truck and could drive."

Passing the joint back to Desmond, he took it, still watching me and nodding.

"Then my grandma: Her husband died when her three kids were small. She raised them on her own, through some crazy stuff, like really hard stuff. I don't know how she survived mentally. Then my parents got divorced when I was like 13. My dad was around when we were kids, but he wasn't really engaged

Shayela

with raising us. I mean, he supported us financially when we were little, but he wasn't there emotionally.

"I guess I sort of just grew up feeling like you can't really rely on men. If I want to do something, I do it. I mean, I *do* want a man. I *do* want a family. I'm just not willing to put up with… Like I want a man who is my equal, you know? Who adds to my life, doesn't drag me down." I laughed under my breath. It was a lot to take in, but Desmond was still smoking and nodding, apparently listening.

This conversation flowed into talking about home and family. He talked about how fertile the land was there in Dominica, how as a citizen he could buy land cheap. He said I could buy some under his name for that price, and he would cultivate and take care of it for me if I wanted to travel. We talked about running little tours and came up with other ideas on how to make a living. It was as if we were in a make-believe world of our own making, where the trees dwarfed us. We swam in the little pool of fresh water and showered in the falls.

After such a wonderful day, I agreed to Desmond's company for the night. I had been planning on staying out on my own, knowing I would never make it to shore for the 5 am *J'ouvert*. Desmond had proven himself to be easygoing and fun, the perfect ambassador.

I met Anthony at the small dock attached to a bar for a ride back to the boat to shower and eat, letting him know about my plan to go out for the night. When he suddenly restricted my dinghy usage, I left a message with the bartender for Desmond. Desmond got the message and showed up at the boat by skiff, only 20 minutes later then we'd planned to meet onshore. Pretty damn good for Caribbean time.

We started off at Crazy Coconuts, a bar south of the anchorage. After a while, we headed downtown to see what was going on there, about a half-hour's walk. On the way, we came across a bottleneck: a house bumping with music, young people lining the front porch and spilling out into the street in clumps. All this activity slowed the occasional car, and drivers would stop to ask about the happenings in either direction. All the attention I was getting (being the only white girl) was directed at Desmond, which made me feel shy and awkward.

But when he asked me to wait there for him, I got nearer to the music beside the steps and let my hips take over. I do love to jump up.

A middle-aged lady with short, twisted dreads saw me and threw her head back in a huge heartfelt laugh and came to shake her booty with me.

"You want a drink, gurl?" She yelled over the music and then led me up some steps. My shyness was swept away sans my male chaperon, and I shook and bumped my way through the crowd, meeting everyone's stares with a melodramatic surprised look. Inside the old ladies and little kids were sitting around watching the festivities on TV in the front room. The middle-aged crowd was near the kitchen around a table full of alcohol and mixers. Lana went in to get me a glass, sharing roars of laughter with everyone who thought me a funny catch. On our way out, she stopped us in the living room to show off how I could dance and, try as I might, I couldn't get the little girls, who were clearly interested, to join in. Turned out Lana was Desmond's aunt: Throughout the night, his cousins, uncles, and aunts were everywhere.

Continuing our walk into town, we were against the tide of people streaming the other way. We could hear the music leaking out onto the wide, modern street along the waterfront where the cruise ships came in. It got louder. We moved past some car blockades and into a block of shabby, three-story buildings, the street lined with stalls of bars and food vendors, trash all over like confetti. I could tell the open establishments, not by signs and big storefront windows, but by the blaring beat, like echo-location.

Like water searching for a low point from the city of Roseau, everyone seemed to be doing what we were doing: sloshing back and forth looking for the party. We had drinks here and there, found a bench with a view to sit, smoke and chill, and danced every chance we got. The wee morning hours crept closer and we made our final pilgrimage into the center of the city.

For a foreign girl during an all-night street party, having Desmond as my escort was a relief: A guy to fend off other guys and lead the way made it easy to relax. He had my back, it turns out, quite literally.

While the morning was still just a faint brightening behind the mountains, people flooded into the city streets, filling them like canals. There were a few double-decker buses that moved slowly along pumping out music so loud it drowned out thought. It was a simple two-beat Caribbean dub. "Don't hit yo

Shayela

brada," in a militant pounding beat. "Yes fada. Take it easy, fada." And in a joyous singing chant, "*duh duh duh duh duh J'ouvert!*" Each of these buses moved along at a snail's pace with people crowded around and chugging along in their wake. Most women had a man hitched on back like a caboose; everyone was sweaty, pulsing bodies stepping one-two in unison, along with the bus.

Desmond latched on behind me like a hot outboard, his arms circling me and creating a bow fender to thrust us through the crowd, as we were often going against the tide. I mostly let myself be buffeted along, enjoying the physical closeness of all these people co-creating this churning sea of celebration. Occasionally, when we came to an empty spot along the sidewalk (often straddling the deep, trash-filled gutter), my hips would get shaking and winding to the music, my arms thrown to the side, my chest pulsing, as I whipped my short skirt into a parrot-green frenzy.

The crowd was mostly locals: comfortable couples stepping along with the buses, butt to crotch on their yearly big night out; old ladies accompanied by grown daughters, also butt to crotch; middle-aged single guys bleary-eyed with too much drink and smoke; grandmas holding babies on the sidelines for young mothers who were relishing the partying opportunity; packs of skinny young guys roving around in sagging pants and oversized shirts; groups of girls in sexy store-bought police-woman or baseball-player outfits; an occasional white face among the mostly black crowd. But the ones I got the most attention from were the clusters of cool, my-kind-of-funky, get-down, bad-ass girls who obviously were hot shit and knew it. They would pull up alongside me and just cock a pose like "damn girl," and watch in approval this white girl who could move like a black one.

The sun came up and it got hot within the seizing mass. Shirts were stripped off, and the collective energy simmered down, and kept on a low boil till 9:00 or 10:00 in the morning. Then people began to disperse. Desmond led me down a grassy path along a river. We ended up at a private pool behind some big rocks to chill out.

By now we were super comfortable in each other's company; we stripped down naked and let the streaming, cool water wash over us, both appreciating the beautiful contrast of his dark chocolate skin to my gleaming white. We shared a joint and luxuriously made love in the warm sunshine. *J'ouvert!*

I initiated the walk back, knowing that the Captain would be waiting and I would have to plead my case as if I were a teenager with an overprotective father. This was a new experience for me, since my father was far from protective (let alone *over*-protective) and barely around during my teenage years.

In a zombie shuffle, the dub beat, "take it easy, fada," still pulsating in our heads and the glare of the sun oppressive with no sunglasses, we headed south across the botanical gardens and toward the water. Once we were alongside Anthony's boat in Desmond's skiff, we whispered our goodbyes with downturned heads. He silently mouthed, "Should I say bye to the Captain?" I shook my head no.

Anthony was waiting for my return so he could pull up anchor. He wanted to leave right then. I hadn't argued with him the night before because I didn't want to put my Carnival plans in jeopardy. But now the time had come. I chose my words carefully: "Before we got here, you were talking like you potentially wanted to buy land here, and we were supposed to spend a few days and check it out. You haven't even been to shore besides the market and that one night at the restaurant. There's so much of the island to see. It would be a shame to let your initial disappointments stop us from seeing more." Hallelujah! He agreed on two more nights until the end of Carnival.

After sleeping all day, I acted as guide for that night, taking Anthony out to experience the festivities and then, with Desmond's help, arranging for a car and driver to tour the east side of the island the next day. This wasn't easy, with everyone caught up in Carnival. But our tour guide had a budding political career and seemed to know everyone, as well as the best places to take Anthony. We ended up driving over the curvy mountainous roads, through abundant rainforest, to The Citrus Plantation: a beautiful, well planned, ex-pat community being built on a river by the sea.

In my deliberations with Anthony, I also recommitted to stay on as crew until Panama. But making such a deal when I was so desperate to stay was stupid. I didn't bargain high enough. I was damn valuable crew and I sold myself short.

Dominica to St. Lucia

February 17, 2010

Desmond pulled the skiff up to the boat as the sun was just starting to blaze. We'd already said our intimate goodbyes onshore, so I gave him one last quick kiss and stood up to climb onboard *Shayela*.

"I'll wait for you," he said. "I'll work hard."

As soon as I pulled myself up and over the lifelines, Anthony cranked the engine and motored slowly forward without a word. Fighting guilt, I went up to the bow and untied the mooring line. Looking up I saw that Desmond had gone off a ways but was idling, soaking up the last sight of me. Oh, Desmond. It was hard to leave him.

It was a rough passage to St. Lucia: straight into the wind, which is the only direction a boat can't sail. So we slogged ahead under power, the 20 to 25 knots kicking up whitecaps and occasionally spraying over the bow. Skipping Martinique completely, we headed for the Port of Castries, on St. Lucia, about 70 miles away.

Once underway, I was free to melt back into the lush, dreamy landscape of Dominica and Desmond. He was just a skinny kid—or at least, that's how he seemed at first. Not someone I would normally find attractive right off. But the way he dreamed with me, and listened attentively; the way he took care of me, just in small ways, always making sure I was okay; he had really grown on me.

During Carnival, a few hours into our first night while we were walking around the dark streets, music pumping out of cars and random houses, following the flow of partygoers, occasionally finding dark corners to relax alone and smoke, he'd been making little comments about how hard it was not to kiss me. But he was never pushy about it. Then, finally, the invisible barrier I'd maintained shifted and he intuitively leaned in to try. But the kiss was hard and sucking, so I pulled my head back.

"Teach me," he whispered, letting his full lips barely brush mine.

"Pay attention," I whispered back, as our lips pressed softly, small wet openings, licks of warm tongue, slow and tentatively building heat, sparking the kindling to make a bonfire.

Then at the top of some stairs behind a cement building, "Give me a lap dance," he'd said. I laughed and obliged. On the dark beach on a table under a tree with muffled voices of guys hanging out nearby, he went down on me, his hot mouth and probing fingers making me come. I couldn't make him, though I tried. "Not yet," he'd said, not letting me have my way. "You have to wait."

I waited until after our night of chugging along with the masses, dancing and cruising and having so much fun, until the next morning in the river, so sensual and luscious. His skinny body was beautiful: muscular, well-proportioned, nice big cock. He was playful as we sat on the smooth sunny rock, massaging my feet, dribbling cold water on my belly. He seemed to always be reading my vibe, pulling back when I was still nervous. Not in any rush. We lay entwined in each other, his fingers trailing over me until I was so hot, my back arching. Then he finally let me have it, slid in so deep. Oh, Desmond! *J'ouvert!*

The final night of Carnival, after I'd taken Anthony in to the festivities and on our island tour the next day, I'd thought ahead and convinced Mina, a 50-something female solo sailor who was anchored nearby, to join Anthony and me. Together, we waited 20 minutes where we'd agreed to meet Desmond, but I'd forgotten to bring his number. Anthony was getting impatient. "Desmond is probably already at the party, we should just go," he declared. This made my heart drop in that old familiar disappointment: being let down by a man. I walked up the hill one last time and there he was, in the back of a pickup coming down the hill, arms up above his head.

It was so nice to feel like someone was attentive and making an effort. I know, I know, I can hear someone—maybe my mom?—saying, "Of course he is," like that's what I should expect from guys. But the reality was, I hadn't had much luck with men for the past few years. No one had made it so clear or been so sweet and openly loving in a long time.

I liked how communicative he was in general, always checking in with me, staying connected, and how open and straightforward he was talking about sex. While dancing, he'd made the comment, "Don't get too wild," which reminded me of an ex who was always trying to restrict my enthusiasm. But when I'd reminded him that it was Carnival, he replied, "Yeah, you're right. I'm sorry. Get wild, gurl, go crazy!"

The chef from The Citrus Plantation had said, about Dominicans in general, "They can teach you how to love." I was beginning to see that. People seemed

Shayela

to appreciate this out-there white girl. The guy who'd given us the tour had told me, "You have a place." And another lady, Angie, with whom I'd only talked for a few minutes had said the same, "You have a place with me."

Desmond had taken me by The Rasta Spice Café, where I felt immediately at home. I could've sworn I'd been there in a dream. The guy working there, long dreadlocks down his back, had held my hand upon meeting and said sincerely, as if reading my soul, "You look tough, but sweet, too. Come back and see me. You're welcome here."

Sitting in the cockpit, pounding through the chop toward St. Lucia, I knew it was silly, falling so fast. But if I had money, I would have turned around; I'd buy land with Desmond. I'd stay. Maybe he wasn't a great fit for the long run but, for the first time in a long time, I didn't feel like projecting into the future. I didn't care about Mr. Right. Dominica felt like a place that would embrace me, where I could make a home, create a satisfying life. Maybe I'd never find a true, life partner—a man who could fully accept me for who I am. I wasn't ever going to shrink myself for a man again. And maybe I was just too much, too independent, too free. But maybe that was okay. I could be embraced by a community and make a life. Desmond might not be Mr. Right, after all he was young and I didn't know him very well, but he could definitely be Mr. Right Now.

~

We anchored along the coast in the dark, and in the morning light made our way into the big, protected harbor at Port of Castries, St. Lucia. It was busy with cruise ships and hundreds of boats; the whole waterfront was wall-to-wall with marinas and hotels. Apparently there was a major drought going on, and the island, whose hillsides were stripped bare of trees and vegetation, was buying water from the cruise ships, which had huge desalinators. It was a complete contrast from Dominica, which was so fertile with flowing rivers, wet green forests and even bronze taps along the sidewalk where you could get all the water you wanted.

The Captain went to shore to clear in with immigration while I stayed on the boat, filled with a renewed energy, like my heart had been jump-started. I straightened up our living space and got in the water to finish the job of cleaning the bottom that I'd started in Portsmouth. Later, once on land, sitting outside an internet café, the first thing I did was call Desmond on Skype. immediately

I felt stupid: What was I going to say? I missed him, but I'd left. I left a message that I'd call him back and hung up.

I started chatting with a girl at the café, told Anthony I'd be back in an hour, and followed her down the dock to meet her friend. She led me through a gate that needed a code, onto a private dock and introduced me to Jay, a Canadian guy who lived on a fancy, 48-foot catamaran. He invited us aboard, poured us drinks and started telling me all about his plans to build a castle on Dominica, which apparently was well underway. He pulled out blueprints and gushed on and on.

By the time I got back, I was late meeting Anthony and he was mad. I felt like a captive and realized that I wasn't made to be on other people's boats. This was not my kind of traveling. I was trapped. If he had carried on with his anger, I would have jumped ship and caught a ride back to Dominica with Jay. But he didn't. We left for Bequia that morning at 3:30 am, timing it to arrive during daylight.

Bequia

February 22, 2010

We pulled into Admiralty Bay in Bequia just as the sun was setting. For a small island, there were a lot of boats anchored in the crotch of the mountainous bay. With a channel for big ships down the middle, shallows on one side and unmarked ship moorings on the other, it was a little tricky getting in. The depth sounder said 20 meters (about 60 feet) of water. I was mildly glad when the anchor dragged like it was set in butter, because we were too close to the boat behind us. But then, with a forward lunging jerk, it hooked up. Pretty deep and pretty cramped, but we were set.

In the morning we went ashore. As we nosed up between the other dinghies to reach the wooden wharf, I stepped off with the painter, but my foot slipped and I fell forward. Desperate not to fall in, I latched onto the dock and got a bruise over my heart. Right from the get-go, Bequia got me where it counted.

We walked around for a bit and Anthony commented, "I don't know why everyone loves Bequia so much. There's nothing here." Then we split up so I could survey the jewelry-selling scene. There were lots of little stands by the dinghy dock selling crafts, most of it Asian imported plastic crap, and it was going at artisans' prices, so no room to mark up my stuff. It didn't take long before Anthony and I ran into each other again because the waterfront was so small. We walked to where the shady road narrowed and there was a string of real craftspeople along the small, tree-dappled beach.

Molinda, who looked like an African queen, sat at her stand selling jewelry and crocheting Rasta hats and bikinis. A young mother of three, she was sweet and welcoming. She gave me a taste of some marijuana wine and explained to me how she made it. Warmed by such a pleasant connection I continued on, Anthony in tow. This was obviously a hang-out. Guys were sitting along the curb, smoking or rolling up in every direction.

I had one more exchange: a guy with a lion-like mane of dreads and a huge smile. I quizzed him on his turtle shell bracelets, which looked like plastic to me, and then made a comment about his carvings and what a hard worker he was. He looked me deep in the eyes suggestively and told me how hard it was to find someone who worked as hard as he did.

"I know," I agreed.

After that I hurried Anthony to the internet place, then dropped him like a heavy bag. "I'm going off. I'll meet you back at the dinghy dock at 6:00."

I immediately walked back to the people who had made an impression. Molinda was breastfeeding her six-week-old and I didn't want to intrude, so I struck up a conversation with Eversly at the next table. He seemed interested in my jewelry, so I unrolled my display, and while he took a look, I hit up one of the hang-arounds for a puff. I let go of selling anything to anyone, and was just happy to share with another artist and have a smoke. But Eversly suggested that he could watch over my stuff or, even better, he invited me to set-up and sell it myself.

"It's okay, we all free here," he assured me.

"Really, no one will mind?" I asked.

"You welcome here, gurl."

"Yay! I'll be here tomorrow morning at nine!" I enthused, tickled.

The rhythm of the bongos had improved down the way and I went off to investigate. Noel (the hard-working guy with the mane of dreads) and some other artisans were playing drums and a bilimboa (an unusual Brazilian instrument made from bamboo and a gourd). The Italian local who made palm frond hats suggested I play the tambourine, but I shook my head.

"My body is my instrument." I smiled and waited for the drums to coalesce into a danceable groove.

"I never seen a woman who could dance like that," Enos said, before I even got going. He was a big, dark-skinned guy who looked like his ancestors were from India. I was standing near his table looking at the cute, coconut husk boats he made. He tried to give me a polished shell with a loop to string it. I told him I preferred the natural ones, carefully picking out four from a basket that would be good for earrings. He laughed, scooped up two of his big hands full, and gave them to me.

The drummers got their beat down and I shook it. A man with light, buttery, brown skin and exotic green eyes began singing a song, "She's a Caribbean woman, she loves the Caribbean life, she's a Caribbean woman, she wants to be a Caribbean wife," seemingly just for me.

Their music and my dancing caught attention from the tourists who were walking past. I could tell that, though they didn't stop in front of the tables of jewelry and crafts, they *did* want to stop. I tried to convince Noel that we should open up the tables and create a more welcoming space, but his lazy Caribbean soul wouldn't have it.

"I guess you're not as hard a worker as I thought," I teased. "You'd never keep up with me."

In the morning, I set up my stuff on a table Eversly rustled up. I'd never been that fond of selling my jewelry on the street. When I was 18 and traveling around the States and Mexico, I would sit down on a blanket. I always felt like people saw me as a beggar as they walked by looking down on me. But this felt different. I got to work putting together feathers and shells, twisting wire and making earrings. People strolled by and occasionally someone would stop to talk.

I had some especially great conversations with sailors. There was an Israeli who came back with a beer for me and told me of his extensive world travels and adventures moving other people's boats. And a Brazilian family: two little girls with their young and vivacious dad and mom. One of the girls was about eight years old with thick glasses and a sheepish smile. Shy trying to find a common language, she kept getting her dad to translate. We discovered that we could communicate if I spoke Spanish, since it's so close to Portuguese. She asked her dad for money to buy a tiny, shark's tooth pendant. I strung it for her, prolonging our exchange.

Then two guys about my age in matching navy blue tee shirts and tanned like sailors, walked by with a bunch of teenagers. I'd seen the big schooner in the anchorage and had already chatted with a few of the kids, who turned out to be students on an awesome sailing adventure. I figured these must be the instructors. One of these guys caught my eye; he was cute, but that wasn't it. When he turned and saw me, he started staring too.

"Davina?" he asked.

"Oh my god, it's Chris, right?! I thought I recognized you! Man, it's a small world!"

We chatted about what we had been up to since last we met, back in Key West, when I was 22 and had first bought my boat. The weird thing was that I'd only just run into Jasmin, his girlfriend from back then. This was in Colorado within the past year and she knew all my cousins in Carbondale. I'd say it was serendipitous, but I don't believe things happen randomly. The Universe is a magical place.

As I was sitting with Eversly and chatting to passersby, an older white lady, wearing high-end linen clothing and lots of makeup, stopped to talk to me and asked if I was from Bequia. Then she went into a tirade about how it was illegal for all of the artisans to be there, and they were hurting the business of her shop next door. Since I was a foreigner, I couldn't get away with it. She was so rude and uptight that I was stunned. As soon as she walked away, Eversly and Molinda got fired up.

"You should have asked her where she's from," said Eversly. "She's from Sweden."

"Yeah, and nothing in her shop is local," jumped in Molinda.

"Nobody likes her," Eversly assured me. "It's always the foreigners who want to make up rules." Then he started thinking up all the things he would say if she came back. It struck me that they saw me more as a peer than a foreigner, which made my heart swell.

But that old give-and-take awareness was still active within me. Making money was not my priority, it never is, but because Eversly had invited me to

Adventures of a Pirate Girl

sell my jewelry alongside them, I felt a slight guilt when I sold more stuff than he did. I gave him a big shark's tooth and bought him a beer. He keep reminding me, "Chill out gurl, feel at home."

A cute blond kid, about 13 and covered in paint, came by. When I asked, he told me he had been busy painting his father's church. They were Southern Baptists from North Carolina. "Wow, I never met a real missionary before," I said.

Later I made the acquaintance of his younger brother. A 10-year-old, tanned, blond boy with no parents around stuck out, so I asked, "Hey, are you Zack's brother?" After that, he sat glued close to me and we spent an hour or so chatting.

When the locals were talking directly to me, they made their heavy accents clear enough for me to understand, but among themselves I could barely tell they were speaking English. And to my delight, this little white kid from North Carolina turned to me and started talking in this island patois, as if he were a middle-aged Caribbean black woman, which had me cracking up in laughter.

It struck me that the missionary life was hard on him and, once we'd established a connection, I started talking about God from my point of view: how God is such a huge idea that it's hard to find words to describe it. The fact that every tribe and race of people around the world *do* describe it, in their own words, seems proof of something. Like that each of us has a puzzle piece and, instead of fighting over whose puzzle piece is right, it would be better to appreciate that we all *have* one. Sharing our piece with others and noticing how they all fit together would get us farther in our quest for knowledge than fighting over whose piece was best. Noticing that my voice was increasing in volume—a common trait of mine—I apologized for getting excited.

"Oh, I'm used to it," he assured me. "My dad does that all the time." I had to laugh!

Bequia has a strong seafaring history, and still does a traditional whale hunt once a year. I happened to be reading (more like trudging through) *Moby Dick* at the time, so the subject was already on my mind. I am against killing whales. The only exception I make to that stance is for the Inuit people of the Arctic who rely on whale blubber to keep them alive. In the Caribbean, with plentiful fruits growing on trees and fish in the sea, I couldn't understand why they would want to kill such advanced beings.

Shayela

The next day I got into a heated debate with a bartender about this. I was at the Whaleboner on the waterfront where I'd gone to send some emails. The barstools were made from gigantic whale vertebrae; whale rib bones created an arched entrance and encircled the bar. We got into it and I got riled up. She had to tell me to stop yelling and was on the verge of taking offense. Together we scared the tourists from Kansas, who got up and left. But in the end she bought me a beer and schooled me on the history and practice of whaling in Bequia: Once a year, guys would go out in little wooden sailboats and try to harpoon a whale. Sometimes they wouldn't catch one for years. When they *did* get one, the whole town went crazy. They'd have a huge celebration and everyone would share in the meat. Even though I still didn't agree, it felt more important to connect with these people and respect their culture than it did to be right.

Spending time with my new friends filled my love tanks right up. The guys, especially, showered me with attention. Noel told me, in a serious voice, how he had land and thought he and I could be a great couple; we could work the land and raise kids.

"I want to marry you," interrupted Enos, grinning, a huge hunk of a man whose mellow energy was comfortable and supportive. He rolled me a joint and fed me some grilled fish. Someone else ran off to fill my water jug. I loved all this unabashed attention, these guys just put their heart out there, come what may, in contrast to how most American guys act. Though some of the younger ones were just being silly, I felt a true sincerity and respect from the others. Eversly told me that I could always come to Bequia, that he had a place I could stay and I could sell my jewelry. He said he liked having good women around.

Molinda, for once unencumbered by her two little boys or the baby, patted the curb beside her, "Come sit with me for your last." She poured me a glass of marijuana wine and let me take her picture. We joked that she should have nice photos of her and the baby for sale, since everyone wanted one.

I had been there for only two days, but I felt so welcomed and at home in Bequia. As I left them to meet up with Anthony, a girl who had looked at my stuff waved, the Rasta man selling veggies called out to me, and a few guys passed, saying, "Hey, dancing girl."

We were leaving that night and the bruise above my heart ached. Oh, how I wished I could stay. I could learn so much about the balance of give-and-take from these people who gave so much.

Adventures of a Pirate Girl

Grenada, Prickly Bay
February 25, 2010

With a good buzz on, it was strange to leave in the evening. The sail was the best we'd had: The moon was bright, the wind was a perfect 15 knots on our beam—an ideal point of sail. My watch was from midnight to 4 am, and the sea was so flat calm that I couldn't see the horizon. We were floating in a seamless void, buoyed only by phosphorescence billowing out from underneath the boat like puffs of glowing smoke.

Surrounded by this wonder, thoughts of give-and-take floated into my head. What was this anxiety about making sure I contributed enough? Like when Jen and I were in Sint Maarten, I probably bought her more beers than she did me, though she wouldn't have even noticed because the cost was nothing to her. Or the feeling that I owed Eversly for his kindness. Wasn't I enough? I wasn't someone who took advantage of people. I gave in heaps of ways. So why did this feeling keep coming up? Did it have to do with self-esteem? Was I overcompensating?

Grenada, "the spice island," was one of the bigger islands we'd visited so far. In the morning light we could see the jagged shoreline along the southern end, which created various bays all filled with anchored sailboats. The land seemed parched and brown. We pulled into Prickly Bay and dropped the hook. It was quite built up: From the dinghy dock there were plenty of bars, restaurants, big hotels, the boatyard and a Budget Marine. To get farther afield, minivan "buses" were abundant, driven by opportunists who swung by wherever someone happened to be walking to pick them up. People in Grenada seemed friendly and at ease with their white visitors.

I was determined to do some active things and decided on a hike at Grand Etang Lake. The bus/van that stopped for me was filled with locals. When I saw how packed it was I shrugged and said, "I'll wait." But everyone urged me in, "Come on, gurl, there's room."

There wasn't really, but apparently, being pressed against strangers and half sitting on each other's laps was normal in Grenada.

As we made our way inland, the congestion of the coast petered out. We wound up curvy roads, with houses here and there: some elegant, with big white porches, others small and shabby with rusty tin roofs. The island glistened with overgrown, lush, green foliage. The van had emptied out along the way, and only

Shayela

I remained when the road ended at the top with a sign for the national park. The lake was surrounded by green hills, and I hiked up and around to a boulder overlook. It was beautiful but I wished I had company. On my way back down the trail I came upon three young guys smoking a joint and laughed, "There you are!" as if expecting them.

"Hey," they called as if we were old friends and we spent the rest of the day together, hiking and getting high.

~

Another day I hung out with some sailor guys I'd met. We motored over on Pete's sailboat to nearby Hog Island, a tiny outcrop just off the jagged shoreline of Grenada. I did some snorkeling while Pete and Ben kite boarded. As we were heading back, I saw *LoneSilver*, the first boat on my trip. She was underway, but Troy must have gotten a glimpse of me, because he circled around close. My gut reaction was to duck—which I did—feeling silly. But I was too chubby to want an encounter.

When I was first on his boat, I was as thin and fit as I'd ever been. Once in Sint Maarten, of course, I'd slacked off and the pounds crept on. Troy had made a rude comment about how I was gaining weight even though, at that point, I had probably gained only a few pounds. It had been only a small comment in passing, but it stung and I remembered it.

Pirate Girl loved her body—but I had to learn that; it definitely didn't come naturally. No matter how bad ass or beautiful a woman is, none of us escapes the insidious voice of body shame. At best—if we are lucky or have done our work—it lies mostly hidden, deep within our subconscious, and only strikes when we are vulnerable.

During my early teenage years, that voice was loud and in my face. I starved myself, then binged and tried—unsuccessfully—to become bulimic. I was relentless at putting myself down, constantly reminding myself how fat I was. I would watch *Spring Break* on MTV and lust after the girls, not to *have* them but to *be* them. To be that sort of sexy, fat-free, totally lovable, skinny body.

But then this book came to me. In my memory it sort of appeared out of nowhere—a big hardback, coffee-table book with a glossy cover picturing a voluptuous woman in stylish, bright clothes. Turns out it was my mom's book and it was a paperback. But the affect it had on me was solid. The author's whole message was to learn to love yourself, no matter how you look; to quit dieting, and actively work on changing negative self-talk so the voice in your head whispers words of nurture and love instead of insult. The book made a huge impression on me. I had been about to drop out of high school in the 10th grade, but had just gotten accepted into a Middle College program where I could attend classes at a local community college for my last two years of high school. Supplied with the concept of self-love gleaned from that book, I worked hard all summer to shift my inner dialogue and simultaneously did a Jane Fonda aerobics workout every single day. By the time I started at the new school, and got a job at the local coffee shop nearby, I was a little hottie and knew it, with an abundance of flirtatious suitors to reinforce that belief.

By the time I was 22, I was living on my boat in Key West and *still* knew it. I had no TV or magazines, severely limiting the bombardment of ubiquitous advertising that informs us women of what it looks like to be happy and fulfilled. Even my mirror was tiny. Instead of being brainwashed from the outside, I rowed my dinghy to shore and back, pedaled my bike everywhere, and was completely focused on following my dream. The brainwashing came from within: I was a bad ass and had a bad ass body. And *that* is how a Pirate Girl feels about herself!

But, no matter how bad ass, that insidious voice remains buried deep within us. It turns out, learning to love yourself is not just a lesson—it is a practice. And at that point, facing Troy's judgment, I knew I hadn't been keeping up with it.

After five days in Grenada, Anthony flew home to England to see his first grandchild and I was left with precious time to myself. I immediately bought a pile of chocolate, holed up in the solitude of *Shayela* and sank comfortably into depression: eating, reading and hiding. When I reemerged a few days later I felt ready to face the world again.

The situation with Anthony was on my mind. He was a good guy, but our mode of travel was way too different. I wanted to explore and get to know people; he wanted to do our chores, have a drink and move on. Plus I found his negativity draining. I wanted to get off his boat but I'd committed to helping him get to Panama. Once there I'd be free, so I began putting feelers out to line up my next ride.

Shayela

I went ashore and felt like I was in the flow because I immediately connected with the *Mistress*'s Captain, who had announced that morning on VHF that he needed crew. He and his wife were older and didn't drink, so not a good match, but I took an instant liking to Itimar, their departing crew member. He was a young Israeli with long, flowing hair and gentle energy and was doing the same thing I was: hitchhiking on boats. We made plans to meet for happy hour.

That evening, I picked up Itimar in the dinghy and we motored over to De Big Fish for happy hour. Itimar and I had a few beers by the time his friend Richard walked in. He was from New Zealand, 40ish, thin and muscular with short brown hair and an edgy, don't-fuck-with-me vibe. He pulled up a seat beside us. His tough demeanor faded when he found out we had a lot in common. In fact the conversation between all three of us was exciting: big ideas about how to help the world and creative schemes to make money. We were all eager to let off steam about frustrating captains and situations, but didn't want to do it in the bar with all the ears, so I invited Itimar and Richard back to *Shayela* for dinner.

All of us crowded into the inflatable, towing Richard's behind us, and bounced along noisily, getting soaked. Once onboard, I whipped up some pasta with the few fresh things I had left. We each kept a hand on our wine glass, as the boat rolled heavily from side to side, and kept up our enthusiastic banter. They were both well read, well traveled and intelligent. I was happy to have such good company in my own space. Itimar was relieved to have some young friends and a drink, after crossing the Atlantic on a dry boat with old people.

There was an attraction between Richard and me, which, along with his sharp edge, caused some friction. He was pushing my boundaries and I almost kicked him out before dinner was over. We got past that, however, and returned to intriguing topics like God, energy, human society, and good books. Finally, at 3:00 am, when we all started to yawn, they climbed in Richard's dinghy to row back to their respective boats.

Anthony's Return

I strode onto the sand to enjoy my last few hours before Anthony got back from his week in England. I hadn't been to this part of the island. A big guy around my age with long, tidy dreads and a clean, white jumpsuit got up from finishing his lunch and called out, "Hey, sweetie, you want some company?"

"No thanks, darling," I smiled and waved, continuing happily along my way.

The beach curved around the bay and I could see the cruise ships down at the other end. Barely lapping the sugary white sand, the ocean was so crystalline it looked like bathwater. I made my way past groups of older tourists huddled together on lounge chairs under the shade of the occasional tree.

Then a middle-aged, black-as-night man with dreads wrapped in a knit cap, approached me. "Five dollars for a lounge chair," he said.

"No thanks, I don't need one," I smiled.

"What do you need?" he asked, in a salesman-like way that I admired. If only I could peddle my wares like that.

"I'd love to smoke some marijuana."

"How much do you want?"

"I don't want to buy it," I explained. "I just want to smoke a little. I'd pay you for a joint but if not, that's cool, I'll just walk. I'm sure I'll find someone who's smoking and doesn't mind sharing."

"I'm Clarence," he said, offering me his big, rough hand. I shook it. "You're a strong woman," he declared.

"I know," I smiled.

"Sit in the chair. I'll be back," he said and ran off.

"I'll rent it out for you if anyone's looking," I called after him, lounging back and enjoying the luxury I wouldn't pay for. He returned quickly and handed me a little bundle in a rolling paper.

"Aren't you gonna smoke with me?" I asked.

"Yeah, I don't usually smoke while I'm working, but I'll smoke with you," he said, flashing a gleaming white smile minus one tooth. We sat in an out-of-the-way place and talked of his Rasta religion, and I showed him my jewelry. It was easy and relaxed, and I wasn't surprised or offended when he said, "I want you to be my woman while you're in Grenada. When you come here, I want to be your man, I like your energy, gurl."

I neither encouraged nor discouraged him, but when he tried to stop me from walking off down the beach I said, "Ya see, this is why I can't have a man. I gotta do what I want."

Shayela

"You should feel free to do whatever you want," he quickly assured me, handing me his number. "Just call me… if you want. I'll treat you right."

"I'm sure you would, Clarence," I said with a wink, and sauntered off down the beach.

With a bag on my back, a skip in my step and a parrot feather earring flapping about my head, I grabbed a bus back toward the marina where I was going to meet Anthony. Earlier, two guys—one with honey brown skin, the other dark chocolate, both baby-faced—were welding metal jack stands used for holding up boats in dry dock. As I'd passed the chain-link fence that separated us, they had both stopped working, tipped their welding helmets up, and graced me with their beautiful smiles. I'd laughed and teased, "Back to work, boys."

Now as I walked by the fence again, they both jumped up in unison and came over.

"Hey," I called in a fun and flirtatious voice, stopping to chat. One of them was not only gorgeous, but had been to Europe and wrote poetry. Their smiles and eyes lit me up, and I felt dazzling like a faceted jewel.

"Ah, boys," I said as I walked away, "I'd keep both of you if I could."

At De Big Fish, the bar directly in front of the dinghy dock, happy hour was just getting started and the place was filling up fast. Anthony arrived. I gave him a hug and bought him a drink. He was keen to hang out for a bit before heading to the boat. There was a blond guy about my age I'd noticed before, tying up his dinghy. We got to talking and I told him I was writing a blog. When he asked what it was about I answered, "Oh, it's like *Sex in the City* for the sailing set."

At this, his energy completely changed. His polite, upright stance relaxed into a sleazy slouch. He tweaked his eyebrows at me and sidled up closer, as if addressing a call girl in a dusty third world country. I held up my drink, "Cheers dude," I said with a sarcastic smirk and turned away.

Then I saw Lorraine, and made my way over to the table where she sat with her son, a little blond cutie about 3-years-old. I'd been to their boat and gotten to know them a little while Anthony was away. She and her husband had cruised for a few years before she'd gotten pregnant. She was also a diver and sorely missed having the freedom to dive much since giving birth. She'd made me laugh with her honesty about being a reluctant mother.

Adventures of a Pirate Girl

"So, have you found your next boat yet?" she asked, while absentmindedly dancing some little toys in front of her boy.

"Yeah, I think I'm gonna go with John," I told her.

John was a hopeful prospect back in Sint Maarten, a guy who had been hanging out at my old haunt, Lagoonies, and had heard about me through mutual friends. He was looking for one to three crew with experience and good cheer to sail to New Zealand. After three emails and a Skype conversation, we were discussing splitting the cost of a ticket for me from Panama back to Sint Maarten so we could sail together. He was young and active, into diving, windsurfing, and kayaking. If I went with him, I'd have to pay my own way. But he made it clear that it would be *our* trip, not me helping him on his. We would both take part in finding and choosing more crew.

"He's the young one, right? The guy in Sint Maarten?"

"Yeah, that guy. Though he might meet me in the Dominican Republic."

"OOOH," she cooed, "is he hot?" Her eyes flared, "Maybe he's gonna be the one."

"No, it's not gonna be like that," I assured her. "A friend of mine in Sint Maarten told me by email that he's alright, but seems desperate to find a girlfriend."

"But I thought that's what you wanted."

"Yeah, well, a part of me does. I mean, I do. I did? When I was in Boulder, all I wanted was a partner. But I think my feelings are starting to change. These Caribbean men love me, I feel like a rock star everywhere I go. I'm not sure I believe there's one single man out there who can keep up with me. I mean, if I meet him, awesome, I'm totally into that. But until I meet someone like *that*, well, I don't think that's John, and anyway, being single in the Caribbean is way too much fun."

Grenada to Curaçao

March 13, 2010

Curaçao lay 400 miles to the west of Grenada, and the rhumb line on the computerized chart marked our intended course well north: past all the Venezuelan islands—past poverty and heartbreak. In places like this, where the divide between rich and poor is a gaping chasm, where politicians (as usual) are in

Shayela

the pockets of big money, and regular people are pushed into corners and over edges, pirates still exist. These were—no doubt—desperate people taking drastic measures. We had heard of boats being boarded while at anchor in the middle of the night and treasures being stolen (cameras, money, passports). There would be a sudden splash when the crew awoke as the pirates went over the side and into the water. While sailing off the Venezuelan coast, my friend Richard was approached by a small boat carrying seven men. His round of shots fired into the sky persuaded them to change whatever plans they had in mind. Sure these people, these *pirates*, were doing bad things; I don't condone that. I certainly didn't want to be pirated! But when their crimes were set in comparison to the crimes of the illusive 1%, the big money, whose manipulation of the world's resources have caused such extreme hardship in the first place, whose ongoing decisions have pushed our planet to the brink, one understood how someone might do something drastic.

We are in this together, us humans. Yes that 1% has all the money, and the entire system is designed to keep the rest of us under control, but we are the 99%: the numbers are on our side.

I would have liked to have seen Venzuela, but not with Anthony.

The week apart from each other had done us both good; things felt easier between Anthony and me and we were both looking forward to getting back to sea. I had accepted this trip as his. I was staying on because of my commitment to help him reach Panama. After discussing this, he agreed to pay my expenses. The islands we would sail past and the insufficient time we'd have in the few places he was planning to stop no longer bothered me. This southern stretch of the Caribbean circle would hold the joy of sailing. The intrigue of landfall would have to wait until my next trip.

We left in the morning after tea and coffee, in no hurry. Since this first leg would take a few days, we didn't try to time it; there was no telling how fast we would go and no point in making arrival plans that would likely change. Once we had set the Genoa and cleared the sandspit island to our port, the busyness and chores of land faded as the islands became silhouettes in the distance. We both relaxed into our anticipated three to four days at sea. It was a downwind run, and we were sailing under the big headsail alone. Up till this point we had mostly been beating into the wind and *Shayela* seemed a cow; now she was doing an easy six knots and seemed more like a bird. Apart from occasionally rolling in some of the sail when the wind picked up and rolling it out again when it slacked, and the few times we jibed so as not to sail dead downwind (a touchy point of sail), there wasn't anything to do but scan the horizon every five minutes and enjoy.

There *were* two unusual occurrences that made me think of pirates.

One was billowing smoke: It looked like a ship on fire. I got Anthony up to take a look. Should we call them? What if they were in distress? What if it was a trap? Luckily Anthony didn't get caught up in my imagined drama, and we just held steady and watched as the smoke turned into a small fishing vessel chugging along in desperate need of a smog check. The other was when Anthony woke me for my night watch. I came out on deck and saw two vessels far apart, both so lit up they looked like the field lights for a football game. Heading directly between them, we were about to score a touchdown. I could hear them jabbering away in Spanish on the VHF and tried to follow the conversation. I heard one say, "Should we do it now?" One thought yes, the other guy wanted to wait, for what I couldn't tell. Pretty unlikely that pirates would be advertising on an open channel like that, but it still seemed shady. My worries were unfounded: We cleared the goal posts unmolested and kept on going.

Without an immediate landfall to muck up the rhythm of the days, time shifted into a more fluid dimension than that measured by the steady hands of a clock. Everything slowed down and I spent hours languidly watching the ocean.

The sky and the sea have an intimate relationship, as if they are lovers. Sky starts where ocean ends. Where they collide is the fluctuating friction of partnership. Each time I stepped on deck was totally different from the previous. While sitting in the cockpit searching the horizon for ships, the shifting duo of water and sky played with me: her swells growing to big rounded hills that threatened to cover me; his gusts blowing off the tops so the rushing sound startled me. Then she would slide underneath laughing, lifting us up, surfing us down. Sometimes she was boisterous, the wind whipping her up into little frothy blue peaks that danced and sprayed. One night while he gently teased our sails, she was dreamy, her surface smooth and thick. With heavy sighs, she expanded and contracted…as if breathing. Grey smears of clouds blocked the stars and the horizon became like that murky place between waking and dreaming.

I loved the night watches. A tiny part of me thought it rude to be awakened at midnight, forced to leave my warm bed for four hours, but that part didn't stand a chance against the awe of being alone with the night sky at sea. With seven billion plus people on this planet, and all of our accessories, being the only human soul, without a manmade object in sight for as far as the eye could see, bearing witness to the enormity of the twinkling night sky—it was like a private viewing of the galaxy's most exquisite masterpiece, with only the internal Divine as your guide.

It became clear on the third day out that, if we continued our progress without alteration, we would arrive at Spanish Water Bay, Curaçao, in the middle of the night. This harbor had a tight, unlit entrance; it would be reckless to attempt the passage in the dark. Anthony decided to shorten the sail to a triangular handkerchief, reducing our speed to .7 knots and continue toward the lights of the island. When he woke me at midnight, we were rolling around like a kid's punching bag weighted at the bottom. We'd get pushed over and popped back up to one side or the other, over and over. He was anxious to have me take the wheel because, with so little forward momentum, the self-steering mechanism was having a hard time maintaining our heading and required constant vigilance. To me, it seemed silly to work so hard to stay pointed in the right direction when we were barely moving, but, when I commented that it would be easier just to drift, he tensed up and said, "If you're not going to do it, I will!"

"I will, I will," I assured him and climbed out, annoyed to sit behind the wheel and steer, going nowhere. When I woke him at 4 am, he pulled out the sail and started making way, figuring it would take the two hours till dawn to get us to the mouth of the inlet. And, sure enough, he woke me at first light from a deep, dream-filled sleep, just as land was closing in around us. He started the engine. I climbed out, barely awake, to take the wheel, and groggily threaded us past unseen reefs, following turns and missing rocks.

As we slowly crept into the long corridor to Spanish Water Bay, the land was vastly different from the other Caribbean islands we'd visited. There was a raised coral lip at the water's edge and bone-dry rocky hills with cactus plants. Once the huge bay opened up, I steered us to a spot behind a fleet of cruising boats, and Anthony dropped the hook. As soon as we were safely anchored, after four days at sea, I crashed back to bed and left Anthony scurrying around with boat duties. When I awoke hours later, we rowed the dinghy to the dock and headed into town by bus. The peaceful, easy feeling we'd shared during our beautiful sail smashed against the bureaucratic stress of land like a ship against a reef.

Adventures of a Pirate Girl

Adventures Ashore

Curaçao
March 14, 2010

Curaçao is a Dutch island, the last of the Netherland Antilles. The people are mostly of African and Hispanic ancestry, although there are also white people of Dutch descent, and plenty of white tourists. The kids learn Dutch in school but the majority of the people speak Papiemento, a musical blend that starts off sounding Spanish then slides into Portuguese with instrumentals of German, Dutch, and French, creating a rhythmic ensemble of history. Most people could speak English, but I found Spanish to be a better bet. The roads were wide and smooth, and the residential area around the bay was posh, with big tile-roofed houses surrounded by gates. There were no corner shops or cafés, just high-class suburbia. The long bus ride into town took Anthony and me past a parched landscape before coming to the old, compact houses of the city.

Clearing into customs and immigration was a bureaucratic runaround that took all day. With each inconvenience Anthony constricted, mumbling complaints about how inefficient the system was. I tried not to get caught up in his frazzled stress, but by the time we finally figured out which bus to take back to the harbor, Anthony was simmering in negativity. The next day we rode around in the dinghy and got soaked searching the shoreline for a place to get on the internet. The bay was vaguely shaped like a roadkill octopus. In the different "arms" we found a yacht club for guests only, a shack windsurfing school and a deserted bar. Other than that it was wall-to-wall houses like southern Florida. We finally figured out that paying the people on the catamaran, *Isis*, $10 a week was the thing to do for internet onboard and we moved our boat embarrassingly close to them.

That whole morning heated up into another ordeal for Anthony: his debit card had prematurely expired, he kept getting cut off from Skype as he tried to sort out the debit card issue, his new satellite phone stopped working... again. His frustration was at a rolling boil when he hopelessly whined to nobody, "Ooohh, what can I do?"

"Have you ever heard about the power of positive thinking?" I gently asked.

"Yes, I have. And it doesn't work."

Shayela

Just then a friend's boat anchored beside us. "Works for me," I cried, jumping up and dashing away in the dinghy to say hello, desperate to escape Anthony's negativity and tickled with the synchronicity.

The next day I was doubly blessed. Not only did I have the boat to myself, but the reason Anthony left was to pick up new crew from the airport, a Scottish woman named Heather.

I had just finalized my plans to fly to the Dominican Republic and get on John's boat once we reached Panama. Heather had been crewing for a friend of Anthony's, but she had jumped ship in Grenada. She was middle-aged and from the Isle of Skye—a professional sailor on holiday. She seemed generally cheerful and cool, which would be a godsend because with just Anthony and me, Panama seemed a lifetime away.

The dinghy dock was located among the fishing fleet. In the boatyard nearby, small cabin boats with rounded, wooden hulls stood on blocks in various stages of repair. Nearby was a bar in a small, yellow, prefab box with benches and tables outside under a corrugated shade. It was so low-key we had overlooked it on our extensive search the previous day. Richards, the entrepreneurial owner, was a big, middle-aged guy of Venezuelan and American descent, animated, friendly, and immediately engaging. He understood that the abundance of cruising boats created a captive audience. Besides the bar and restaurant, he had a washing machine and was getting internet installed within the week. On Friday nights was a happy hour, so Anthony, Heather, and I went in to check out the social scene. I met a handful of cool cruisers and ended up having a wild, late night out, dancing.

～

We didn't want to stay in Curaçao long, but the weather had other plans. It was blowing 25 to 30 knots and, with the infamously rough waters around the knob of Venezuela, we weren't going anywhere. Used to provisioning for big charter groups, Heather took on the job of cataloguing our food supplies and shopping for the Pacific. I helped but felt like a third wheel. When I cracked a beer at noon out of boredom, I knew I was going downhill. By email, my mom suggested that I get off the boat for the day. I took her advice.

Adventures of a Pirate Girl

While I was motoring around in the dinghy, I lucked upon Maria and Don, a mid-30s couple from Miami whom I had met at the happy hour. They waved me over from their cockpit. Turns out they were having guests over and invited me aboard for a drink. Score!

The pineapple rums lubed the conversation, a blend of Spanish and English among the three bi-cultural couples. Richards, the bar owner, and I were the only singles, and there were eight of us crowded into the cockpit. I was feeling vulnerable, bored, and no longer needed on *Shayela*, so I welcomed Richards' flirtations; it's comforting to be wanted. When the party was simmering down, I got his hopes up by volunteering to take him ashore, motivated by the thought of chocolate from his restaurant. He gave me a few Snickers bars, some peanut M&Ms, and a big hug—professing his love to me for the umpteenth time.

"Now you have to tell me something good," he said, expectantly.

Clutching the chocolates to my breast, I declared, "I loooove these chocolates!"

The next day I struck out alone for the city by bus. It was good to be free and on my own, but by the time I got back to the dock, I had deteriorated into melancholy. Richards' bar, where the food was good and cheap and where I'd be enthusiastically welcomed, sounded just right. When I walked up, Richards grabbed me and flipped me upside down, making me squeal and instantly shifted my blah mood. The bar was swamped with locals and Richards pointed out a pale-skinned guy with black, curly hair and a blue scrub shirt, saying, "That's my doctor. Ask him what's wrong with me."

Daniel was a wound-care physician and manager of a hyperbaric chamber, a pressure chamber used to save divers who get the bends in Curaçao. He was Colombian, 41 and cute. He bought me a beer. I joined him and his friend, a gregarious, caramel-colored guy with one gold tooth in his genuine smile. They were volunteers for the rescue team. We had a lot in common. They were both divers, good conversationalists and concerned about how humans were impacting the environment.

Anthony and Heather were supposed to give me a ride back to *Shayela* but I'd been at Richards' bar for hours and couldn't hail them on the VHF. Daniel and I both wanted to hang out but I hesitated, "I might get stuck onshore is the only thing. I'm just worried about missing my ride."

"We'll figure it out," he assured me. "It's not worth worrying about. If you miss Anthony you can sleep…" he hesitated for a second, having already informed me about his pending divorce and kids at home, "…in my minivan?"

I shrugged, smiling, and off we went for a midnight tour of the sights, smoking a joint in each place: an old stone fort turned restaurant overlooking the main inlet into the harbor, and another fort with a round tower that we climbed in the dark. Then there was an old stone building where, back in the 17th and 18th centuries, human beings from Africa—who'd been stolen, brutalized and shipped far from home—had been quarantined. I walked slowly into the barn-like room. I could almost see all those people chained to the posts like cattle. The eerie weight of tortured souls was palpable.

It was a sinister and disturbing place, reminding me of how damaged humans are under the weight of thousands of years of collective trauma. As we continue to demand equal rights and justice, let us focus on healing ourselves. It is the ones among us who continue to perpetrate torture on others—the ones whose brains don't even hold the pathways that recognize love—that are the most wounded and need the most help. Healing ourselves is healing the planet. We are all in this together.

Daniel parked his van in a deserted perch overlooking the bay and made room to sleep. We lay down, nestled together. He turned, as if compelled by expectation, and kissed me. But with the gentle pressure of my hand on his chest, he relaxed back and we both slept remarkably well, without sheets or pillows, on the floor of his family van.

In the morning Daniel went to work: Anthony, Heather, and I got underway.

Last Leg with Anthony

Curaçao to Panama
March 25, 2010

Anthony's original itinerary had included a stop in Cartagena, a port in Colombia that I was excited to check out. I could just imagine sultry nights in the historic port, an open-air restaurant in a stone plaza, a live salsa band and the hot-blooded Colombians who knew how to dance. He had also intended to stop at the San Blas Islands, an isolated group of sandy isles along the gulf coast of Panama that apparently were relatively untouched by progress and where the native people still had authority. But we were nearly a month past the Captain's original timetable and there was a weather window of opportunity in the Pacific before cyclone season became a concern. So Anthony was feeling the pressure. And I was feeling the pressure of this last leg with someone I'd already energetically split from, which would have put a real damper on visiting those places anyway. So I contented myself to just sail the 690 nautical miles to Panama.

It had been blowing hard for the past week and was still rushing past at 25 knots. The sea was steel gray and seething, rough and rolling with a massive swell. But whatever weird feelings I'd lodged in the crevices between us three were whipped away by the wind and water. We were a crew with a mutual goal and I think we all felt the same: It was good to be back at sea.

Like a downwind sleigh-ride we were going with the wind. So even though the big messy swells came up behind, towering over us for a second before sliding under our stern, lifting us up, up, up, where at the tip top I'd catch my breath for a second like the drop of steep hill, before sliding waaaaayyyyy down—it wasn't terribly uncomfortable. I got somewhat used to it. Though once, while in the cockpit on watch, writing in my journal, I looked back and squealed! The wave was shockingly large and, instead of benignly disappearing under us like the rest of them had, this one slapped the stern of the boat and crashed into the cockpit. Yikes!

There had always been a whirring motor within me, a man-made machine that churned out expectations each day and kept me motivated. "Without me," it argued, "what would force you to be productive? What would keep you from becoming a vegetable?"

I, of course, argued back. "There is a deeper Source. And if you would just shut up, maybe I could hear it! Anyway, even a vegetable grows toward the sun."

I'd go through periods of defying this whirring noise by giving myself over completely to doing nothing...for days. Forcefully doing nothing, all up in its face, waiting for the machine to lose its grip and let me go. But it was persistent and nearly indestructible. At other times I'd quiet it with meditation and sport, drown it out with alcohol and pot, but its nagging would eventually return. Its attempts to prod me into action usually backfired, instead making me feel guilty and depressed because of my inaction. That whirring motor (the voice in my head) worked on the shame of not being good enough and on the fear of death. There was only so much time to make something of myself. It was possible that it helped with production levels and the bottom line, though I remained skeptical. Who says that's what I needed anyway?

I believe that each of us is a direct link to the Divine. We are all made out of the same stuff. *Everything* is. At the tiniest level, with the highest-power microscopes, physical matter doesn't even exist, it's all just vibration. Pure Life Force. I wanted that electricity to power me. When the motor was quiet I was a hollow vessel. Then whatever moved through me, whatever I was inspired to do, whatever thing I created, welled up organically. It was pure. Uncontaminated. Straight from the Source.

The first day out on our voyage to Panama, I could feel the motor fighting to hold on. I was restless. It was too sloppy to sit in the cockpit with my computer, but I was nauseous sitting below, staring at the monitor. I couldn't make jewelry because the little bits scattered with the motion of the boat. I wasn't hungry—and eating didn't count as being productive anyway. Finally, the sea salt began to warp the machined fittings of this man-made contraption, the constant motion bent its precision teeth, and its noisy expectations eventually slowed to an irregular sputter.

At sea there was space: only the sea and the sky—and I was suspended between them. I was freed from both the distraction of external clutter and the whirring of that internal motor. If I did nothing of consequence but keep watch and occasionally adjust the sails, I was still traveling toward my destination. I was still doing something.

On the fourth night out I awoke to my alarm at 11:55, crawled out from my bunk, braced against it and pulled on my foul-weather pants. When I climbed the few steps and came out on deck, I thought my eyes were playing tricks on me. I rubbed them and shook my head. We were surrounded, as far as I could see, by massive, smooth, rounded, gray hills, each illuminated by the moon with a golden sheen.

Heather and Anthony had much more in common than Anthony and I: They were closer in age, from the same part of the world, and even had a similar diet—meat, potatoes and veggies—while I was a pescatarian. I never completely got their dry, English humor, but on the last afternoon we were all feeling great. Heather and I were in the sunny cockpit enjoying a drink. We had a laugh about something and she said, sincerely, "Now I wish you were staying."

Anthony was down below, making dinner in the little corner galley right inside the companionway. He had the veggies cut, potatoes boiling, onions sautéing and steak for Heather and him ready to put in the pan when zzzzzzzzzz...the fishing line we'd been trolling for days without a nibble, suddenly sped out. A tuna! Anthony came out on deck as if he'd been expecting it, pulled it in, killed and filleted it, and wham, slapped the steaks straight into the hot waiting pan. Now that's fresh fish!

After five days out, motoring early the next morning, we were getting close. I was looking for the channel through a misty silver drizzle, the sea thick like oil. Then the silhouettes of monstrous ghost ships materialized around us, all of them at anchor, or so we prayed as we anxiously looked for signs to reassure ourselves that they weren't underway. Stories high, they dwarfed our little craft, and we didn't want to get caught too near one. I picked our way through them and found the channel into the Shelter Bay Marina on the Atlantic side.

CHAPTER 6

Between Boats

Treating Myself to a Lover
Shelter Bay Marina, Panama
March 30, 2010

    It was a refreshing change to tie up to the dock in a marina (we'd only ever anchored through the Caribbean) and this was a nice, modern one. There were clean showers with hot water, a pool and a hot tub, a bar and restaurant, and more new construction for shops underway. Yachts from all over the world were docked here to make preparations either to transit the canal from west to east, or, having just done this, to begin their journey into the Caribbean.

    The Panama Canal is a 48-mile (77 km), man-made waterway connecting the Atlantic Ocean to the Pacific through the Isthmus of Panama. Because the sea levels are different on the two sides, locks raise or lower ships accordingly. Each vessel is required to hire an official pilot and have four people onboard to handle the long lines used to tie each corner of the boat. Meanwhile, on-shore, guys either let the long lines out as the water level drops or pull them in as it rises, keeping each vessel suspended in the middle of the lock's towering walls and swirling water. Sailors take turns volunteering on each other's yachts and Heather had gone off for a few days to help with this line-handling chore.

    The best part of staying at the marina was that I could just step off the boat anytime, without having to negotiate with anyone about using the dinghy. On a night watch while still out at sea, I'd decided to take a lover while in Panama; I hadn't had one in a while, and I deserved one, I told myself. I needed a little fun, so was keeping my eyes out.

Adventures of a Pirate Girl

Our neighboring boat in the marina was a 78-foot Choy Lee motor sailor. Onboard were nine Americans from Minnesota who were planning on going through the Northwest Passage in the Arctic Circle. They were loud and brash, not from my tribe, but after being with a subdued Englishman for so long, I found comfort in their company, my naturally loud voice blending perfectly with their vociferous milieu, never causing anyone to politely signal me to lower my volume. On a whim, they took me to dinner in Colon. One guy, Craig, reminded me of an ex-boyfriend: strapping, but quiet. A "do anything for you" type, if a little dull. While swapping stories, the extent of his offering was a gentle "very cool, very cool," while nodding his head. He seemed to gravitate toward me. I was, after all, the only unattached female. I thought he might be my hook-up.

The next night there was a potluck dinner for all the cruisers; Anthony and I went, since it was our last night together. Afterward he went to bed and I went to the bar. Craig was there and bought me a drink. Then Potter, a young blond, showed up and saddled the stool on my other side. We all chatted a bit, then Craig up and left, not interested after all. Potter asked if I wanted to get stoned, so I followed him to the boat he was on: a 40-footer.

Like the three bears, there were three American guys onboard, all blond surfers. The big one was maybe 50, the middle one in his mid-30s, and the baby one was Potter, who turned out to be 21. As we stepped down into the cabin, the other two casually looked up and nodded at me as if I was a frequent visitor. The yacht had been built in the same boatyard in Taiwan where my boat had been built and had a similar interior. This conjured a warm, familiar feeling in me. We all gathered around the table and shared in the ritual of smoking pot. Funny, I kept directing my conversation to the Papa bear, assuming he was the Captain, though he sat there mutely. It was the guy closer to my age who spoke up and engaged with me. We had a nice conversation about wooden boats, Reuel Parker (a boat designer I knew personally), surfing in Costa Rica (I had some experience)—we seemed to hit it off. It wasn't until later, after Potter and I left, that he informed me that it was this guy, the middle bear, who was the Captain. Apparently his fiancé was scared shitless of sailing. Huh. In retrospect, I'm glad I didn't know. I might have gotten my hopes up.

Potter, it turned out, had ulterior motives. Normally I had radar for this sort of thing, but he seemed so young and harmless, I hadn't counted him as either predator or prey in my "take a lover" game. As we slowly wandered around the marina grounds smoking his last joint, it began to occur to me what he was about and I was having fun watching to see if, and how, he would make his move. We strolled past the complex still under construction; the shops with glass fronts were empty, but otherwise complete, the doors unlocked. One of them caught my attention and I lingered, smiling coquettishly. It struck my imagination like a match: All four interior walls were lined from floor to ceiling with mirrors. He must have seen the flare because that's when he cornered and kissed me. I laughed and pointed out, "It's like we found an amusement park for sex sports." I suggested we get in the hot tub, which was in the vicinity. Still in a playful and teasing mood, I swirled around the tub in my now-see-through panties, not letting him pin me down. After a bit he said, with a hint of sulk, "You're teasing me, and I'm getting horny."

"Oh, you poor little boy with a hard-on," I thought to myself, my passion somewhat dimmed. "Whatever are you going to do?" It occurred to me that a hard-on was like a crying baby, something a woman was expected to deal with. Granted, I was batting him around like a little mouse. So once he forcefully grabbed me and made it clear what he had to offer, grinding it scrumptiously against me, I decided, oh yes. I wanted it. And so yes, I would have it.

I led him back to the mirrored room. First he held me up against the wall—no having to maneuver for a good view there! And then I was straddling him on the floor and he still managed to pound upward like a jack hammer. Oh damn. These little boys. It was light and easy and fun, like an ice-cream cone you've been craving on a hot day. And safe—of course we used condoms—but also emotionally safe, since he was too young for me to wrap my heart around. Regardless of this, there always seemed to be a few stray heartstrings that would get attached. As a woman I think this is just part of the energetic transaction of taking a man into your body. But I was pretty good at ridding myself of them quickly.

The next morning I packed my stuff, gave Anthony a hug, and got in a taxi.

Adventures of a Pirate Girl

Dragonfly

Panama City, Panama
April 3, 2010

The marina was located deep in a national park. It took nearly an hour in the taxi to wind through the jungle before finally breaking out from the tree cover, crossing a small bridge by the locks and arriving at the bus station in the city of Colon. I'd been warned that this was a dangerous area, so I stayed near the ticket booth until my bus came. We traveled southeast, across the skinny Isthmus of Panama to a hostel I'd found online, Casa del Carmen, in Panama City.

The place was a quaint, yellow house, and the lady who ran it was welcoming and genuinely friendly. I dropped my bag on a bunk in the tidy dorm room and wandered around the rest of the place. There were big, colorful, shared spaces: a lounge with couches and a TV, a computer desk area, a well-stocked kitchen—but the best part was the back patio, surrounded by a high wall topped with coiled wire to keep the dirty city out. The inner walls were lined with banana trees, birds of paradise, and other tropical plants. Birds darted and swooped around feeders and a mosaic fountain, and a tame green parrot sat on a perch. The dining area was on the patio, right outside big sliding doors. It was covered and tiled, with brightly painted tables.

Free and autonomous once again, I was filled with the sense that everything was perfect—exactly how it should be—that I was beautiful and capable and totally on top of my game. Life was amazing and I was stoked to be living it.

I ventured out to the grocery store just down the street and I felt like I was in a perfume ad: a top model sauntering down the street in heels, with a tantalizing aroma wafting from me in a cartoon pink cloud. Seriously, I was turning heads. The taxi driver, diagonal from me across the busy intersection, leaned his body out the window and watched me as he drove by. A guy walking his dog across the street stopped and whistled. I laughed and waved flirtatiously. Two guys walking toward me, deep in conversation, were stunned into silence as they parted to let me through, both turning to watch me pass.

If I didn't make this clear earlier: I was not a drop-dead gorgeous woman. I was well-proportioned and healthy. Not bad looking; cute. Nowhere close to gorgeous. But life force was emanating so strongly from me, it was like a magnet.

Between Boats

That evening I was hanging out in the lounge, chatting with various people. I met Stephen, who struck me instantly as from my same ocean tribe. He was a surfer kid: well…32, but had that never-grow-up, lost-boy vibe that I love (I had Peter Pan tattooed on my shoulder when I was 15.) He was from Florida, and had the same variety of freedom I did: Borders didn't hold him in. He was surfing in Panama regularly *and* had gone on annual surf trips to Hatteras—my home for five years—and knew the same local surfer boys there that I did, so we had plenty to talk about. I was excited to meet someone who felt like he could be a real friend; I missed and craved friendship more than anything. Maybe it was that craving that got me all full of swagger, talking about how man-crazy I'd been. I told him the first section of the blog I had been writing about sailing in the Caribbean was called "A Man in Every Port," like I was bragging. But after a bit I found my own eagerness annoying so I opted to play cards with some American girls, where the subjects of books and feminism were lighter and I didn't have to face my patterns with men.

That night I had a dream about Stephen: that I wanted his attention but didn't ask for it.

The next morning I went on a run and found a huge park 10 blocks away, with hills and trees and walking paths. Then I spent the day on my computer, sending queries to magazines, trying to become a real writer by publishing articles.

My energy was sinking a bit, so I read Liz Clark's blog, hoping for inspiration. She was a badass surfer chic who was sailing the world and living the dream to the fullest, but within my awe of admiration there was jealousy. She was way too cool, too beautiful, with outside financial backing and the glossy surfer magazines following her story. She had the know-how and support to really live big, which made my life feel paltry and slightly pathetic.

That's when I noticed my slow slide downhill. I took a nap, took the cute Rottweiler puppy that was chained up in the deserted side-yard for a walk, made friends with a girl from Switzerland. Though we didn't have much to talk about, we spent the next morning touring the Casco Viejo, Old Town in Panama. It was near the sea, with historic wooden house fronts refurbished and painted in different pastel colors. The classic colonial Spanish architecture was juxtaposed with crumbling buildings and a run-down ghetto. It was eerily quiet, like an empty movie set. We went to the one café we found and, upon leaving, were warned to stay on that side of the street; apparently the other side of the narrow lane was dangerous.

I was trying to stay upbeat but I kind of wanted to go to sleep… forever. I didn't know if I wanted to go sailing with John. I was supposed to meet him in the Dominican Republic the following week, but I'd just gotten word via email from my friend Dennis back in Sint Maarten that he didn't like John. He had a small-man complex, Dennis said, and when they'd met through mutual friends at Lagoonies, John had gotten all negative and fired up about politics. Fuck. The thought of being trapped on another boat with someone I didn't know was eating me up. It's as if I'd been blindfolded and spun around: Which direction should I take? I'd already committed to sailing with John. He was on his way to meet me, and I had the ticket.

I tried to rally against the lazy gluttony in my soul, but it was so hard. Frickin' depression: Is that what kept me from being like Liz Clark? I went to the grocery store, not to buy healthy, whole food like I had the other day when I was flying high, but to buy as much chocolate and ice cream as it would take to numb this horrid expanse of nothingness that was spreading inside me. My life felt meaningless and I was totally alone… in this life, in this country. All of my dreams and hopes felt futile and pointless. And you know what? Not one single person noticed me, proving attraction isn't all about looks. It was as if I was completely invisible—which was good, because I couldn't stand to be seen in this state. I just wanted to grab my sugar, slither under a rock and pig out.

In the park, lying on a blanket finishing off a pint of Starbuck's ice cream in the muggy city heat, I had written about my dilemma. I talked about it in the kitchen of the hostel, while a glossy clean American couple listened with compassion as they cooked dinner. When Stephen showed up after being gone for three days, I discussed it with him while stretched out on the couch enjoying the comfort of a movie in English and his familiar vibe. But still I could feel this intense energy in my throat, like I was wearing a choker. It hurt to swallow.

The next day I wanted so bad to hang out with Stephen; to spend the day with him, away from the hostel.

"Oh come on, Stephen. Let's just go do something."

"Ah man, I'm tired. I guess I'd be up for going to the mall or something," he offered.

Between Boats

"I don't want to go to the mall," I got all puffed up. "We're in Panama, let's go do something, like, I dunno, go to the botanical garden or something."

Instead of just admitting that all I really wanted was his company, I ended up going off on my own. I took one of the buses and sat huddled on the bench seat, alone.

The buses in Panama are a sight to behold: They are usually old school buses, but totally tricked out. They seemed to be privately owned by the drivers, because each of them is a work of art with full, intricate, colorful murals completely covering the outside, and various decorations: stuck on jewels or little trinkets along the dashboard, and velvety material or fringe on the ceiling inside. Mine had blaring music.

I half-heartedly headed to the botanical gardens, but it was getting to be late afternoon and the lady I was chatting with warned me that it might be hard to get a bus back. As we drove past the Panama Canal museum, overlooking one of the locks of the canal itself, I jumped off the bus when it stopped for someone else. I'd already been through the canal on a boat years before and had toured a different canal museum, so I wasn't interested in this place, but I went anyway just to kill time. Then, feeling like it would be even more pathetic to just go back to the hostel, I went to the mall.

While I was eating donut holes, waiting for my movie, a big studly black man, an ex-pro baseball player, approached me, chatted me up and then joined me for the movie. We ended up hanging out for hours afterward, drinking cans of beer in the back seats of various party buses and touring the city. He was nice. Interesting. Good looking. He even searched me out the next day and tried to stay in touch. It was fine. He was cool. So I fucked him.

This time it was more like eating a chocolate bar after I'd already had a whole tub of ice cream. Normally, the chocolate bar would be satisfying but I didn't really appreciate it because I was already too full. In fact, it made me slightly sick.

The next morning at the hostel, I was sitting on the patio having my third cup of coffee. A German girl joined me and we continued an earlier conversation about our adventures. She immediately tuned in to where I was at:

"Okay, I want you to do something," she said. "I want you to imagine calling the Captain and canceling. Just feel what that feels like."

"When I think about that…"

"No, don't think. *Feel* it; take a minute. Close your eyes. Feel it. What is your heart telling you?"

It didn't take a minute, I already knew. "It feels like utter relief. Like a weight off my chest."

"Okay, that's it. You've already made the decision. Your head wants to analyze it, but you know what your heart wants."

And, just like that, the sharp scratchiness in my throat was gone. It was like the dam between my head and my heart had washed away and the energy was flowing again. I didn't owe John anything. He had another crew with him anyway, so he wouldn't be totally stranded. And I didn't have to figure out what I wanted to do instead. All I had to do was steer toward what felt better.

I still had the ticket to the Dominican Republic, and Sean, my old friend who owned a bar there, had been arranging for someone to pick me up at the airport and set me on the right bus to visit him, before joining John's boat. The thought of this made me feel loved; what a relief it would be to hang out with a friend who cared about me. Plus Sean had a girlfriend. We had a bit of history together, but her presence would keep things solidly in friend mode. After giving myself a tummy ache with the over-indulgence of meaningless sex, that was just what I wanted.

The morning I was to leave, Stephen and I made lunch together at the hostel. He had found me a tiny joint and walked me out to the end of the street where it ended in an overgrown ditch, so I could smoke it. When the cab showed up, while I was struggling with my backpack, the lady who ran the place nudged him, friendly but forceful, "What's wrong with you American boys? Help her!" Which he did.

Safely in my window seat on the refrigerated plane, the journey was underway. Whether by boat, plane, train or automobile, movement without a thing to do but sit and stare always satisfies me. I was leaving the old, embracing the new. Contentedly, I gazed out the window, while within me a swirl of fresh experiences coalesced into positive memories.

Then, out my window, I noticed a dragonfly clinging to the top edge where the glass met the hull. A good sign, I thought. As the plane began to roll away from the gate and down the runway, I realized the dragonfly was committed. Its tiny hair-lined arms gripped the lip of steel and, with a sailor's knowledge of the elements, it turned its body into the wind. It had big dreams... it wanted to fly high with the plane. Our velocity increased and its wings started to vibrate while its fragile body twisted and flapped. Maybe it was dead; its dried-out shell stuck on by some death goo. But then I saw it scramble to get a better position. What if it's stuck? Its big dream would rip its wings off, tear it to pieces. A dream can do that. But right as the bow of the plane lifted, the dragonfly let go. Under its own power it glided away.

And so, like the dragonfly, I let go. This dream could lift me if I let it go. I spread my wings and with the power of inspiration, I glided away to see where the wind would take me.

CHAPTER 7
Dominican Republic

Luperon, Dominican Republic
April 10, 2010

    I took the bus through the Dominican Republic, a lush, verdant country of rolling hills, patchworked with many shades and textures of green. There were roadside fruit stands everywhere with pineapples, mangos, bananas and oranges, and there were guys getting on the bus to sell anything from nuts and homemade sweets to phone chargers and cheap sunglasses. We passed small towns that reminded me of the Wild West, with packs of guys loitering in front of dilapidated wood-slat houses, their motorcycles crowded out front like horses. I was instantly swarmed when I got off the bus in the small town of Luperon. Apparently the motorcycles, called *motoconchos*, were the common transport for anything from two adults sandwiching a few kids to a guy carrying a queen-sized mattress. I walked.

    And finally, after days of traveling from Panama by plane, car and bus, I spotted the sign—Shaggy's Barstool Sailor. Sean greeted me, with his tousled reddish hair, scraggly goatee and thin frame, he strongly resembled Shaggy from Scooby Do.

    Shaggy's was in a cement courtyard fronted by a low wall, yellow and blue, with a rectangular cement counter encircling the seating area, shaded by a palapa roof. The kitchen was a basic, cement-block building with living quarters behind it.

    After catching up with Sean, Camilla and Lynn, his mom, I moved aboard Sean's 36-foot boat *Capitana*. She was more of a shell than a fitted-out yacht, with no proper galley or head. She was anchored in the large, protected harbor.

Dominican Republic

The water was thick and green, and nobody swam in it. It was so full of nutrients that the noise of the crustaceans against *Capitana*'s hull made it sound like the boat was afloat in a bowl of Rice Krispies. Motoring through it at night created a phosphorescent wake of light as if the dinghy was lit from underneath. Whatever my accommodations, I rejoiced being alone on a vessel once again.

I set down the 22-ounce bottle of Bohemia beer—the only size available at Shaggy's. Then I pumped up Sean's old inflatable—I needed transport back and forth from his boat—and began the chore of patching and painting its bottom. But after I'd finished, air was still escaping. This was how I felt. I could hear the small hissing sound of my enthusiasm for travel and adventure, for doing something admirable and interesting, slowly leaking out of me.

Sean and I had talked about my working for him, and I did, a little. But it wasn't a very busy time of year; it felt more like hanging out at a bar and occasionally grabbing someone a beer. It didn't provide any kind of routine or structure that may have helped my mood. I felt adrift in a sea of no plans: my enthusiasm steadily leaking—tttssssssss.

I made friends with two preteen girls, Skye and Ciele (pronounced sail), whose parents were the quintessential barstool sailors: They lived on a boat, but day and night you could find them at the bar, sucking down alcohol, leaving the girls to fend for themselves. One morning the girls and I went on a run together. Then they took me to a non-denominational church in the beautiful, western-style home of the white English pastor. There were folded seats set in rows on the terrace and maybe seven people, one of whom was a Haitian man with the darkest skin I'd ever seen, and a bright, humble smile. The pastor was giving his sermon and I was absentmindedly enjoying the beautiful views overlooking the harbor, when his words trickled into my awareness. It was the story of Onesimus and Philemon.

"Excuse me," I interrupted. "I'm sorry, I'm just trying to understand."

"Yes, go ahead, my child," he allowed, patiently, happy to be leading one of his flock.

"Are you saying that Onesimus was in the wrong for stealing?"

"That's right, he ran away and stole from his master. Stealing is a sin, but he was forgiven."

Adventures of a Pirate Girl

"But, I mean, he was just trying to save himself. Doesn't the sin of enslaving a fellow human being trump the sin of stealing to survive?" I asked, shocked.

He tried to explain that slavery was different back then. I pointed out that if the guy was trying to run away, he obviously wasn't happy with the arrangement. I was appalled and said so. It was especially offensive to hear this from a white man on an island that included Haiti, the poorest country in the Americas that had just suffered a catastrophic earthquake, which nobody seemed to be talking about.

The pastor's face began to swell like a balloon, growing red with the pressure.

"I'm sorry, this just strikes me as totally racist and cruel; I can't sit here. I'm gonna go." I stood, tentatively smiled at the girls and shrugged. They popped up and followed me out.

~

I was borrowing an old fiberglass shell of a skiff until I could get Sean's inflatable to hold air. It would have looked more at home washed up sideways onshore and filled with sand. It had a little outboard engine from the '50s. To make it go, I had to take the cover off the engine, wind the string around the flywheel just so, and then pull with all my might, which worked about 40% of the time. Otherwise, I took to standing in the bow and paddling her with the one oar, gondola style. But *Capitana* was a long way out.

I tried to stay positive but, without some plan to cling to, I could feel myself sinking—and those 22-ounce beers weren't helping. I grabbed onto ideas as if they were pieces of floating wreckage. A young guy I met at the bar was one. He was heading to Puerto Rico that evening, but his engine was running at a high rpm. He didn't have much experience so I offered to help. Turned out he was happy for me to join him, and for a minute I would have, but he was meeting up with a girl in a few weeks and then that would be that. I'd made friends with a family on *Free Spirit*, who would've loved to have me as crew, but they wouldn't be going for months, and I couldn't wait that long. For a day I dreamed up the grandiose fantasy of fixing Sean's boat and circumnavigating Cuba, while creating some collaborative artwork. But Sean vetoed that in a heartbeat because of the legalities. That was good because, though the idea of it buoyed me, the reality may well have wrecked me for good.

Dominican Republic

My big, cool adventure, my impressive feat of bravery—it had all been done. Back when I'd owned my boat, it was so much more than just a floating hunk of fiberglass and wood. It became a part of my identity: proof of my strength, determination and worthiness. It was my ticket into the "I am doing something extraordinary with my life" club. Being an adventurer was the same—it was how I saw myself. But maybe it was time I got off my high horse and admitted it: I wasn't actually that great a traveler. So what made me happy anyway? Meditation. Dance. Writing. Being physical. I hated to admit it, but some sort of routine. Friends—that was a big one. Being with people I loved.

But I still clutched at scraps of buoyant debris: I could go to Cuba by plane, or at least travel around the Dominican Republic. The voice in my head was telling me, "You have to *do* something."

But I peeled its fingers back one by one from its grip and released myself. "You don't have to be a star, Davina. You don't have to have some claim to fame. You are lovable and worthy just the way you are. You can just go home." Sitting under the palm-frond roof at Shaggy's, way too early to be starting on my second Bohemia, I opened up my computer and decided to look into it. But—one, two, three, four—the Universe had other plans.

First I contacted Taylor, the manager at my old, beloved workplace: the Walnut Café in Boulder, Colorado. She instantly wrote me back, prodding me gently to not let go of my dream, but opening her welcoming arms all the same. She was about to leave for a dive trip to Thailand and, if I could get there by May 15th, I could cover for her at the Walnut and step back into the life I'd left. She was doing the schedule right then and needed an answer. Pressure. That would have barely given me three weeks, and even though I wasn't doing anything, it didn't seem like long enough.

Second, I got an email from a girl I'd met briefly in Curaçao. We had been keeping in touch because of our similar paths: she had been crew and jumped ship as well. She was now in Panama at the same hostel where I had stayed. She informed me that she had just signed onto a boat heading into the Pacific. Shit. She hadn't made the loud declaration to sail around the world like I had; she was just going sailing. In the Pacific! Just doing it. Damn.

Then third, I filed my tax return online and found out I'd be getting a refund of just over $1000. I would put this into a separate account and not use it for day-to-day expenses; it would be my safety net money.

And fourth, the most compelling email arrived from Louie. He was someone I had been in contact with since Sint Maarten. Originally, he and his wife, Carrie, had contacted me from the crew site 7Knots.com, looking for paying crew. They wanted people to pay a charter price for an all-inclusive adventure trip aboard their luxurious, 48-foot catamaran *Cariño*. I had gracefully declined, explaining my completely different mode of travel. But they did seem cool. Carrie was involved in a non-profit in Zimbabwe and had mentioned an affinity with my obvious spiritual nature. Louie had stayed in contact through the past few months, chatting with me on Skype and sending me links to other boats and other opportunities. At one point he offered to lower the price, but I declined.

"I am looking for people to cover *my* expenses, just like you are," I said, putting it as clearly as I could. Now, in this email, Louie was finally speaking my language. Carrie was working on her non-profit in Africa for three months and he needed help aboard: He would pay my expenses and, when he got a charter, I could make money.

And with that, the small hissing sound stopped and my energy seemed to expand as if being inflated with a hand pump. Joining Louie was the ticket: I was going to sail the Pacific!

In Love with Love

I had a bit of time before I'd fly out to get on *Cariño* so I decided to accompany Lynn, Sean's mom, to Samana, where she was meeting a friend to help him sail his boat to Puerto Rico.

I had known Lynn in Beaufort back in 2000 and, though I was in the Dominican Republic to visit her son, I felt more connected with her. She and her late husband had lived on *Suits Us*, a 28-foot Bristol Channel Cutter. When he passed away, she'd carried on. Sean and Lynn had stuck together, each on their own boat, but, since opening the bar, the tension between them was coming to a head and I was stuck in the middle, hearing both sides of it.

Lynn was a strong-willed, single-hander and her vessel, *Suits Us*, was moored right beside *Capitana*. She had been ferrying me back and forth, feeding me breakfast and coffee, and generally making my stay aboard *Capitana* possible. Sixty-seven and still agile, she had short, white hair, strong hands, and a face that didn't give a shit about cultural expectations of how a woman should look.

Lynn was tough. She knew all there was to know about boats and getting it done, and enjoyed her self-appointed role as mother of the harbor, even though she enjoyed bitching about it just as much. She kept tabs on everyone, making sure the boats that left got to where they needed to go and the ones that arrived got what they needed to get. In this country, every price was negotiable. I'd be proud of myself, having bargained something down to half what was asked; then Lynn would inform me that it was still five times too much. She didn't speak a word of Spanish but she got her point across.

We left early for Samana. It took us seven hours squished into the beat-up, four-seater vehicle called a *guagua* (pronounced wa-wa), sitting crooked and sideways with seven other sweaty bodies not including the driver. After traveling northeast from Luperon for several hours, we finally reached our destination, a bustling tourist town. Right off the beach were two small, round islands jutting up and covered in luscious green jungle with bridges stretched between them, attaching them to the mainland. Lynn and I took a walk across them and stopped to take pictures of some boys jumping off.

"I'd be scared to do that," I was just saying to Lynn when the oldest boy, probably about 15, rich brown skin and in tight black boxer shorts, noticed my obvious interest.

"*Tu queres saltar?*" he asked me.

"*Si,*" I answered, smiling, "but I'm scared!"

I could jump from outside the railing, he explained, saving maybe four feet on the 50-foot drop.

"No, if I'm going to do, I'll do it all the way."

I climbed up on the sturdy cement handrail, not stopping long enough to give hesitation any time to elongate, this boy at my side. I could feel the thrill of it in my stomach, heart and throat: "*Uno, dos, tres,*" we jumped! Free falling, and then the sharp slap of the water on the bottoms of my feet. The younger boy came right after. When we swam to the base of the bridge to climb up, he swam underwater and placed my foot on a little notch between the sharp shells.

Looking up at the bridge, a string of cement arches, I realized the climb back would be the scariest part. The boys wanted to somehow hoist me up, which would have been so much more dangerous. I assured them I could do it if they led the way. So we scrabbled up the first concrete mound, and then inched

Adventures of a Pirate Girl

along up the arch, swinging out around each supporting pillar until we were right under the walkway. At that point there was an overhang up to the railing. I channeled all my rock climbing experience, slapped away their helping hands and pulled myself up. The boys were so stoked; jumping around, they hugged me and told me I was the first *"gringa que hizo eso"* (white girl who did that).

After that adventure, Lynn's friend, Chuck, met us, and I stayed with them aboard his 28-foot yacht for two days. Chuck treated us to dinner with a lovely couple, an American and his Dominican partner whom he had met online. Dave and Doña owned a restaurant/night club on the Samana waterfront and invited me to stay at their house once Lynn left.

I spent the night at their house—a brand new stucco abode built more to American scale than Caribbean. But from the interior décor, it was obviously more a depot than a home; between the haphazardly-placed brand new couches were piles of stuff that had been tossed there in Dave and Doña's hurried comings and goings.

I woke up on my 35th birthday and decided to take a bus to the *Cascada Salto del Limon*. On the side of a small road through the rainforest there was a rickety stall, like a makeshift lemon stand. I let the guy convince me of the need to hire a horse ride to the falls, but was disappointed when the guide led my pony by a rope as if I was a little girl at the fairgrounds. I could have easily hiked it for free. But the site was magnificent. A thin white sheet of water cascaded down a velvet-green wall of rock that wrapped around a natural blue pool where I took a swim.

Afterward, I was planning to get my stuff back at the house and take the bus to Cabarete. But Alfonzo, the chef in Dave and Doña's restaurant, who was also staying in their house, was in the middle of putting together the metal frame of a bed for me. "Don't go yet. Hang out with me, it's my day off."

I thought, what the hell, it'd be nice to have someone to spend my birthday with. He asked me what I had done on my last birthday and I explained about 420 in the States: How in Boulder on April 20th, thousands of people gathered on the college campus for this baby holiday that was growing in momentum. At 4:20 pm, everyone sparked up in unison and clouds of marijuana smoke drifted over the sea of people. It being my birthday, I was the self-appointed Queen of 420.

Dominican Republic

So Alfonzo decided that's what we'd do: Get some weed. To do this, we walked and walked and talked and talked, which was great practice for my Spanish. Once we'd obtained the goods—behind some shack way up on the hills—we made the long trek back down through the town, across the bridges, to the second island, where there was a cement platform and pavilion, the ghost of a restaurant that never was, now crumbling back into jungle. From there, we could just make out the land across the bay. Breathtaking. We smoked and, of course, the mood shifted and he sidled up a little closer. So I laid down the law:

"*No estoy interesada*," I explained. "I'm celibate." This took some work to translate, but when he finally got my meaning, he acted as if I were a nun sworn to lifelong celibacy. His face grim with the thought of it, he asked how long it had been.

"About two weeks," I answered, struggling to stifle a giggle.

We went back to the restaurant, which was closed, and Alfonzo made us dinner while I sat on the chest freezer, watching him and drinking beer.

"Oh," he cooed, like he'd finally figured it out, "You're in love." He was close. I had been staring off into space, daydreaming about Stephen from the hostel in Panama. This was one of my bad habits, not anchored in anything real. I knew that. The make-believe Stephen was an idol I'd conjured up to produce feelings of love and comfort—the emotional equivalent of meaningless sex.

The next day I caught the bus for Cabarete, a tourist town on the north coast of the DR, feeling back to myself, or at least the self I preferred: the fearless, not-worried-about-it, world traveler, rocking out in my seat with my iPod, the hot wind in my face. At the local hostel, I got a beautiful little room all to myself for $15 a night, proud for getting it down from the $35 the lady first quoted. It was in a little round palapa hut surrounded by gardens, complete with a beautifully tiled bathroom. After a seafood dinner in the house restaurant, which was *delicioso*, I retreated early to my lovely little space.

If I had my own pot I could happily hang out with myself, like a parakeet in front of a mirror, for hours. The need for other people completely dropped away.

In *What the Bleep Do We Know,* a documentary exploring the connection between quantum physics and consciousness, one of the scientists explains that feelings are actually chemicals, like heroin, that our bodies can produce on demand. We get addicted to them. Well, with a little smoke, the fetishized fantasy of a man, some music, sexy panties and a mirror, I could happily entertain myself all night long. I would imagine each little phrase he'd utter: "Excuse me," when he got a phone call; the smile when we'd pass in the hall; "We roomies again?" his brilliant smile flashing. I'd use my imaginings to sculpt a false idol, and this idol and I would fall in love. With this romance novel in my mind and tiny circles on my clit, I could produce a rush through my heart. Not the overwhelming tidal wave of an orgasm, but the continuous, trickling flow of a river. I was definitely addicted to this chemical and I knew it.

I thought of the movie *Cold Mountain*, set during Civil War times in the U.S.. Nicole Kidman only meets Jude Law a handful of times but then, once he's away fighting, she holds him in her imagination and fantasizes about him for years to come, writing him letters and pining. I definitely found it easier to love someone from afar. When I was a teenager and had my first real boyfriend, we were totally in love for a while until I told him I wanted to see other people. After our break-up, I dedicated a journal to him and kept it like a make-believe relationship into which I could pour all of my thoughts and feelings. With Stephen, I'd subconsciously ensured that I could use him to manufacture this fantasy by putting up a wall, a false bravado, presenting myself as a man-eater and connecting with him like one of the guys, protecting the vulnerable and lonely girl inside. I doubt he had any idea that I had a crush on him.

I can trace this pattern back to my childhood. As a kid, I emulated my dad's way of being in the world. There was no doubt his was a safer model: emotionally unavailable and looking out for himself first and foremost. He seemed more free and powerful than my mom. When they got divorced he felt free to drop his successful business and become a poor writer living a Bohemian lifestyle on the beach in Santa Cruz, while my mom struggled and slaved to support us four kids. I didn't want to be vulnerable. I wanted to be tough. But, of course, it's a lot tougher to be vulnerable than it is to be cut off emotionally.

I knew I needed to quit doing this relationship abstraction. When Stephen popped up on Facebook, I tried to get serious: "Maybe we could meet up on my way back through Miami?" He made some crude sexual joke about going at it in the janitor's closet at the airport, which, of course, had been prompted by the way I had presented myself to him. But my feelings got hurt, I took offense and unfriended him. I also dropped the fantasy.

Women

Luperon, Dominican Republic

My stomach clenched and I grabbed desperately for the five-gallon bucket, my head spinning. Once I purged from the top end I sat, hunched over on the same bucket, and squirted my liquefied insides out the other end. I didn't even have the fortitude to set that foul pail outside; the distance was too far from the cabin floor where I lay. Inside the boat was a sweltering miasma, my body leaden and slick with sweat. I didn't have the strength to crawl forward and open the hatch to let in some air. All I had left to drink was a warm swish of water at the bottom of a plastic jug. I was alone in this state for what felt like days and I imagined myself dying there, with no water to drink and no way to shore. My body had revolted against the lifestyle I'd been living, cleansing itself of my crutches: men, food, alcohol, smoke.

It was women who rescued me.

Lynn came by in the afternoon to check on me, since I hadn't answered her early morning VHF call for our regular coffee and breakfast on her boat. Once she found out about my condition, she brought me a five-gallon jug of drinking water and alerted Laura, who lived on *Free Spirit* with her husband and three, preteen sons. Between them they cared for me, bringing me bland foods and making me as comfortable on *Capitana* as I could be. When I was barely well enough to venture out, Laura sent her eldest, Blayde, over in their aluminum skiff to fetch me. Sprawled out in their main cabin, plugged into the laptop with headphones, I watched a movie while the boys scurried around, reluctantly doing their daily chores. I was feeble but content to be surrounded by this inspirational family.

Free Spirit was an old-school, pirate-looking ship: 60-foot, gaff-rigged, with no winches or sail tracks. Blayde, Valin and Drake were excited to have me onboard because my reputation as a wild pirate woman had preceded me through their friends, Skye and Ciele. Blayde (14) was tan and fit with long blond hair, who wanted "more surfer guy than grunge rocker" when I offered to trim it. He introduced me to the boat, pointing out its features with maritime lingo and the exaggerated maturity of a budding teenager. Valin (11) was slightly chubby like the rest of the family, with dark hair that hung in his eyes. He was into so many things he had a hard time focusing on any of them: an avid reader, an intellectual with a witty sense of humor and a passion for baking.

Adventures of a Pirate Girl

When I got a little better he began making me elaborate desserts whipped up with flare, if not technical know-how. The third son, Drake (9), was so sweet and pudgy I had to hold myself back from cuddling him and pinching his round cheeks. They all spoke Spanish because, for the first time in their lives, they were taking time out of their home schooling routine to attend the local school in Luperon. I admired the way Laura and her husband Tamer spoke with their kids, honestly explaining things like marijuana and sexuality as these topics came up; also the way each boy had responsibilities and chores. The jovial way they joked, played and worked as a family on their pirate ship filled me with joy.

I loved her family, but most of all I loved Laura. She was fun, embarrassing her kids by stopping in the street to shake her booty when the speaker truck passed by blaring earsplitting music. She had a logical, accepting, and think-for-yourself way of going about life. They were from Alaska and were Christian "because they needed a story," but she was curious about my pagan spirituality. We found we had more in common than not. They had a government contract and were able to work from afar, but they weren't rich by any means. Still, she was making this self-sufficient and adventurous lifestyle work.

When I left the Dominican Republic on my way to Panama to meet up with my new boat, I had a 12-hour layover in Ft. Lauderdale, Florida, and a list of things to do while stateside. It had already been six months since I had left the country, and might well be years more before I returned. Again, a woman was there for me. A friend of Lynn's gladly picked me up at the airport and toted me around to do some shopping and other errands. We got it all done while sharing our stories, and then relaxed over margaritas for *Cinco de Mayo* while we chilled by her pool.

Something was shifting, thank the Goddess. Suddenly I was attracting all these awesome women. Men (at least for me while on this trip) were like candy and I definitely had a sweet tooth. And though we all need sweet things to make life worthwhile, women were my health-food: wholesome and life-sustaining.

Growing up I preferred the simple camaraderie of boys, but I usually had one or two really close girlfriends. In the third grade my best friend Marianne and I would skip around holding hands, even though other kids made fun of us, calling us "lesbos." Even so, we were happy in our own little, imaginative world.

When she moved away in the fourth grade, I was stuck with the remaining gaggle of girls. I still remember how they would take turns picking one of their own to hate for the day. Abolishing her from their little group, they would make a game of taunting the poor girl. I thought it was cruel and stupid, and I would always make a point to stick by the outcast's side. Until it came to my turn—and no one stuck by me. This kind of behavior dissuaded me from fully embracing girl culture and my femininity.

It starts young, with the monotony of the color pink in the girl's toy aisle, where there aren't a whole lot of other options specifically for young females if they aren't into playing princess, Barbie or housewife. Then, as they get older, popular media encourages a catty, judgmental, backstabbing culture: magazines pointing out which movie stars gained two pounds and which looked like skeletons; the close-up, candid shots of jiggly thighs and the ultra-computer enhanced women with airbrushed skin. The patriarchal machine—by constant bombardment through ads, TV shows, the music industry—stuffs girls into the girdle of a shallow, beauty-obsessed femininity, squeezing us into unhealthy relationships with ourselves and with each other.

I had a close circle of girlfriends in my early teenage years. In the eighth grade we began to differentiate ourselves from the bubblegum pop culture at our school—listened to different music and got creative in how we dressed. We also got curious about witchcraft. With books from the library we delved into ancient European herstory—our buried pre-Christian roots. Paganism, before it was slanted by Christianity, simply meant people of the earth. Together we experimented, creating simple Goddess ceremonies, attempting to reach a deeper connection to ourselves and the divine in a way that felt authentic to us.

In my early 20s, in Key West, Florida, I got involved in a Wiccan circle where we gathered for full moons, solstices and equinoxes, creating rituals that honored the rhythms of our earth and our connection to her. My beliefs about a higher power have always been my own. But for me, these reawakened rites that honored the sacred feminine as essential and powerful (as well as the male), come closest to revealing the magic that lies just beneath the surface of our world.

This stuff helped me grow into and connect with my feminist roots passed down to me by my great-grandmother. I began to fully appreciate my girlfriends and to understand the strength and support that comes from the women in my life. It was transformational for me to learn to love myself, to love my sisters, to connect and uplift, to value myself, to understand and feel my power. In this life and on this journey, I know I am blessed because of all the amazing women who love me. And I look forward to all the ones I have yet to meet.

CHAPTER 8

Cariño

Manifesting

Balboa Yacht Club
Panama City, Panama
May 6, 2010

    I had been busy for the past week aboard my new boat, *Cariño*. She was a high-end luxury yacht, much fancier than the average cruising boat, and with so much navigational equipment, the nav-station looked like an airplane cockpit. She also had AC, a deep freeze, a dive compressor, an inflatable dinghy that could pull a wake-boarder, a sailing dinghy, two kayaks, and on and on. She was a power hungry but beautiful boat. Louie, the Captain, was a pirate in the best sense of the word. He had lost his previous plywood trimaran in the South Pacific when it had broken up around him and his crew; they narrowly escaped with their lives. Now, a few years later, he was returning to the South Pacific on a $750,000 yacht bought for him by his girlfriend. His job was to make it pay.

    After my layover in Florida, I'd flown on to Panama. Louie's local driver, Martin, had picked me up from the airport and driven me the few hours through the rainy night back to the same yacht club where I'd said goodbye to Anthony and left *Shayela* the month before. On board *Cariño* I had a good night's sleep and, the next morning, Louie immediately put me to work. Over the next week, I wired a new shore power switch, did some plumbing, wired the new inverter, replaced water filters and helped with the massive provisioning we needed to prepare for crossing the Pacific. We also moved the boat through the locks from the Atlantic to the Pacific side. In exchange for my expenses, I had also been cooking and cleaning for him. Being busy was just what I needed. And so far we got along great.

Louie was maybe 50, a big guy from Texas, his brown hair balding slightly on top and long in the back. He had a rich brown tan all over, a Polynesian tattoo down the middle of his back and was mostly toned with a smooth, round beer belly. While transiting the Panama Canal he had proven himself social and fun, doing the can-can for the gathered onlookers and the web cams, in nothing but his thonged bikini bottoms. It was empowering for me the way he trusted my competence, explaining what needed to be done and then leaving me to do it.

We'd anchored *Cariño* in a bay at the end of a long peninsula that stuck out from Panama City. Along the road ran a nicely landscaped walkway where the locals came to ride bikes, jog and stroll. The high-rise cityscape was in the distance, and there were a few posh restaurants, bike rentals and bars near where we landed the dinghy. Farther out on the peninsula was a fancy marina full of sports fishing boats and big glossy motor yachts.

Louie and I were doing some emails at the Balboa Yacht Club when a familiar face walked up. She was young, tanned and blond, with striking pear-green eyes and a muscular neck and shoulders. I pointed at her and declared, "I know you from somewhere."

"Costa Rica??? No... I know... Hatteras, the Orange Blossom."

"That's it!"

Her name was Rebecca. We hadn't really known each other, but we knew all the same people.

After talking more the following night at happy hour, Rebecca and her Captain, Craig, brought their swanky, 69-foot steel motor yacht called *Kokomo* around the point and anchored near us. She and I spent the next few evenings hanging out, our respective Captains always in tow. In between the boat talk, sea stories, and general banter with the boys, she and I would occasionally get a moment alone, and she would slip out of her tough, redneck demeanor and expose her feminine side, the side that believed in organic tampons and was concerned about how our food was processed in the States.

She had grown up fishing and surfing with her dad in Virginia and Hatteras and had been a mate on a charter boat since she was 15. She had won fishing tournaments and had fished commercially on a tuna boat for a few years. During that time, she was on the top-producing East Coast tuna boat. The girl was a bad ass. She had been engaged to the Captain of the commercial boat, but realized that she was miserable, both in the relationship and in Hatteras. Wow, could I relate! Then Craig, an old fishing buddy, had called her up, insisting she get her butt down to Puerto Rico for an opportunity she couldn't refuse. He even sent her the ticket. She was now getting paid big bucks to crew with Craig around the world. The owner had taken off for two months, but urged them to take his boat out, go fishing and have fun. When Craig was around, Rebecca said, it was more like family than work. He even did some of the cooking. It sounded like an ideal situation.

After a long week of preparation, Jill and Steve, an active and adventurous middle-aged couple from Washington state, joined us on *Cariño* as paying crew, basically charter guests who were happy to work. We had one night on the boat and a morning of orientation, which was cut short by electrical problems with the autopilot. Jill and Steve were eager to help, but their faster-paced energy, continuous flow of questions, and need to be doing something collided with our slower, more mellow process, and only made the job harder. Also, their tight schedule created a lot of pressure and, by that afternoon, the exhausting week had caught up with Louie and me. We were both worn out, and I was desperate for some free time—some girl time. Louie dropped me off at *Kokomo*.

Rebecca had just finished her chores for the day and we decided to take a walk. Craig took us to shore on their "dinghy," a 20-foot V-hull center console that made it obvious they weren't your average cruisers. As we approached the rough, wood and iron edges of the floating dock, Rebecca and I hung our legs overboard to fend off. One of them remarked, not for the first time, "We need to get some fenders."

Rebecca and I strolled toward the marina on the wide, paved walkway as people on four-seater bicycles, like Flintstone cars, pedaled by. By this time we had gotten to know each other a bit, and being without our Captains, we were free to take out more intimate pieces of ourselves and our experiences, not only to share but also to re-examine in the light of a new friendship.

At the end of the road, behind a lot piled with machinery and metal boat jacks, we wandered down a path strewn with trash and found a small rocky beach out of the way of the bustling marina. On flat stones we made ourselves comfortable and rattled on about our lives.

Cariño

Rebecca noticed a wayward fender bobbing just off the beach, just what she and Craig had asked for! She jumped up and walked down the shore to get it. I followed with the stick of bamboo I'd been playing with. She tried to hook the fender with the bamboo, but it twisted around and got sucked back out. She was up to her calves now, balanced on unstable stones. Seeing how intent she was, I waded out to help. The fender eluded us both, as if purposely staying just out of reach.

We gave up and went back to our perches up the beach, seamlessly yakking about guys and relationships. Right as we sat down, the fender edged up and, like a skateboarder catching the lip of a half-pipe, stalled out on a rock. It had our attention now and we both watched it.

"You know it's just teasing us," she remarked.

"Yeah, as soon as we get up, it'll go back out," I agreed. "Just like a guy. It shows off just enough, then moves out of reach as soon as it's got our attention." We laughed at this analogy. I went on to reflect how I always, incorrectly, called fenders "bouys," and my last Captain, who was British, pronounced it "boy-ee." Rebecca took it one step further, remarking how her ex was dragging her down. A good relationship, we agreed, should hold you up, help you float. And, like a fender, ease the chafe and rub of life.

We continued our conversation, not giving in to the taunting "boy-ee." It gave up on its fake-out tactic and started slowly up the beach toward us, poking along five feet or so offshore. We watched, but got caught up in the current of our conversation; both of us took turns, going off on tangents before flowing back into the main topic.

I was trying to keep my focus on Rebecca when the buoy, now in front of us, but still out of reach, caught my eye again. Then I decided to test a theory of mine. I believe that we are energetic beings and that we manifest our lives through the law of attraction: "Like attracts like." According to Abraham (channeled by Esther Hicks), we are co-creating everything, and the extreme contrasts in our world help us clarify what we really want. It's all about focusing one's thoughts. If you want something, and stay in the feeling of craving, all you get is more wanting. The trick is to feel like you already *have* what you want, experiencing the emotional satisfaction without needing the thing first. Appreciation is powerful.

I was about to suggest this experiment to Becca, but she wasn't at a good interrupting point, so I began on my own. In my mind's eye, I saw the fender there on the beach. Knowing it to be there, feeling it there. When she paused I told her, "Help me manifest getting that buoy. Feel it, everything perfect just the way it is, like it's already in our possession."

For a second I felt completely in tune, like every wavelength in my being was vibrating at that perfect frequency. Just then…there it was, the buoy, sitting on dry land directly in front of us.

I believe in this power. I see proof of it in my life. Of course, it's always harder when I'm emotionally attached, or when I have complicated and unconscious feelings about what I want, like with money or love or accomplishing my dreams. This journey of mine was an experiment. I was perfecting the art of defining what I wanted and at the same time letting it go. I got that fender. I was on a luxury yacht, expenses paid, heading into the Pacific and having fun. That buoy was mine.

Into the Pacific

Panama to Galapagos
May 18, 2010

Finally, after two weeks of hustle and bustle preparing for our voyage, we headed out into the Pacific. With the blare of tropical sun and the sea slick and flat, the day was a bright white haze. We motored out past the congestion of anchored cruising boats, out past massive cargo ships, out past a gargantuan three-masted sailing ship, until the city was just a faint outline in the glare. And—just as land slipped completely away and there was nothing but the great, blue, breathing ocean—a whale emerged from the deep, peering at us with an ancient, intelligent consciousness. Then we caught three fish right in a row, two mahi-mahi and a tuna, making our paying guests happy. We were off to a good start.

Jill and Steve were great crew: They had boundless enthusiasm for tasting this different lifestyle, one that Steve was keen to hook Jill on. Jill kept busy cooking and cleaning (taking over my responsibilities), and Steve was always fishing or picking the Captain's brain for details about how all the fancy equipment worked. They were pleasant to have around, just a little over-eager.

Cariño was a catamaran and so had two pontoons, or hulls, with a wide, bridging deck connecting them. The main salon contained the galley and dining table surrounded on three sides by a cushy couch that could comfortably seat eight. The navigation station was in a corner. A sliding glass door took you through this center cabin into another sitting area outside, like a patio, with a table under a hard roof.

From the inside of the cabin, you stepped down a few steps into one or the other of the pontoons. The Captain's master bedroom was in the aft part of the starboard side, with the head that had an electric toilet, sink and teak-lined shower, up forward. On the port side in the back was the cabin where Jill and Steve stayed. Just forward of that was the food storage area, and in the triangular bow was my little cabin, which, apart from a little space for my stuff, was mostly filled with bed. On either side of the hull above my bunk were portholes, making it nice and bright while we were in calm seas. One of them was a big opening window only a foot above the water line. From it, I could peer across to the other hull while we were cutting through the waves.

Louie was extremely relaxed about our watches; he didn't impose a strict schedule like every other boat I'd sailed on, and he trusted heavily on the radar. During the day no one in particular was on duty; the boat was on autopilot steering itself and we casually kept our eyes out. At night it was fine to be curled up inside watching movies, with just an occasional peek outside. The watch would just stay up as long as they could; when they caught themselves dozing off, it was time to wake up someone else to take over.

I was on watch the second night and hadn't yet slacked off into Louie's way of doing things. I was outside, sitting at a swivel seat behind a steering wheel; there were two, one perched on the very back of each pontoon. We'd had light wind since leaving, then it died completely—the sails luffing, the boom wagging back and forth. I had gone inside to pour myself a cup of coffee when the radar alarm went off. Seconds before I had done a visual sweep of the entire horizon and saw nothing but pitch-black, a still night. I couldn't figure out how to turn off the alarm, so I woke up Louie and went back out to resume my watch. After he'd dealt with the alarm, Louie leaned out the door to check on me and I noticed the flag gently waving in the breeze. Suddenly, without any warning, the sails filled with a bang and the boat sprang forward like a greyhound out of the starting gate; the wind was blowing 25 knots. At this Louie howled like a wolf in heat. Then, a black wall of wind and pelting rain hit us like bricks, and it was blowing 50. You can't heel over a catamaran like a monohull to drop the wind off its sails, so I quickly switched off the autopilot to steer her into the wind, while Steve (who'd come up to investigate) and Louie pulled down the canvas. The storm passed by quickly; we got through it, and after that it was beautiful sailing.

My sunny sleeping space became an adventure in itself. The window was no longer above the water line. In stronger winds, as the boat launched off waves and slammed back down, speeding over the top of the sea, the water rushed up and over my porthole, making me feel like I was in a torpedo sub. The motion was completely different from what I was used to when sailing in monohulls. It felt like an old-fashioned, wooden rollercoaster: shimmying, vibrating, jerking and slamming in a way that seemed too stressful on the boat. After a few days of this, I noticed that my bed was feeling damp, and realized some of the ocean rushing by my window was making its way past the seal and dripping down into the compartment underneath my bunk. I had to wait for a calm day to take care of the problem.

The more time I spent with Louie, the more he grew on me. He was easygoing and warm, sharing his space as if we'd all chartered the boat together and were on equal footing. Engaging naturally in conversations, he never overrode anyone or acted like a know-it-all. He was open to opinions and happy to show anyone how things worked. He was fun and silly, getting us to laugh and feel connected. In short, he was a pirate in the best sense: on a boat he'd convinced his girlfriend to buy, with people who were paying him *and* who were doing lots of the work. He inspired all of us to take care of him.

I liked him, but he was careless. It didn't take me long to step into the role of gently nagging wife, since Carrie wasn't there to do it. Time and time again, he would set his glass of water on the nav station table. If it spilled, the water would wreck havoc on all the expensive equipment. When I'd tell him to move it, he would without protest. He would pee off the side of the boat—a big, flat, moving platform—with only one elbow hooked around the wire rigging, his body twisting and bumping around the stay while he pissed into the wind. I'd heard that was the most common way fisherman died, their bodies found in the water with their pants down. Also he pushed the boat harder than most cruisers would, leaving up lots of sail to go fast instead of reefing early—the more prudent choice when you want to preserve your rig.

Cariño

I woke up once at 5 am, Jill and Louie dead asleep on the settee. Some watch.

"God, Louie, did you even give them a briefing on how to do a watch? How often did you tell them they needed to check the horizon?"

"I didn't," he answered innocently. "I just said have a look around."

When I asked her, Jill figured every half hour or so was sufficient. I'd been taught that a tiny light on the horizon can become a cargo ship on top of you within 10 minutes and shared this information with Jill.

The previous night on my watch, I had been going over and over in my head how slack the watches were. I was obsessing about it when, for the first time in days, there was a ship that appeared as a small light on the horizon. I must have manifested the alarm again as confirmation that it was truly working. After that I began to adapt to Louie's more relaxed watches, lying inside writing and reading and only going out every 10 or 15 minutes to stare into the darkness.

We were getting close to the equator and, for all of us except Louie, it would be our first crossing. Jill made us an amazing dinner—pasta with marinara sauce, salad, roasted garlic butter and freshly-baked bread—and we talked about silly things we could do to celebrate the moment we actually crossed. This is a sailor's tradition that goes way back. In the end, we cruised over the invisible line at 2 am without any hoopla. Even the watch was probably asleep.

On another night Louie and I stayed up talking. He was starting to feel like a true friend, sharing with me his emotional challenges of having bipolar disorder. He also told me how Carrie was jealous that he'd taken me on as crew. It sounded like they were struggling as a couple: She wasn't as stoked on the cruising life as he was, and he wasn't sure they were going to make it. It put me at ease that he was so comfortable in himself.

One night after our talk he gave me a hug goodnight. Then, while watching a movie, both of us sprawled out around the settee, our legs comfortably touched. Again, when I was in his way, he put a hand on my hip to gently move me. All of this felt totally natural, like we were friends. But I was glad to have other crew onboard and I closed the door to my cabin at night. I knew the sex thing would come up, and I hoped that when it did, the conversation would be easy.

Steering

I lay in the sun just in front of the cabin—away from everyone—to soak up the peaceful feeling of solitude. The Pacific Ocean rushing beneath me through the netting that connected the pontoons on the bow completely filled my senses. I was alone and free to contemplate. I'd been thinking a lot about the concept of finding balance, something that didn't come easily for me.

I am an extreme person. Whatever I do, I do it head first, all the way. At 13 I became a vegan and stopped eating all animal products for two years. At 18 I went to Europe to begin my traveling lifestyle, buying a one-way ticket into the unknown. And at 22, without a clue about sailing, I bought my boat and moved aboard.

I went extreme with trying to get healthy too. After months of overeating and drinking I would think, "Tomorrow I'm starting a cleanse," then proceed to stuff my face with every bad thing—ice cream, candy, beer, bread, cheese—and make myself sick. I would do this with marijuana too sometimes, compulsively loading the bowl, even though I couldn't get any higher, just to finish the bag so I could quit. It was as if I wanted to separate out the part of myself that I didn't like, like tipping an egg back and forth until the white comes away and only the rich yellow center remains. It doesn't work though. It only polarized my extremes and made being happy less sustainable. I had to accept and love the whole egg.

I thought the better tactic to finding balance might be to think of it like steering a boat. There is an ingenious, self-steering device called a Hydrovane that works without electricity as long as the wind is steady. Part of it hangs off the stern with its own little rudder in the water; the other part is a frame stretched with thin sail material that can be adjusted to the angle of wind desired to stay on course. The Hydrovane took over steering by moving back and forth just enough to keep the wheel at the same gradient to the wind. That's how I felt living in Colorado. It was almost effortless: a little exercise, a little smoke, a little meditation, a cold beer with friends. Once I got myself on course, it didn't take any power to maintain my heading.

But since I'd been traveling, the unpredictable winds and currents had been buffeting my hull and, without a daily routine to keep my sails full, my self-steering had faltered. There's a tendency to oversteer on a boat. You turn a little one way and, when the boat doesn't react right away, you turn a little more. Then, all of a sudden, the vessel is way off course, the sails either too tight or flapping. That's what I kept trying to do, over-compensate for my months of mild depression and over-indulgence by enforcing an unrealistic health plan: no white flour, sugar, beer or cheese and exercise whenever possible. In the Dominican Republic, with no refrigeration or the ability to cook, when Lynn or Laura offered to feed me, of course I was thankful, regardless of what they served. When we were invited to *Kokomo* for a scrumptious eggplant parmesan, how could I refuse? When I joined in a cruisers' get-together at the pizza joint, or chatted with the welder over a cold beer, the social activity seemed more important to my health than any strict diet plan. I loved this saying and found it to be true:

> *Beer and franks with cheer and thanks*
> *is healthier than*
> *sprouts and bread with fear and dread.*

Not only did I want to sail around the world, I wanted to steer toward happiness. I thought the trick might be to be gentle with myself. Just because I ate too much eggplant parmesan and banana pudding, washed down with rum and cokes, it didn't have to mean I was spiraling downward. I could just point my bow back in the direction I wanted to travel: Take a long walk the next morning and relax into the fluid movement of back and forth. I was not on the straight and narrow of a busy street, cars whizzing past, in danger of crashing if I veered a foot over the yellow line. I was at sea, with plenty of leeway on either side. No vessel steers a dead-straight course. If I just kept bringing myself back to center, toward what felt good, maybe I could find moderation, even within the changing conditions of my traveling life. Maybe I could relax, balance the helm and once again, leave the steering to the Hydrovane.

Galapagos

May 26, 2010

On the morning of our eighth day at sea, the low-slung, gray-brown island of San Cristobal came into view. Steve and Jill went into action; they had only a week in the islands, and they weren't going to waste it. Out came all their dive gear, and they got to work rigging up their tanks. I drank my coffee and watched as Louie hand-steered us toward a massive landmark called Kicker Rock, an obtuse triangle of stone like a utility blade that stuck out of the sea. They were in full wetsuits and ready to go as we approached the rock, which now towered above us. A small boat was already there. Without a permit, we knew we weren't supposed to be diving, but that wasn't going to stop Louie. We pulled up close to the crag and, with the stern blocked from view of the other vessel, Jill and Steve slipped covertly off the transom like Navy seals. We circled slowly around the massive protrusion and took pictures. Then Louie said I could snorkel a bit too, so I dove in. There were sea lions lounging around on the outcrop, but none of them joined me in the water. The wall was loaded with fish, though the visibility wasn't great. I mostly liked the stealth part.

Afterward, we motored into San Cristobal's harbor. Once anchored, the port Captain came out to *Cariño* and explained that, since we hadn't purchased the necessary permits in Panama that would allow us to visit all three of the main islands in the Galapagos, we would be restricted to staying on San Cristobal. Louie was coming at this discussion from all angles, making the port Captain explain it over and over again, getting me to translate even though the guy spoke English. Suddenly we noticed a thick white trail of smoke started to twine its way up through the nav station equipment.

Louie jumped on this and yelled, "We have an emergency!" as he started pulling out cushions to access where the smoke was coming from. "We were planning on going to Santa Cruz, but our charger started causing problems and we were forced to stop; now it looks like it's going to catch fire!"

The Universe smiled on us because this bought us a day to check out San Cristobal. We all went to shore to register with customs. Once back on the boat Louie stretched out on his belly, accessing the charger wearing nothing but his flowery, pink-and-purple g-string. Jill, Steve and I left him to it, and returned to land to rent bicycles and go exploring.

The local sea lion population was making good use of every available space wherever we looked: a bunch covering a derelict vessel in the harbor; one on a bus stop bench, which didn't move when I sidled up and took a picture. After returning from our bike ride through the dry and somewhat barren landscape, we discovered one had made itself cozy on *Carino's* swim platform.

That night we sailed to Santa Cruz Island, the hub of the Galapagos and home to their international airport. The unprotected anchorage at Puerto Ayora, on its southern shore, had a swell rolling through it and was extremely busy with all sorts of vessels: Big live-aboard motorboats that took tourists on three- to five-day cruises to the various uninhabited islands; cruising sail boats that were all using two anchors—one from the bow and one from the stern—to hold them into the swell; yellow water taxis roaming in and out among the other boats, trolling for customers; big inflatables ferrying people from the tour boats; fishing boats and dive boats coming and going. And, a steady stream of big, steel barges pushed by launches moving everything from volcanic rock for building to piles of propane tanks, trash, provisions and even brand new trucks.

Puerto Ayora was a lively tourist town. The main road along the waterfront was wide and paved with octagonal red bricks. Like any tourist town, there were knick-knack shops, tour operations, restaurants and high-end jewelry and art stores. But here there was a cohesive design: The buildings tended to be stucco in light colors—white, orange, pink, blue—and have terra cotta roofs, accented with wooden terraces and trim work. The curbsides were sculpted and with the brick work, created decorative walkways. Around one corner there was a tortoise statue in raised garden beds. Along the ocean there was a big open square with volleyball nets where the locals would play. Extending into the water was a covered pier with varnished handrails. And further along the waterfront, where the fishermen tied up their small blue skiffs, was a space with built-in blue cement counters where they would unload and fillet their catch, with plenty of resident pelicans and seals begging for scraps. The town wasn't overly planned or uptight; it retained a loose, organic feel. From the sea, the land was mostly low profile, though there was a gentle incline behind the urban center to the ancient, dormant volcano in the middle of Santa Cruz Island.

The Ecuadorians had created a model of tourism in the Galapagos based solely on their natural assets. After the trash-strewn Caribbean islands, I appreciated the Galapagos for the clean towns and beaches, recycling bins in the main squares, and solar-powered streetlights around the docks. I respected the fact that tourists were required to hire a guide to enter the national park, which constituted most of the landmass of the islands. Everything was regulated (no diving without a dive boat; no fishing without a permit) and tours cost a lot. Still, being a person with only slightly more than $500 to my name, with the whole, wide, uncertain future in front of me—I did what I could.

Jill and Steve had limited time and they provided the motivation, which, I had learned, counts for a lot. The water taxis were cheap and always cruising into shore and back out through the anchored boats; this made it easy and convenient to come and go as we pleased. We went to the Darwin Institute in

Santa Cruz to see Lonesome George, the 100-year-old, last-of-his-tribe land tortoise, who had lived most of his life on an outer island, but was brought to Santa Cruz to breed with a close relative.

We rented bikes and did a 50 km ride. Passionfruit grew like weeds along the sides of the road, and I kept finding the intact bodies of little yellow finches that had been hit by cars. We rode out to Tortuga Ranch to see the massive turtles in their natural environment. For only $3, we hired a guide to accompany us through tall grass and trees. He pointed out the sizable, rounded shells of this slow species, not that we would have missed them. Down the hill from the ranch we happened upon the entrance to a lava tunnel and poked our way through. These tunnels were created by molten lava cooling and crusting on top while the hot part kept moving below. We saw pink flamingos wading in shallow, brown pools; walked the long stretch of white beach with turquoise waves called Tortuga Bay; snapped pictures of black marine iguanas lounging on the white sugar sand and of blue-footed boobies diving into the surf like kamikaze fighter planes.

Louie wasn't going to let the rules hold us back, so after a few days on Santa Cruz we made plans to leave for Isabella Island at 4 am. But, after a late night of drinks and munchies on our boat with some fellow cruisers, we pushed back our departure time to a more respectable hour. Isabella was only a 40-mile day sail and we stopped on our way for another stealth dive. This time it was my turn. Jill let me use her gear, and Steve, a dive master, gave me a brush-up course since it had been years since my stint as mate on a dive boat in Hatteras.

That afternoon, we pulled into the protected anchorage on Isabella where there were only four other cruising boats and one fishing boat anchored. Penguins zoomed around like video game torpedoes, and the lazy sea lions made good use of our back steps as sunbathing platforms.

We invited the whole anchorage over for drinks at 5:00 and had a great evening getting to know the other cruisers. There seemed to be a younger demographic in the Pacific compared to the Caribbean. The Caribbean made it easy for retirees to cruise down the island chain; the Pacific took a lot more planning, guts and know-how to traverse the long passages. I loved that Louie was so social. The stories and color of the different seafaring people we met added so much to our journey and was in stark contrast to the isolation I had felt with my previous two Captains.

Cariño

The next day Steve, Jill and I took a paid tour to see the second largest volcanic crater in the world. Louie was not interested in any of our active excursions. He'd become discouraged with the growing list of boat repairs and seemed a bit depressed.

"Hey," I prodded, "why don't you come with us? Exercise always helps me when I'm depressed."

"The only things I like to do are sail and fuck," he said. "And I can't do either."

So he dropped us off on shore where we climbed into the back of the tour company's truck and were bumped and jostled along the dirt tracks on the hard, wooden seats to where our hike would start. Instantly I bonded with the girl sitting across from me. An American about my age, Kelly was in the Galapagos for a few weeks working for an international environmental agency. The job took her all over the world.

We spent the entire trek together, walking up through lush, green foliage to the lip of Sierra Negra, the caldera, which was like a giant's vast, green, soup bowl, six miles across, filled partially with solidified black lava porridge. Sierra Negra was the most active volcano in the Galapagos; its most recent eruption was in 2005. From there we hiked down to Volcan Chico, where hardened red, yellow and black lava rock had overtaken any green growing thing as if we were on the moon. From this high vantage point we could see the gradual sweep of land, down, down, down and out, all the way to the sea.

It was a treacherous hike. I hadn't gone on a run since the Dominican Republic, and my knees ached on the descent. When a woman rode by on horseback and declared loudly in English to the whole group that she was having a birthday party that evening at the Casa Rosa bar/hostel, Kelly and I tuned in. Having this to look forward to gave us the energy to hobble the rest of the way into the sleepy town. Once there, I tried to back out, because my knees were complaining like never before. But we stopped at the Casa Rosa and were instantly seduced by the scene: Kids were playing volleyball on the beach; an engaging Italian guy with a spastic afro arranged some rickety lounge chairs for us and got us passion fruit daiquiris; a young English girl (with the same lopsided, skater haircut I had worn at 13) entertained us with her travel stories. I was persuaded to come back that night for the party: it was on. On my way back to the boat, down the sandy main street of the miniature town, I ran into our Captain and easily swept him into the plan for the evening.

Adventures of a Pirate Girl

Louie and I returned to the Casa Rosa as it was getting dark. The crowd turned out to be mostly in their early 20s. The birthday girl, the woman on the horse from earlier and the owner of the place, was a middle-aged, hot mama, the kind that was not letting her youth go without a fight. She had four teenage kids, all stunningly beautiful, along with an entourage of hot, young men. It was hard to tell if they were her kids' friends or hers. Kelly showed up with Ricardo, an extremely sociable Ecuadorian from the mainland of Ecuador. He was on Santa Cruz making wooden signs for the park service. When I told him I liked his hand-painted "Surf Galapagos" tee shirt, he pulled it over his head and gave it to me.

We were having a great time but Louie was ready to leave. Kelly assured me I could stay in her hotel room so I didn't have to depart with him. Before she left, she explained how to get to her hotel. Later, Ricardo and I wandered around searching the few streets in complete darkness—there were no streetlights or ambient light—but we couldn't find the hotel.

I felt comfortable with Ricardo, so thanked him when he offered to pay for a hotel room. He got us a room with two beds and didn't protest when I sent him to his (though in the morning, I slipped under his arm for a little wholesome cuddling). He took me to breakfast, and we spent the whole day wandering around laughing, hugging and carrying on like we were sweethearts on vacation.

I'd mentioned that I wished we had some pot, and Ricardo procured it, though he didn't mention that he had never smoked. He also didn't tell me he'd never been snorkeling. We discovered a protected, deepwater pool and slipped in for a swim. What to me was a magical mermaid lagoon, where we could dive deep and examine interesting rock and coral formations among darting fish, was to him a terrifying first experience, stoned out of his mind in an alien underwater world. It wasn't until we were safe in a restaurant having lunch that he admitted this. He also told me about his dad's sign business and his 12-year-old daughter who lived with him full-time. He was sweet, smart, mellow and appreciative and treated me like a queen.

I made plans to meet both Ricardo and Kelly back in Santa Cruz and, at 3 am the next morning, we pulled *Cariño's* anchor to return. It was a beautiful sail back; we watched for an hour, delighted, as dolphins played under our bow. We caught three yellow-fin tuna. The thrill in Steve's voice every time he called out, "Fish on!" reminded me of a little kid's.

Cariño

The first thing I did when we got back to Santa Cruz was open my computer and press the ON button, but nothing happened: No color lit up its face, no harmonic chord greeted me, no fan whirred. There was only a persistent beeping and a dark screen. Fuck.

As soon as I could, I took a taxi to the only computer repair place on the island. I wandered into what looked like a TV butcher shop piled high with black carcasses. The guy there did all the things I had already tried—plugged it in, turned it on, took the battery out—with the same result. I was relieved when he admitted he didn't know anything about Macs. I wouldn't have felt safe leaving my prized Mac Book with him. I searched for some diagnostic help online on a PC at the internet café, but with a slow connection and an unfamiliar screen all in Spanish, I got nowhere. Louie swore he'd had the exact same problem; he had had to buy a whole new motherboard that cost him $300. I needed my computer; writing was my project, my semblance of structure. Fuck.

Jill and Steve were returning to the States the next day and offered to take my laptop with them. Their nephew used to work for Mac and was a computer whiz; they would get it fixed and send it back to me.

How would I pay for the repair? The international shipping? I did get my tax refund, but I was determined to save that money in case of an emergency. By the time we got to Tahiti I'd be on my last dollars. Thinking about the future felt overwhelming, so I stuffed my face with chocolate and gave myself a pep talk: "Really, Davina, if thinking about the future is daunting, don't do it. There really is no point. You cannot foresee the future, and worrying about it is NOT going to help. Just be here now. You are fine and fed and taken care of now. Things will line up; they have so far."

I didn't have much time to make the decision. The next morning, I dressed it up in its wetsuit skin and dry bag, handed it over, said my farewell to Jill and Steve and let it go.

Adventures of a Pirate Girl

Daggerboards

Santa Cruz Island, Galapagos
June 2, 2010

Now that our paying crew was gone and it was just me and Louie, I decided to clean the bottom of the boat in preparation for our next ocean crossing to French Polynesia. I donned snorkel gear and gloves, tied a scraper and scrub brush to my bikini bottom with longish bits of string (experience had taught me this would save time retrieving them when I fumbled), then dove into the bright turquoise water. Oh, it was cold. You'd think with the clear, bright color and being on the equator, the water would be warm, but the Humboldt Current, which brought nutrients and fed the plentiful biodiversity, was bloody cold in May.

Because the boat was a catamaran, the underwater surface was shallow compared to a monohull. I dove under, holding my breath, and scraped off the slime that had begun to take hold. This boat had daggerboards: Two, huge, fiberglass boards—about two feet wide and 12 feet tall—that went down through the boat in fitted slots and into the water underneath. They could be lifted when in shallow water or for maneuverability when motoring, but while sailing we'd drop them down to counterbalance the sails and prevent the boat from tipping or pushing sideways when the wind was blowing hard. I dove down to give them a good clean but they weren't there! I saw nothing but the rounded hulls sitting like two parallel canoes. I popped back up, laughing at myself. I'd have to yell to Louie to drop them. I looked up to where they should be protruding six feet above the deck.

"Huh?" I gasped. They weren't there. I dropped my head back under the boat to check again, then swam underneath and peered up. Both daggerboards were sheared off right where they came through the hull. Fuck.

I climbed up the small swim ladder that hung off the stern, climbed the few steps and peered into the cabin.

"Uh, Louie?" I said, hesitation in my voice. "Uh, the daggerboards? They're gone."

"What?"

"They're broken off. They're not there. They're gone."

He immediately jumped up, went to the steering station and pushed the button. Sure enough, the boards ascended above deck but stopped about three feet up. This was the part of the boards that sat within the fiberglass sleeve from the deck through the boat down to the water. I followed him forward, and we both grabbed the top of one, gave it a yank and up popped the snapped-off fiberglass board.

"Shit. Ah, fuck. God, when did this happen?" he asked, half to himself.

"I don't know. I didn't feel anything. Steve and I put them down when we were at sea."

"You're not supposed to put them down all the way."

"I didn't know that."

"It's my fault, I saw that you'd dropped them, and I didn't say anything. Ah, fuck."

"What are we going to do?"

"Ah, fuck. I had to replace them when we first bought the boat and it cost $20,000."

"I mean, can we sail without them? Or, I mean, are we going to have to get them fixed here?"

"I don't know. I don't know. I've got to think." Shaking his head, he turned and went back inside.

When I went back in, he was sitting at the nav station, staring blankly at his screen, not even flinching when I said his name. My mind was racing in defense of myself and I had to get off the boat. I readied the kayak and paddled to a little, out-of-the-way beach. I pulled up on the sand beside a sea lion rolling idly in the surf, letting the water wash her round body in and out, back and forth.

For a few days Louie was in this black mood; he was sullen and quiet and it made me want to run. I stayed as far away as I could: I explored the jagged coastline by kayak. I wondered, while scrabbling up along the volcanic rock near the beach, whether I was still wanted. There I found a sinkhole of clear, cool, fresh water. The steep rocky sides were 20-feet high and the pool, made by moving lava, was an eight-foot channel. I breast-stroked through what I thought was a secret spot but, when I came around a bend, I saw people diving into the water from the high black wall. I tried to reassure myself that the daggerboard situation wasn't all my fault. I went for a run to clear my head. If I had to, I could find another boat; there were enough cruisers around, I'd find something.

Back onboard, I kept to myself. I'd moved my stuff into the now-empty bigger cabin, since Jill and Steve had left, and stayed there, curled up with dinner and a book.

On the third morning, when I came out for coffee, there was the Louie I'd grown to love, sitting up straight and alert. "Right. So today, we're going to take what's left of the daggerboards to a yard where they build fiberglass boats. I've talked to the guy and he thinks they can build new ones."

A slow smile spread across my face. We have action!

We hoisted what remained of the stubby daggerboards into our favorite water taxi and then into a taxi onshore: a brand new, extended cab pickup truck. After a 15-minute drive, we pulled up to the yard, attracting the attention of the young guys, who came out from behind electric sanders, pushing their white masks up on their heads, smiling in appreciation of my Spanish or my short green skirt. Victor was in charge; he shook our hands and directed the boys to unload the boards. I explained the project, not needing much help from Louie, being well acquainted with this kind of work and understanding what needed to be conveyed. Then we returned to *Cariño*. There was nothing more for us to do but wait.

Between my two new friends—Kelly and Ricardo—my social calendar was full. Both of them had also returned to Santa Cruz Island after short visits to Isabella, so we met up. Kelly (from the volcano hike) had only a few days left in the Galapagos and we spent them together. One night, after joining Louie and me for dinner on our boat, she and I took blankets to the trampoline netting on the bow and made ourselves cozy. It was a dark, warm night. We could hear faint music and see lights dancing on the water: White anchor lights with their counterpart reflections bobbed and swayed while the red and green on the water taxis laced through them, zipping here and there. We talked about men and love.

"I always seem to be on islands," I explained, "back in the States, in the Florida Keys and on Hatteras, through the Caribbean, and now here. I meet these guys, island boys. Some of them are lovely men and, who knows? Maybe if I stayed, it could work out. But they're a part of their place. When I sail away, that's it; I'll never see them again. Even the last few American island guys I went out with were stuck. They couldn't follow me."

"I know exactly what you mean," she assured me, taking a sip of her drink. "It's the same for me. I'm always traveling too, but if it's meant to be, it can work out. I met my boyfriend in Belize," she reminded me, stretching out to set her glass down on the deck before cuddling back into the blanket.

"Tell me about him."

"Well, he's amazing. I mean, when I met him, we had this amazing connection, a hot, whirlwind romance while I was visiting Belize for a week. I didn't think it'd go beyond that. He was a small-town boy, how was he going to keep up with me? But we stayed in touch and then he came to visit me. I helped pay for the ticket. The connection was still there, super strong. And then I went back to Belize to see him. And then he moved to the States. Now he lives with me. I sometimes still get on his case, like, how is this ever going to work? You don't have any goals in life. You're not driven. But it's just me being crazy. He's working in construction, putting himself through night school on top of paying for his little sister and brother to go to a better school in Belize. He's so loving and solid. He teaches me a lot, actually, about what love really means."

"Hmmm," I nodded, taking it in.

"What about you and Ricardo? He seems pretty great."

"Yeah, he's cool; though he's got his daughter full-time so, unless I want to move to Ecuador…"

We carried on our conversation and after a while fell to sleep.

Ricardo had found *Cariño* by water taxi once he'd returned to Santa Cruz Island; it wasn't hard to recognize the big glossy catamaran with yellow sail covers. He was a city boy and over the next few days he'd taken me out to various restaurants and bars. I was on a restricted budget and enjoyed getting a chance to check out some of these places.

However, I was more of a nature girl and preferred to explore the island. I still hadn't seen any of the iconic, blue-footed boobies up close, so one day I made it our mission. We hiked along a well-cared-for path, through the scrabbly brush, small trees and towering cactus until the dry dirt turned to sand. Black marine iguanas, some up to three feet long, sunbathed along the path; often they lay every which way on top of each other. We came to the shore and I posed for a picture in an old, washed-up wooden skiff, a cactus tree with plate-sized pads behind me. There was a sea lion lying in the strip of shade the boat provided, a couple of big iguanas right beside the sea lion, and I spotted a sea turtle a short way down the beach in the water.

Animals here seemed completely at ease with their human visitors and never bothered to move away. I could see the blue-footed boobies in the distance, dive-bombing the sea, so I went to get a closer look, stepping from rock to rock. This white-bodied, black-winged, gray-beaked, common looking seabird elevated to exotic by big, baby-blue webbed feet. Ricardo followed. Ever the gentleman, he kept trying to hold my arm, as if I needed support to manage the uneven terrain. Finally, after being handicapped by his help, I said in Spanish, trying not to let annoyance leak into my voice, "Ricardo, I can't walk across the rocks with you holding onto me."

"I'm only trying to help," he responded.

"I know. You're just being sweet but, Ricardo, I've sailed across oceans, I've climbed sheer cliffs with only ropes to catch me. This is easy; it's just a few rocks. Really."

When we'd met on Isabella Island, playing boyfriend/girlfriend for that first day was fun. Had it ended then, I would have always remembered it as a romantic tryst. But hanging out with him for a week, I began to realize I'd jumped into being romantic too fast. I did enjoy his company but, now that he was around consistently, his kisses were getting annoying. One night, after a dinner he cooked for a group of us at Kelly's friend's house, we were alone on the dark patio and he took my hands in a serious way, then poured his heart out about his deep feelings for me. A weak smile on my lips, I let him speak. But, in the end, I had to tell him that to me it felt like more of a friendship than a love affair.

───～───

Louie, being the social butterfly, also kept me busy while we waited for the daggerboard repairs. *Cariño* was a great boat for entertaining, and he was always happy to use it as the anchorage's social hub. Drinks aboard became the happy-hour custom, and we had our regulars. There were the five Aussie blokes with an 18-year-old daughter in tow who were taking two catamarans back to Australia. One morning, we zoomed around in their inflatable looking for surf and ended up on a thrill ride, zipping right in front of waves and then, just before they threatened to flip us, we'd cut out over the side, making my heart stop a few times.

Cariño

There was Curly, an old New Zealander with a big, bushy, white beard and a jolly laugh, who was delivering a rickety little catamaran across the Pacific.

And there was Milo, a single-hand Norwegian who was making her second attempt to sail to Antarctica. She'd had her steel boat designed and built specifically for this voyage, but had had to turn back due to weather on her first attempt.

Louie was always in communication with the cruisers around him. Through networking he lined me up a few jobs diving into the cold water and scraping the barnacles and furry growth off the bottoms of boats, which earned me a few hundred dollars. He was often on the single-side-band radio, chatting with people back in the Caribbean and all over the Pacific.

"We'll find you your next boat," he often reassured me, which made me feel cared for, like I wasn't so alone on this journey.

Any fear I'd had that the sex thing would come up had dissolved. By now we were solid friends and, besides that, Carrie and Louie were doing well again, always on the phone. He'd never made any moves on me, and I no longer worried that he would.

Ricardo invited us to a Father's Day barbeque that his sister was arranging. After the meal, all of us satiated and lazy, I hung out with Patito, a 6-year-old boy who, after engaging me in his games for a bit, snuggled into my lap in the hammock. He was so sweet and cuddly that it tugged on my heartstrings. Those baby cravings were still there.

There was an open-air produce market every week, and every week Louie and I went. We'd stock up on fresh fruit and veggies as if it were our last chance. We kept ourselves busy as much as we could but, despite all of this activity, we were anxious to go. Maybe the daggerboards would be done soon and we could go, though after a few weeks, we were greeting the vendors like friends. Were we ever going to leave?

Finally, after three weeks, the guys from the boatyard brought our daggerboards out by water taxi. We were ready and waiting for them with our Australian friends, who'd offered to give us a hand. We lifted the first massive board from the water taxi with the halyard, me cranking the winch at the base of the mast to hoist it and the guys guiding it up and over the lifelines and into place so I could lower it into its slot. It went down promisingly for the first few feet, then stopped. The 12 feet of fiberglass had to slide through a seven-foot slot. It had to be perfectly straight, and wasn't. But Louie and I were so ready to go, our conversation went something like this:

"They just need a little sanding. It's no biggie, just a little sanding here and there and they'll go right in."

"Totally, we have sanders. We'll be at sea for weeks. We'll have plenty of time, we can just work on them while we're underway."

"Yeah, there's plenty of space on deck. It'll give us something to do while we're sailing. It'll be fine. We could totally do that."

"Yeah, no problem. We are going today. Everything else is ready. We are outta here!"

Everyone else onboard looked at each other knowingly, shook their heads to themselves and kept their mouths shut.

We strapped the daggerboards to the deck, pulled up anchor, waved goodbye to our friends and got underway. This was going to be the start of a clean, healthy passage with lots of salad and fresh food. Then Louie mentioned the chocolate he'd bought and so, my arm duly twisted, I baked brownies and while they cooled I went to my cabin for a nap. A few hours later I peeked out the sliding door into the blare of tropical sunshine and realized we were heading back to Santa Cruz.

None of our friends in the anchorage looked surprised to see us pull back in and drop the hooks. Louie had been on the satellite phone, so the moment our anchors were set, the guys from the yard were stepping off the water taxi with sanders at the ready. They were on deck until 10 pm; the boat glistening with a layer of fine powder like toxic snow. It finally became apparent that the boards were warped: a much bigger problem than a little sanding could fix. It was back to the boatyard to start again.

Somehow, after that, all the tension and anxiety we'd built up in our desperation to leave Santa Cruz Island dissipated. It was what it was—and we let it go.

Victor

Santa Cruz, Galapagos

I needed to stock up on some reading material, so I took some books and walked over to a bar where I knew they had a take-one, leave-one shelf. Once I found a few that looked interesting, I headed to a friend's house. He was a local surfer, maybe 50, whom I'd hung out with a few times. He dug out another book for me and we said our goodbyes. The daggerboards were due soon, possibly the following day.

I stopped at a stall to buy a pair of coconut-shell earrings I'd been wanting and was on my way back to the *muelle* (moy-ye, the dock). It was just past sundown, and a guy sitting alone on a bench stood up as I passed, "Hey, *chica*," he said. It took a second to realize who it was: A cute guy who worked at the dive shop on the corner of the main square. We'd been playing eye tag from afar for days, stealing glances at each other that sometimes intersected with a jolt.

"Oh, hi," I greeted him, both of us smiling at this chance to finally meet. He offered me a swig of his *caña* liquor from the bottle, but I declined.

"I would totally have a drink with you, especially since it's probably my last night here, but not right from the bottle," I explained in Spanish.

He responded, impressing me with his good English, "Ah, it's your last night! Yes, let's definitely make it special!" So we walked to where he worked and got some plastic cups, ice and lime. Perfect.

Then we went back the way we'd come, away from the lights of the main square. As we walked, he talked with enthusiasm about diving, adventuring, and life on the island. He was gorgeous, with caramel skin, a sparkle in his eye and an enticing smile, engaging and full of life. Suddenly he stopped and bowed slightly, his arm formally parting the nearby bushes as if he was a concierge parting curtains to show me to a private room, only it was a small, neglected dock concealed from the street. As I admired the spot, looking out over the water, he poured our drinks and put on some music. The reggaeton he chose made me want to dance and, as he handed me my drink, he put his other hand on the small of my back, pulled me in and began to move his hips in time. Ah, I love dancing, and a man who knows how is especially hot. He did, twirling me around and falling back into the Latino reggae rhythm that I loved. I set down our drinks to take full advantage of such a skilled dance partner and he pulled me right back in until his leg was between my thighs. I pushed him back a little for some space and asked how old he was.

"Twenty-seven," he said, then spun me around, pulled me back close and said, "Nah, I'm 33."

I laughed, then with his hand securely behind my shoulders, he dipped me, leaned in close and said, "But what if I'm 23?"

"You're just being silly, which one is it?"

"I just want to check how my age affects things with you," he answered. Laughing, we kept dancing.

"What does it matter anyway?" he asked. "We're obviously attracted to each other and I've been working on attracting someone like you. I mean energetically, have you heard of the law of attraction?"

That *really* got my attention. Could it be we had more in common than just a major magnetic pull? I let myself relax closer into him until our bodies were pressed up against each other, our hips moving together—slow, fast, push, pull—to the beat.

"I used to be a real player," he told me, looking into my eyes.

"Nooo, you?" I joked. "I couldn't tell." He dipped me low and I threw my head back laughing.

"There's so many girls visiting the island," he said, pulling me back up so that our faces were almost touching, "and I just wanted to have fun."

"Mm hmm, tell me about it," I said, nodding. He spun me around and then back close, face to face. "Sailing from place to place, it's the same thing," I said, "So many hot guys, it's been a lot of fun."

"But I'm getting bored with that."

"Yeah?"

"Yeah. I'm building a house. I want someone serious. Someone who could be my partner. I want to have a family."

I couldn't help but giggle; he spun me around hard and then whipped me in tight.

"Why are you laughing? Aren't you getting bored with it too? Don't you want a family? Kids?" With this he stopped moving, holding me up against him with his arm tight behind my lower back, challenging me with his eyes.

"Yeah, I do," I admitted. "I do want kids. I've gotten bored with it, too. I've been celibate actually. I don't want to fuck around anymore. I want something real."

Standing there, the electricity between our bodies was intense. All the dancing and flirting had built up a static charge; you could almost see it sparking between us. He just stood there staring into my eyes. My lips, with a mind of their own, yearned up toward his, but then he swooped his hips around again, moving me with him, and we danced like this, both his arms wrapped around me, both mine around his shoulders, our faces cheek to cheek, our breathing getting heavier.

"I want to see your house."

"I want you to see it, too."

"Let's go, let's go see it."

"If I show you tonight, you won't see how beautiful it's going to be. It's a mess, all I do is work lately, and it's a mess. There's no electricity yet, no drinking water. I'd rather… Let me show it to you tomorrow. Give me a chance to clean it up. It's all wood. It's going to be beautiful when it's done."

"Tomorrow, then?"

"Yeah, tomorrow. How about at noon? That'll give me a chance to clean it up. Meet me at the entrance to Tortuga Bay"

"Okay, I'll bring a picnic lunch."

"Okay, I'll bring something, too."

Then, finally, he leaned in and kissed me. When our lips came together the charge leapt up and whooshed through my entire body, burning away all thought, any remaining resistance. It was powerful and left me a little stunned.

I barely slept that night, I was so excited; and still I popped up the next morning eager to start the day. For once I was thankful that the boards weren't ready. I made muffins, danced, invited Milo over for coffee and eagerly awaited my date with Victor. After a shower, freshly shaved legs and a cute outfit, I walked to the edge of town where the stone walkway started to Tortuga Bay. I sat and sat; the minutes ticked by. And that old familiar heft started to press down on my heart: Being let down by a man adding its weight to a lifetime collection of similar disappointments. I tried to let it go, but I'd really thought he would be there. And that fucking kiss. Damn.

Adventures of a Pirate Girl

After 40 minutes, I started down the path that I'd walked so many times before: a long, stone walkway with a short wall on either side that went on and on through the short, scrubby brush trees and towering cactus. I meandered, not entirely ridding myself of the hope that he would show up, on and on until I finally arrived at the glorious sandy beach. In a corner away from the few people there, I set up my blanket, had my picnic and tried to hold tight to my pleasant day, probably the last one on Santa Cruz Island. By the time I walked back to town a few hours later, I allowed the sadness and disappointment to creep in. I got a beer and was about to go back to the boat when I decided, "Fuck it; I want to see him one more time."

So I got a taxi, but the driver and I couldn't find the place. He stopped and asked a few people, but nope. Nope. So, finally, we turned around and picked up this little old lady. I jumped out and helped her load the huge sack of limes she was carrying into the back of the taxi. Another lady got in and the driver asked them if they knew of a young Victor building a house; neither of them did, but they both got involved in the story. The one lady was adamant, telling me it was time to stop adventuring, I should settle down and have a family. Otherwise I'd be alone.

My response belied my emotions: "Just because you get married does not guarantee that you won't end up alone. And you can't just decide, 'That's it. I'm going to have a man.' You have to meet one, and it's a natural thing, and besides, I want to. What do you think I'm doing searching for this guy's house?"

She and I got out of the taxi together back at the *muelle*, and she insisted I go by his work, an idea that hadn't entered my mind. By that point I didn't particularly want to show my face, but she pushed me, "*Hazlo, vete* (Do it, go)" and so I went in. The girl at the desk looked up and, without a word, led me around the corner—and there he was. He came up to me and handed me the book I'd left in his bag.

"Here's your book." He seemed like such a different person. Gone the shining, smiley boy: here was a cold, blank man. I looked into his eyes, trying to find the guy I'd met the night before, maybe a hint, but I could only see a wall. "How was the beach?" he asked me.

"Fine. Where were you?"

"I drank until 8:00 this morning. I slept until noon. Then I had to eat. You're leaving tomorrow anyway."

And to think, I'd brought condoms to the beach. "How stupid of me," a part of me thought. But another part jumped up in defense: "You didn't do anything wrong. You were only staying open to the possibilities. Plus, it just makes leaving easier."

The next morning, Louie and I went to check on the boards—and they were done. We loaded them into the taxi and said goodbye to the guys. We had Curly with us, then swung by Milo's boat and grabbed her too. Together the four of us slipped those suckers right in. Louie and I had learned our lesson on patience so well that we went to shore one last time, did internet, got some eggs and green papayas, then returned to the boat. I got in the water, cleaned the propellers, and off we went, a month after arriving in the Galapagos: calm, organized and ready. Of course we backed up over someone's anchor line, I had to jump in again to untangle it, but, aside from that…

Doing and Being

Galapagos to Nuku Hiva
July 11, 2010

We were 11 days out from the Galapagos. Nuku Hiva—our next destination, an island in the Marquesas group—was 1048 nautical miles ahead of us: one speck in a Milky Way of islands dotting the Pacific Ocean like stars in the infinite sky.

Here I was doing it, living the dream. But what was I actually *doing*? The time around us was as immense as the sea. We hadn't seen anyone since we passed *Juno*, a slower sailboat that left the Galapagos a few hours before we did. And *Cariño* basically sailed herself. Apart from bursts of work adjusting or changing sails, between the autopilot, chart plotter and radar, the work of sailing was no work at all.

I let go and accepted the reality of the moment.

On the third day, Louie called me outside. There was a helicopter, like a huge black bug, circling our boat. It pulled up and hovered just above the water, truly only a stone's throw away. Two guys stared at us from behind the rounded windshield; we stared back. I ran and got the camera and we all waved. It was as if we'd found the last humans on a planet of nothing but sea.

Sometimes I could sense the world as a huge blue sphere, vast and mostly empty before me. Did I really want to spend so much time sitting on a boat sailing around it? I got bored. I needed stimulation. I could be *doing* so much more. I should be… Shouldn't I? Was I wasting time? Was it selfish to be doing so much nothing? There were big problems in the world—global warming, corporate greed—the whole structure of society needed reordering. Our entire world view was overdue for an overhaul. All of us going about our lives under the false premise that we exist as separate entities. That the world out there had nothing to do with the world in here.

I set up the flat-screen TV and watched *What the Bleep Do We Know*, to get in a better mind space. It reminded me, again, about how magical the Universe was. That we are powerful creators, we are creating reality itself—us and the rest of the unified field of consciousness.

Then I started reading *The New Earth* by Eckhart Tolle, which I'd read before, to prolong this awareness: "The true purpose of your life cannot be found on the outer level. It does not concern what you do, but what you are: your state of consciousness… Your inner purpose is to awaken. It is as simple as that. You share that purpose with every other person on the planet, because it is the purpose of humanity."

It dawned on me like the radiant sun, how lucky I was to have all this time undistracted by the daily stress and runaround of shore-based life. Like a Buddhist nun dedicating her life to God, I had countless hours to open my awareness of the present moment. Learning to *be* instead of always striving to *do*. And this was useful work, important to the human race.

I sat with this idea. In the chair behind the wheel, I stared out at the undulating blue world, rising and shifting, in constant motion; the light shimmering white on every dancing surface; flying fish zipping out of their underwater reality to skirt above it in bursts; birds dipping and swirling, looking down at us in wonder; *Cariño*'s sails scooping the invisible wind, pulling us toward our destination. For short stretches, I was completely there, any trace of boredom or judgment dissolved. I was filled with an invisible force like those sails. And then, when the internal voice inevitably returned like a child unable to keep still, I'd smile as it chattered on about glorious moments past and possible futures or reminisced over each of my dear loved ones.

This heightened awareness stayed with me for four or five days, and a desire to actually *do* something gently rose up within it, like water seeping into a hole dug close to the surf. One morning I watched the movie I'd left unfinished the night before, then got out my jewelry-making stuff and sat outside. After that there was plenty to do: fishing; my meditation practice; working on my French while working on my tan. I made some earrings, did a little writing and some reading, a little yoga. Food preparation and maintenance took some of my time. Louie and I got so motivated one day that we waxed the cabin sides and polished the stainless. Then we sat back in the sun and toasted ourselves with rum punches.

There was stuff to do—unless I didn't want to—and then there was just now, glorious and simple.

The wind dropped to 10 knots and we put up the spinnaker, like a huge, blue kite pulling a sled.

"The wind's died," Louie informed me, disappointed.

"Cool," I said. "We'll have a nice chill few days."

"Yeah, a bit more than a few days if it stays like this."

"That's fine with me," I smiled, completely in the now and totally content.

Almost There

We were within 200 miles of our destination: 25 hours away at our current speed. Big and bumpy, the sea was tossing *Cariño* around. Sometimes there was a heavy rumbling reminiscent of a train chugging down a track, and occasionally there was the jarring thud of a wave pounding her flat underbelly. The wind was blowing around 20 knots and we were doing seven knots on a broad reach, the wind behind us and a little to the left.

The clock, which hadn't been changed since the Galapagos, said 11 am, but we'd gone so far west that this number no longer corresponded to the sun, which had only come up two hours before. We set another clock to UTC (Coordinated Universal Time) and it said 5 pm, also out of whack. But because we were traveling through time zones and it was inconsequential whether we knew the exact time or not, we let go of this metronomic counting and let time warp as it may.

The weather had been amazing, blowing steadily from the east-southeast at between 10 and 25 knots for the entire 18 days, with only a few lighter wind days and no heavier ones. The only major changes in weather had been internal: the constant fluctuation of my moods. It's curious how, despite the fact that human emotions completely color our experience, we receive little to no training or guidance as children about how to deal with them. My spiritual euphoria lasted for awhile, but inevitably my ego made a stand once again. I was either a successful adventurer or a lazy, useless slob; everything depended on my fickle mind. There was no point doing battle with it, since that only made it stronger. So I surrendered to what was, like I did with the weather—it could be raining or it could be sunny, but there was no point getting overly attached or upset. I kept reminding myself of this and continued meditating.

On one of those down days, Louie got out his huge chart that covered the whole Pacific to show me all of the islands scattered ahead of us. Most sailors relied completely on electronic charts displayed on a small screen. But he and I still believed in having paper charts as a backup; it seemed safer in case the electrical system failed. So he rolled out this big map that covered the table. But the worry about finding another boat plus my lack of funds, on top of an underlying smear of generic anxiety, swamped me. The chart conveyed too much space and I just couldn't look at it; there was too much unknown. I didn't like to consider my future when I felt vulnerable. It was more than I had the energy to handle, which would just muck up my manifesting. I liked to keep my dreaming of the future for when I was feeling good.

I reminded myself of what I'd learned about quantum physics. According to Lynne McTaggart, author of *The Field*, the tiniest particle, when not being observed, acted like a wave and spread out into more than one place at a time. A single particle, therefore, became a wave of possibilities. It was only with the focus of someone's attention that the particle settled into being one thing. That was my future: a wave of infinite possibilities. And I was practicing allowing all of them, instead of narrowing them down with the focus of worry. There were many different situations that could be great—and I wanted them to stay a wave until one presented itself as the obvious and best choice.

Cariño

I also reminded myself of how good I was at manifesting. One recent example was my computer. Jill and Steve had taken it back to the States, and it just so happened that their nephew, the Mac expert, fixed it for the price of Jill's home-baked cookies. Then a cruiser friend contacted Louie out of the blue to say he had to return Stateside but was flying back to his boat in the Marquesas. Was there anything Louie needed from America? So my computer would be meeting me at Nuku Hiva free of charge.

Landfall

Nuku Hiva, The Marquesas
July 18, 2010

After 18 days at sea, we crept into a bay guarded on either side by massive rock sentries that rose up in ridges of towering, green walls. These were the remains of an ancient volcano crater, Hatukau Bay, Nuku Hiva in the Marquesas Islands. It was Saturday and immigration was closed until Monday, so there was no pressing business on land. After anchoring, we spent the whole day cleaning the boat, toasting our arrival with Bloody Marys and napping. In the evening we climbed into the dinghy and headed for terra firma.

A traditional dance performance just happened to be taking place across the street from the cement dock where we tied the dinghy. The lady at the front door spoke French but was easy and smiling when I choked out, in my own halting version of the language, "*Voulez-vous prendre des dollar?*" I was covering for Louie who didn't give a shit and just talked to everyone in English, fearlessly communicating regardless of language.

The dancing was powerful. Men and woman of all ages and shapes were wearing grass skirts and woven tops decorated with feathers and shells. Their deep breath chants and strong communal movements spoke of the tribal life of times past. The place was packed with locals with only a handful of tourists.

The Marquesans seemed quick to laugh. Most had golden brown skin with thick, straight black hair. There were loads of kids running around and the teenagers all seemed stylishly dressed. There were pregnant women, sizable older ladies and studly, warrior-looking guys with tribal necklaces of teeth, bone and shell. And almost everyone carried the local mark somewhere on their body—often covering arms, necks and even faces—the Marquesan tattoo.

After the show, while walking past groups of lingering young people as we returned to our dinghy, I tried out my new word, *kaHOUta*, Marquesan for hello, and was touched by how openly happy and warm these people seemed. "I want to know them," I thought.

The next day began with boat work and by 3 pm, after we had eaten a big lunch, I was too full, tired and shy to go to land. Compounding this was disappointment in myself for not going. I hate when I'm scared, so I started to drink wine. Luckily, Louie jerked me from this slippery slope by suggesting we go meet some people who had slowly made their way into the bay under upside-down, crab claw sails, apparently without a motor, on a native-looking, small and open catamaran. We brought our glasses and a box of wine; as we pulled up the man and two women were just getting anchored and immediately invited us onboard. They had just arrived from Hawaii after 33 days at sea.

My first thought was, "Wow, this boat is about as far apart on the spectrum of seaworthy vessels from *Cariño* as you could get. These people had a *real* adventure." *Aluna's* two hulls were skinny like canoes, and the deck was completely open with only a small bulkhead to duck behind from the weather. The bunks and galley were in either hull and had extremely modest accommodations: no toilet, no fridge, not even built-in water tanks. The rigging was in the traditional Polynesian style, with the tip of the triangular sails pointing down.

Beat (pronounced in two syllables: be-at), the Swiss Captain, had built his Wharrem catamaran design out of plywood (the Tiki 38 with a borrowed Polynesian rig). The crossbeams were lashed to the canoes with rope, the standing rigging (typically wires that hold up the masts) were rope, the rudders and the hatches had rope as hinges. The forward deck consisted of slats of wood drilled with little holes that were laced down with rope. Beat and Beatriz, his Colombian wife, were proving that you could sail long distances with very little. I found myself saying, "I can see myself doing something like this. This is the kind of adventure I could get into."

Beatriz was a professional dancer and Beat a musician and actor. They were in their late 40s and, in their younger years, had traveled around South America doing street theater for a living. After 15 years in San Francisco, where they had been an integral part of the Colombian community, the American government had kicked them out. They were in the Marquesas to connect with the culture doing theater and dance and to make a living.

Cariño

The next morning we zoomed by to pick them up, as we all needed to check in at the immigration office. Louie and I spent the morning on land doing internet and banking. Then we went to see Rose, an old American lady who had come to Nuku Hiva by boat in the '70s and stayed. She had put together a museum of Marquesan artifacts and art, ancient and modern, and ran a hotel.

Back at the boat in the afternoon, I opened up my computer to write—and was faced with the same blank screen and strange beep that had caused me to send it away for repairs. I tried to hold on to positive thoughts, but I could feel myself slipping. I clung to a glass of wine for a handhold. I thought about going back to shore but we were supposed to leave the next day. What was the point? I go past all these beautiful places: It's just another bit of paradise that I won't get to experience. Just as my fingers lost their grip, and I began the slide into negativity, Beatriz, Beat and their departing crew, paddled up in their Polynesian-style canoe.

They were like nomadic holy people who had come to the palace, and I offered up our comforts to them: our plush couches in air-conditioned comfort, our juice with ice for Beatriz and red wine for the rest. We separated naturally—men on the foredeck and women in the main salon—and got to chatting. As night was falling, Louie suggested I make us a big pot of popcorn. Just then a dinghy pulled up.

The celebratory vibe was in the air, so I invited the newcomers aboard. They were a cute guy in his early 20s and a beautiful mid-50s blond: Americans. Someone asked the woman if the young guy was her son, and she threw her head back in wicked laughter before saying, "No, I sold him his boat. I'm helping him take it to Australia and I occasionally sleep with him," and with this she shrugged casually. Louie got out his goat-skinned drum that normally lay dormant and Beat pounded out a rhythm. Beatriz and I danced.

Later, I admitted to Beat that I was bored. He spoke in direct, no-nonsense terms about the ego and how we all suffer, how it is our own self that's the problem. With no one to talk to about my internal struggle for so long—Louie couldn't listen to my problems because he was so wrapped up in his own—it was a relief to engage again in the language of self-growth and awareness. Beat made a passing comment that I could join Beatriz and him since their one crew was departing, and I said I would if I had the money to pay my way. He said, "Well, we don't have money either, and we have to make a living—so we could do it together."

When everyone left, Louie went in to Skype Carrie, and I was alone. I could feel the new circumstance out in front of me. Beat and I hadn't had a serious discussion of my joining them, but it felt like something had shifted. As if the decision had made itself. Drunk but excited, I scribbled in my journal and dug into a tin of cookies. I passed out, right there in the salon, and awoke at 3 am.

The first feeling I had was relief, as if it had all been a dream. I didn't have to make such a drastic change after all! But as I made my way to bed, a little dancing person started bouncing around inside of me and I knew it was inevitable: I had to do it. I couldn't sleep with the excitement. When I woke again in my clean, soft, white bed, with anything I could dream up for breakfast just waiting to be made, I again felt relief. But once the part of me who knew this opulent life was killing me woke up, it got to jumping around again. This was going to happen whether I liked it or not.

I made us a big egg and French bread breakfast and even poured some Baileys in my coffee. Then I confided my potential plans to Louie. He was supportive, saying he thought it was a great opportunity. What better way to travel in French Polynesia than by a Polynesian-inspired catamaran?

We ran into Beat and Beatriz onshore.

"You got my attention last night," I started, slightly nervous.

"I'm not easy to be around," Beat responded, knowing exactly what I was talking about. "I like to push people."

"That's what I need, someone to push me," I replied, way too quickly. I'd already made *my* decision.

CHAPTER 9
French Polynesia

Aluna

Nuku Hiva
July 21, 2010

It all happened so fast: We were all together, standing in front of the walk-up window outside the *Gendarmerie* (police/immigration office). I signed off from Louie's boat and signed on with Beatriz and Beat on *Aluna*. Then Beatriz and their departing crew, Ellen, headed down the street to arrange for Ellen's flight out the next day, and Louie went back to his boat, pulled up anchor and headed out of the bay, underway for Tahiti. Just like that, I found myself alone with my new Captain.

We began to walk down the street, the glistening green slopes rising steeply around us. The yards were well cared for, with bright red hibiscus flowers, mango trees, fragrant light yellow frangipani blooms and other lush tropical vegetation lining the tidy streets.

Beat was Swiss, thin and wiry, with a bald head and expressive face. He was a fiery guy and immediately his fire slammed up against mine.

"Have you ever been in crisis before?" he asked. "This is going to be very hard for you."

"Shit, what have I signed on for?" I thought. Our conversation seemed like a loop de loop interchange on a freeway that went round and round but never got off. It wasn't the normal give-and-take, but a contrived exercise to prove to me how attached to my beliefs I was. He cut me off and dissected my use of particular words, "I think," being an evil culprit, without interest in what I was saying. My beliefs were just *mine*, while his were *the way*. And just when I started to think "what a know-it-all asshole," he told me that we are all mirrors for each other.

He was right. We had started our relationship in a self-help framework, with me confessing how miserable I was living the bourgeois lifestyle and wanting to do something about it. But I hadn't meant that I wanted him to be my guru. I have always been wary of people with this higher-than-thou attitude, and I found myself tip-toeing around words, trying to state things just right to avoid the over-intellectualized headache he was creating. I used the body awareness I learned in meditation to prevent getting swept up into anger and frustration and tried to prove how enlightened I was by letting him be right; that I wasn't that attached to my beliefs; if he wanted to be right, he could. I told myself I didn't care about him or what he thought about me. I wasn't going to fight him.

"You're gonna have to fight," he said.

"Maybe opening is a better way," I said.

"Maybe you have to fight to open. Why is everyone against fighting?"

"Five to 10-thousand years of patriarchy could have something to do with it," I would have said, but held my tongue. I wasn't going to fight. I pretended that I was completely open and calm.

"I don't have any walls up," I said smiling, while deep inside a tiny yellow guy pulled the walls of a tiny fortress around him and stood guard. I can bend, I can open, but I will maintain one small and hidden place where I am still right and you are still an asshole.

Later, while alone, I asked in my journal, "What's scaring you?" I wondered why I couldn't truly let all of my walls down. Was I scared of losing myself? Wasn't losing oneself the road to enlightenment taught by some spiritual practices? What if I could trust that if his intentions turned out to be controlling, I would recognize it and move on, trust that to break down my barriers wouldn't leave me weak and undefended, but would allow the Universe to flow through me. Would allow me the moment of NOW.

Later, when we went out to the boat, its bleak accommodations struck me in a new light. Now that I was to live and sail here, my admiration of their adventure on such an open and extremely simple boat was replaced by concern.

French Polynesia

Beat had been up front about how little sailing experience he and Beatriz had. And *Aluna* was bare-bones. No fridge, no built-in water tanks. No nothing. Shit and shower in a bucket. I could live like that—I did for many years on my own boat, but… my brain started to get frantic.

I had a look over my new vessel and asked Beat questions about the rig and gear he had onboard. The two skinny pontoons held Beat and Beatriz's cabin in one and a rudimentary kitchen with another bunk in the other. Up on deck, between the separate entrances to the pontoons, there was a bulkhead in front and back, each of which had about a foot overhang on top, creating a small central space that provided a little protection from the elements, but no roof. The deck connecting the two pontoons over the water consisted of slats of wood tied to the cross beams, which didn't appear like they'd hold up if, say, a big wave pounded them. The two outboard engines weren't working. We were close to the shore: If the wind started blowing and the anchors didn't hold, our only recourse would be to lift sail. But the sails were lashed along the side. They were made of tarp and strung between two bamboo arms that opened like a folding fan so we'd have to lift the whole heavy contraption and rig it to the stubby mast, not a quick or easy operation. I asked about safety gear: harnesses, life vests, life raft, throw-ring. Beat answered, "Just don't fall over."

They may have made it here from Hawaii, but this apparent disregard for the force of the ocean and the ferocity of Mother Nature struck me as insolent and dangerous.

My mind was verging on freaking out and, without goofy, lovable Louie, who always put himself out there and connected us with our fellow sailors, I felt stranded and alone. If we did find ourselves being washed onto shore, the most efficient action would be to call for help, so I asked for the VHF. Beat went below and, after a few minutes of rummaging, pulled out a Tupperware container. Inside was an old, black, boxy handheld radio that looked like a cell phone from the eighties, and he turned it over as if looking at it for the first time. He screwed in the antenna and told me that he didn't know if it should be set on international or U.S. I tried calling a boat in the vicinity that Louie had been in touch with, first on one channel and then, when that didn't work, on the other. They didn't answer and I would have given up, but I remembered how Louie was always insistent while reaching out to people, never being put off or getting insecure. So I started calling any boat:

"Radio check, radio check. This is *Aluna*. Can anyone hear me? Come back." Again I kept switching the setting and repeating my call, "Radio check, radio check."

Finally someone came back and, in a fed-up voice, said, "We can hear you. Be calm."

I sang out, "Thank you," wanting desperately to play it cool. Explanations flashed through my head, but I knew that anything else I added would only give away how frenzied I felt. Meditation would help, and I looked around for a spot to sit. Beat asked what I needed and scoffed when I said I preferred to be out of the elements with a little privacy, as if my practice was trite and superficial. That night I slept in the cockpit, since Ellen, the departing crew, wouldn't leave until the following morning. Since it was raining, I huddled under a leaky tarp, a yoga mat my only padding. What had I gotten myself into?

Beatriz's company made all of this easier. She was a joy to be around. Her energy was lighthearted and sweet. She stayed out of the tension between Beat and me, but let me know she appreciated my being there and felt safer with me around to help with the sailing. A small, voluptuous Colombian with olive skin, she had a big smile and a little-girl giggle. After 15 years in the States, she still struggled with English—and French was proving a real challenge as well. She was exclusively a heart-centered person, claiming ignorance to anything requiring logic or technical know-how, and I wondered if this was partly her reaction to 15 years with Beat, who was completely in his head.

The next few days were filled from morning to night. Everything took longer without all the conveniences of modern yachts. We started each day with wonderful oatmeal, cooked with powdered milk, quinoa, nuts, raisins and chopped-up mangos that we'd picked up from the ground under trees. We were on an extremely tight budget, so our meals were simple, starch-based affairs with some chopped cabbage or gathered fruit to freshen them up. We all took part in preparing them and (with no refrigeration) we would make just enough. No overindulging as on *Cariño*. I discovered that building up an appetite and sitting together like a family, talking and eating was something I really enjoyed. Between the smaller portions, the more physically demanding days, and the lack of excessive daily alcohol, my body immediately responded, feeling thinner and more energized.

French Polynesia

But my mind kept changing so fast it was like a boat that kept coming through the wind, not staying on one tack long enough to make any headway. I'd feel panic ("How the fuck can I escape this? Abort mission!"), and then my sails would catch the wind from the other direction and I'd tack, feeling social and connected and glad to be involved in such an adventure.

Scribbling in my journal, I talked myself through this: "In this moment, you are okay. Breathe. It's okay. Talk to people, stay connected." So I chatted with cruisers on land, helped a guy with a project on his yacht and kept sussing out potential rides. Also I made a local friend, Gabriel.

Aluna's dinghy was a skinny canoe with an outrigger, like a tiny catamaran with an atrophied pontoon to keep it from tipping over. We paddled it right up onto the small, black sand beach. Gabriel was busy sweeping the grounds on the quay and called out his appreciation for our craft with its traditional Polynesian style. Once landed, I went over and asked him if we could use the tap at the little bathhouse to do our laundry in buckets. When he said yes, Beat and Beatriz went back to *Aluna* to get all the laundry, while I waited onshore, sitting under a tree with my journal. Gabriel came over to sit with me. He appeared to be around 20, with a baby face and long, dark hair pulled back at his neck, and wearing a baggy tee shirt and long shorts.

"Gabriel," he said.

"Davina."

"*Tu veux de la fumée?*" he offered, showing me his hand-rolled cigarette.

"*No tabac, ahhh, juste marijuana.*" I said, which brought a knowing smile.

"*Tu aimes mixte?*" He asked, pulling out a little pouch and showing me the marijuana and tobacco. "*Mixte?*"

"*Ba way!*" I grinned. Yes, now we were talking the same language! Handing over the pouch, he had me roll it, though by now I was starting to suspect that *he* was actually an androgynous *she*. We smoked and then had a great time working out words, Gabriel writing them in Marquesan in my journal and me sounding them out.

Thank you… *kautau nui* was pronounced *kahoota nui*.

Hello. … *kaoha nui* was pronounced *ka OOOO ha nui*.

Adventures of a Pirate Girl

As we chatted, it became clear that whereever s/he lay on the spectrum of gender, s/he was interested in me in a sexual way.

Later, after we got all our washing wrung out, back to the boat and hung up, s/he came out to *Aluna* in a skiff. Pulling up alongside, Gabriel addressed Beat in French, informing him that, "Davina is going to come with me. I will take care of her and feed her and bring her back out to the boat later."

With a huge smile the whole time, I stepped into the skiff feeling like a teenager being properly courted. As soon as we made our getaway, s/he handed me a beer. And once onshore, bought us more beers at a shop. The big bottles and small bottles were the same price, so we got the big ones. Then we went to the beach to drink and smoke and play the communication game.

Gabriel's friends came by, two guys from Tahiti, looking for pot. Gabriel had the hookup, so we climbed in the back seat of their car and drove up the steep switchback road. Once we were high enough to overlook the harbor, I asked, in as many French words as I could piece together, if we could stop to take a photo. The land on either side of the round bay stuck out like the extended front paws of a dog lying on its belly. The three of them were so relaxed, speaking in a blend of Marquesan and French; I was totally at ease, not quite understanding but being included anyway, with laughter and energy.

We went to see Gabriel's cousin, a young guy who'd built his simple house: two small rooms with an open-air kitchen underneath. They were all so patient with me, speaking slowly and stopping mid-story to help me understand a word. The cousin asked if I'd find a Marquesan husband and, for the first time, I didn't jump to explain my mission to sail around the world, but answered, "*Je ne sais pas.*" I don't know what my future holds.

Beat, Beatriz and I spent a day cleaning the boat. Another day we re-anchored. If we had had an engine this process would have taken an hour. But without a motor we did it under sail, which required us to mount the crab claw rig. This was so much work that we decided to take the boat for a spin while the booms and sails were on so I could familiarize myself with how things worked. They mentioned that, since I had so much more experience than they had, I could potentially be the official Captain, freeing them up to do their theater work. Tacking to the mouth of the bay and back, then re-setting the anchors, took all day due to the fluky winds.

French Polynesia

One day we did a long hike over the ridge, through the next valley and up onto the next ridge. We talked about what we saw—the bountiful fruits and apparently high standard of living—but Beat's critical and negative comments got to me. I remarked about the Polynesian culture and how different it was from what I had experienced before and he slashed that, as if with a machete: "There is no culture here. What we see is just the shadow of culture; it's not real, it's been lost." Normally I enjoyed discussions like these, but it was obvious he wasn't open to out-loud pondering. He was convinced of his stance, so I shook my head, laughed, and added another brick to my wall.

While eating breakfast the next day, Beat went through a list of needed boat chores, putting my name or his down as the manager of each one. Beatriz would help us but was exempt from managing because, as they both insisted, she wasn't logical enough. I nodded and pretended I cared, while my mind was desperately scouring possibilities for escape. Even though originally I had been attracted to the opportunity of doing theater and dance, when Beat proposed going to a beautiful, grassy park studded with rock sculptures to begin playing with some ideas, I tried to bow out. By now I was about to burst with the feelings I had been suppressing and I struggled to keep them down and get away before I exploded. But they called me on it, asking me if I wanted to talk.

"No. No, I don't." I said.

"Are you having second thoughts?" they asked.

"Yes, yes, I'm freaking out, totally freaking out! I'm having second, third and fourth thoughts; my mind is going crazy. I don't know if I want to do this. It's like my ego has split in two and has been arguing with itself loudly and non-stop since I got onboard! I just started my period and maybe I'm just totally emotional. Maybe I just need to be alone, meditate and write."

"I don't think this is something you can work on alone; we always think we can but it's with other people that all this stuff comes up," said Beat. "And what is meditating gonna do?"

"I don't care if you think my meditating is stupid," I declared, though I could feel myself go rigid with the familiar block springing up.

"You don't care?"

"No, you're right. I do care. It hurts me when you are so judgmental about something I feel strongly about." Admitting this dismantled a few bricks and I immediately felt the space.

Beat then explained that he had his own conflicted feelings about meditation, and he hoped he hadn't stopped my practice.

My mind tacked through the wind again; I suddenly felt powerfully connected and open to them. Beat explained how he had used theater to examine and work with his own internal conflict, sharing some details about the parts of himself that he'd had a hard time accepting and loving; also his struggle to use "I am" when talking about ego and mind, instead of his usual "you are," which made it so much easier to hear. After talking we all agreed to go to the park and do some improvising.

At the park, we did some exercises that demonstrated how theater could be used for self-discovery and healing. One of these was particularly revealing: The instructions were to be more powerful than the others. Beat talked loudly and maneuvered to be in my face. I stood up proudly, hands on my hips, chin up and looked loftily off into the distance, ignoring him. Beatriz remained sitting, asking innocently if we had already started, claiming she didn't understand. After an hour or so in the park, we headed back to the boat.

I realized this wasn't the kind of situation I could be in if I wasn't totally present. Beat and Beatriz wouldn't allow me to hide. There was no room to anyway; I had to be there 100%, or not at all. But I was finding it hard to fully trust Beat.

The way he was attempting to help me with my inner turmoil reminded me of a past situation. While I was living alone on Hatteras Island during one winter, I started falling into a depression, so I went to stay with my dad and his wife in California. I started seeing a therapist and doing some deep, emotional work and they were supportive. After a few months, I'd made headway and felt healthy and happy and ready to return to my life in Hatteras.

But before I left, they sat me down for a family meeting that felt more like an intervention. They insisted that I was severely bi-polar and should be on medication. I listened and tried to remain objective, listening to their opinions. But when I tried to respond, Dad's wife kept cutting me off, telling me to use "I" phrases and correcting my wording in an exaggeratedly calm voice, instead of just listening to what I had to say.

My therapist strongly disagreed with their diagnosis. She assured me that I was a deeply feeling person, but in her professional opinion, I did not have bi-polar disorder. I didn't talk to my dad for years after that.

French Polynesia

But what if it was true? What if I worked past all these barriers and discovered that I really was fucked up?

"I wouldn't want to be a burden on you," I sobbed to Beatriz and Beat, the tears welling up, my body starting to quake. "I hate to be such a problem." The Universe seemed to conspire with my vulnerable emotional state, because it started to rain. We quickly pulled the tarp over the cockpit and retreated to our separate pontoons. All day the rain came and went, and I alternated between intense therapy sessions with my fellow shipmates and time alone in my dark little cubby of a bunk to write and cry.

All of the pain of self-hatred and depression surfaced that day. Beat was a demanding emotional coach and I cowered and trembled. "I don't know where it hurts," I told him. The great adventurous Davina was so different from the scared, shy and addicted Davina. Maybe he was right: that my self-esteem relied on others and I needed approval and love to keep me buoyant and confident. Maybe that's why I never wanted to fight: Maybe I was scared I would lose. I always wanted to be agreeable, the good guy, the one everyone loved and related to. And now I had a lot of people reading my blog, expecting me to live my dream as I said I was doing, cheering me on when who I claimed to be was a lie. I didn't even know if this was my dream anymore. Why the hell was I doing this? I was so much happier in Boulder. I just wanted to go home.

"Maybe addiction snuck up on you and your body is reacting from not having any alcohol," they hypothesized. I nodded my head in agreement, not confessing that I had a few boxes of wine left over from *Cariño* and I'd snuck a glass each day. What happened to the strong willpower I used to pride myself on? Who was this Davina? When I had left on this trip I thought I knew, but now I was seriously beginning to wonder.

Making this even harder was the thought that sailing with Beat and Beatriz was giving me the opportunity to work on this stuff; this was a chance to learn new ways to connect with people without using sexuality and drugs. If I walked away from *Aluna*, I was a coward, scared to face myself, and I would never be happy. I would wander forever in intoxicated denial and be miserable.

Back and forth, the wind kept catching my sail on the opposite tack, and now it was whipping violently in the storm. Then Beat said something that stuck: If I was 100% in the moment and giving myself to this experience, I would be free to go at any time. As long as I wasn't fully present, I was stuck in fear and couldn't leave.

That night, after the torrent of my tears had stopped, my decision shone through like the sun through clouds: I would go. Louie had been emailing me about all the opportunities in Tahiti to find another boat, and I had just enough money to get myself there. Being on *Aluna* had been an important experience, but I wasn't stuck in it. And though I would continue to work on myself, it didn't have to be torture.

The next morning I woke up early and meditated as I had every morning since getting on *Aluna*, then jumped in the water to clean the hull. Beatriz, despite her confessed unease with snorkeling, jumped in and helped. Beat called us when he had breakfast ready. We joined him in the cockpit for our lovely oatmeal and I let them know I was leaving. I felt alive, energized, and completely in the flow: 100%. However my next step was going to unfold, I wasn't worried. Beat, who was never encouraging or openly appreciative, asked me, just out of curiosity, if there was anything they could do that would convince me to stay.

Rakinui

Nuku Hiva to Tahiti
July 29, 2010

After informing my shipmates of my decision, I shaved my legs and cut my hair, and we paddled in to find out how I was going to make it happen.

The French lady at yacht services, in her I-couldn't-care-less, French attitude, told me the inter-island ferry wouldn't be back for another three weeks and it cost more than the plane anyway. The plane cost $290 plus $40 to get a taxi to the airport. I had $300 left. Totally unfazed, I turned to Beatriz and shrugged my shoulders.

Beat called Thomas, an American guy we'd met who lived on Nuku Hiva and was married to a Marquesan. Over the phone, Thomas informed Beat that the ferry was due back that night or in the morning, and that it was possible to get a cheaper fare, but it was first come, first served.

French Polynesia

"If the ferry shows up tonight," he told Beat, "call me and I'll drive over the island to make sure Davina gets a spot and then sleep on your boat. Otherwise, I'll meet you in the morning."

The ferry came after dark, but it had started to rain and it seemed absurd to paddle back to shore in the deluge. Besides, my cabin was strung with wet laundry and there was no space to accommodate Thomas for the night. If it was meant to be, it would work out in the morning.

Before it was fully light, I stuffed my still-damp clothes into my backpack and we went to shore. The word around town was that immigration normally required a $1500 bond to sign off a boat without a plane ticket or another boat to sign onto (to make sure foreigners left the country), but somehow the *Gendarmerie* simply signed me off *Aluna* and wished me *bon jour*. Then Thomas drove us to the big ferry loading dock, which was full of commotion.

Rakinui was part cruise ship (the back half stacked up like a tiered wedding cake) and part cargo ship (the front long and low, with two crane arms to load storage containers. It made a regular, two-week tour of the islands and was now on its quick, four-day run back to Tahiti. It was docked out of town at the mouth of the bay, and the dirt lot in front of it was packed with trucks and people. There were big steel boxes being loaded onto the bow and forklifts zipping around. I had never been on such a colossal ship before, which to me had the romance and intrigue of the *Titanic*.

Thomas found the man we needed to speak with: a dark-skinned, stern-looking, 40-something hunk named Tony, with tattoos of rams' horns curling around each of his pectoral muscles. He was busy ordering the chaos of loading over a walkie-talkie. Thomas asked in a hodge-podge of Marquesan words and simplified Tarzan English if there was room for me.

"No, sorry. D class is only locals now. It changed," he answered back in English, a little slow, but fluent.

"Come on, you recognize me. She's a friend."

"Please," I begged, lunging forward on one knee and raising my hands prayerfully. "I will do dishes. I will work. I'm a sailor and I've got a boat in Tahiti. I've got to get on this ship." He barely cracked a smile but pulled me up off my knees and made a call. I was in!

"You stay in the back though; no talking with tourists, no eating in the restaurant, and no hanging out at the pool," he said, back to his gruff countenance.

After I paid the $220 ticket, we drove back to the dock in town where the ship's launch was ferrying the tourists in and out by the bus full. Thomas arranged to come onboard and show me around; he had done the island tour on the cheap with his son and knew the ropes. He carried my bag up the staircase at the side of the ship and took me to D class. Right at the stern on the lower deck was a small room with a table, two chairs and a window into the kitchen where I would be fed. From there we went down a dark, narrow stairway toward loud, tinny American pop music and came into a little room lined with bunk beds. There was a family sprawled out on floor mats watching videos on their computer. Like a teacher introducing a new kid to the class, Thomas—again in his mixed Tarzan English and Marquesan—asked where they were going and told them my name was Davina and I'd be sharing the room. I felt so safe and guided. I might be out in this big, wide world alone, but there were angels at every turn.

Once Thomas left, I strolled back down the lower gangway. The steel deck was covered in black rubber matting, with a solid railing, waist high, between me and the four-story drop to the sea. A guy with short, funky dreads was leaning on the balustrade rolling a cigarette. I didn't usually smoke cigarettes, but I asked if I could have one because it made for an easy bridge to conversation. He handed me the pack and asked if I spoke English. His was perfect. He was from the island Moorea, but had lived in the States for years and was a waiter onboard *Rakinui*. He offered to give me a tour after our smoke.

He took me up a flight of stairs to a pool surrounded by lounge chairs. Above that there was an open deck for sunbathing, a bar, and an indoor lounge area, which he thought would be fine for me to hang out in. It had self-serve coffee and tea in the corner and comfy chairs and tables surrounded by windows overlooking the bow of the ship, with its towering crane and stacked cargo containers. Off the lounge area was the computer room lined with shelves filled with books in French, English, German, and the odd Spanish and Italian. Down a flight of stairs was a big ballroom where the passengers from the A, B, and C classes ate.

He led me into the kitchen, introducing me to the staff as we went. There was a tiny bakery in the dark recesses and, as we passed through the different rooms, I caught a glimpse of Tony (who had warned me not to leave the stern area), so I smiled, shrugged an "oops" and waved before hurrying away. Another

French Polynesia

flight down was the gift shop and main desk, where my guide introduced me to Michael, whom I recognized from the launch: a tall, straight-backed, young guy with a large bone tiki carving on a cord around his neck, a gleaming perfect white smile, and great English. They both assured me that if there was anything I needed, I should let either of them know. Their hospitality felt genuine.

Learning a language is intimidating. I felt like a baby learning to walk. I'd rush out into what I wanted to say, then find myself stumbling on wobbly legs, the words I'd practiced in my mind suddenly gone. I'd want to just plop down and forget it, but the person was still standing there attentively, waiting. So I'd grab the only words at hand and use them like crutches, in creative and far-from-correct ways to keep moving forward and finish my thought. Years before in Paris, people seemed ready to push me over if I didn't speak French perfectly. I remember asking a woman for directions in French. She looked down her nose at me and said, "I don't speak English," before hurrying away. But here in French Polynesia, the people I was meeting were cheering me on, standing with their arms outstretched, ready to catch my meaning as I wobbled slowly toward them.

Wandering the decks of the *Rakinui* gave me lots of chances to practice my baby French. My quarters in the stern were near the crews' quarters and dining area, and everyone seemed to hang out back there when off duty. The big tattooed sailors, who worked the massive lines around huge, barrel winches while docking and departing, had plenty of time to talk and were curious about the single white girl in D class.

I really liked these Polynesian men, who seemed to have a healthy masculinity. In the West, the archetype of strong male tends toward the military tough guy, completely cut off from the feminine. More sensitive guys were often too flimsy for the likes of me. These guys were warriors. I had seen it in the traditional dances on Nuku Hiva, where the men's movements were forceful and grounded, their breathy chants emanating deep from their bellies. But they didn't seem divorced from their softer sides: they'd often stick a frangipani bloom behind an ear. They loved their stunningly big necklaces, made of bone and shell. One day onboard *Rakinui*, one of the biggest, bald and tattooed sailors with missing front teeth was wearing a beautiful crown of colorful flowers.

I didn't expect much for food onboard, but I started to get hungry and went to the little window that cut through to the kitchen to investigate. Matahi (mahtah-ee), a cute young guy with Asiatic features and soft facial hair accentuating his authentic smile, was there cutting vegetables for the restaurant and immediately asked me if I wanted something to eat. I attempted to explain my eating habits without the word for meat: "*Juste vegetal et poisson,*" I managed. He took this literally and sautéed me some cabbage and onions topped with a fillet of fish heaped on a china plate instead of the tin bake pan we were supposed to use. Such a delicious meal cooked especially for me and handed over with such a sweet smile tickled me, and I ate in total appreciation.

That morning we stopped briefly at the island of Ua Pou. Among its steep, green mountains, the towering pinnacle rocks stood way up above the island like ancient gods, watching over the tiny humans scurrying through the generations. The family in the shared room had departed, and a drunk had come aboard, who joined me at the small table with his meal. He was loud and sloppy, though congenial. I rolled my eyes at Matahi and asked, "How do you say…?" and did a little charade to learn the word for drunk in French. I tried to continue thoroughly enjoying my breakfast, even if my peace was a teensy bit disturbed.

Later that night, Matahi, after working all day in the kitchen, came down to the D class to give the stinky shower room a thorough clean. Michael came down with sheets, a blanket, and a pillow for me, which normally weren't provided, and hung out for a while to chat. The drunk never came back to sleep in the shared room and later Matahi confessed that, though they knew he was harmless, they had made it excessively clear he'd better leave me alone.

Michael invited me to come and see the *Rakinui* band, of which he was a part; they were playing that evening at the bar. We met up beforehand and I followed him through the maze of narrow hallways to his cabin that he shared with Hiro, my guide the first day. The three of us stood shoulder to shoulder in a closet-like bathroom passing around a joint. Afterward , Michael covered up any trace of the forbidden smoke with air freshener as if he was killing a swarm of flying insects and Hiro passed around the eyedrops. But when I entered the small bar, on the high, back deck just above the pool (which sloshed dramatically with the roll of the ship), I regretted it. My French was even worse while stoned and I felt awkward looking people in the eye. There were six musicians playing stringed instruments and singing in a fast, tropical style, and even though I was feeling self-conscious, I made myself dance. First I faced one way as the floor

French Polynesia

slanted up with the big sea, then the other when it slanted down. "I am going to stop drinking and smoking, starting tomorrow," I told myself.

There was a French girl about my age. Despite my bungled greeting to her, in which I looked away too fast and then worried about how awkward I'd acted, she approached me after the music. Turns out she had lived in Tahiti for a few years and was a therapist specializing in…addiction. That's a sign, I thought, and confided to her in a mix of French, English and Spanish, my growing awareness of my dependence and the intention I had made that night.

The next day we stopped in Rangiroa, a huge atoll in the Tuamotu group. It was more like the outline of an island, with the whole middle part water instead of land. The ship slipped through a small inlet and anchored in a gigantic lagoon. We passengers filed down the stairway and into a barge, which powered right up onto the beach. Again I was totally content. I wandered away from the main group, who were congregating around the few tiki shops under the palm trees on white sand, and found a secluded spot to sunbathe. The lagoon was clear, like bathwater, and went from sandy white to vivid turquoise and finally to a deep, indigo blue.

After that I strolled the few minutes—crossing one lone, empty road—to the outer side of the island. This was a wild, windward beach where the deep Pacific washed up in frothy waves and there was no sign of humans. I combed the shore for treasures and found heaps of weathered, purple cowry shells. When I returned to where the main cluster of people were, Michael handed me a plate of salad from the picnic that I had assumed was only for tourists. Then he introduced me to a white French guy in a sarong with a traditional tattoo creeping over one shoulder, who had lived on Rangiroa for seven years and did paintings in a pseudo-Polynesian style. His art combined the tribal patterns with images of sea creatures and were made with mud and all-natural plant dyes. I liked him right away. After I admired his little gallery he led me out back, speaking in slow and clear French, making sure I understood. He invited me to sit at a table behind his shop with some of the guys from the ship and brought me an espresso. When a pipe came around I didn't hesitate, being so accustomed to bonding over a smoke. When I said goodbye, my host offered to house and feed me if I ever wanted to hang out on Rangiroa for a while.

Back onboard, my dropped intentions gained momentum as they plummeted downhill; I took the beer Tony offered. Back at our tiny dining area, the drunk was playing a ukulele with a guy who had caught my eye earlier. One of the sailors, he was a big, broad shouldered guy with silky, cinnamon skin, thick, black hair and full yummy lips: the perfect South Pacific specimen. Earlier, when I had stepped from the stairway into the launch, he'd helped me with a hand on my side and held on for a few seconds too long. We locked eyes now. Thinking I'd give them my last box of wine (since I intended to quit), I went to my room to get it. But when I returned, the drunk was gone and Johnny told me we were going to drink it together. So, instead of making plans for the next day when the journey would end in Tahiti, instead of talking more to the French therapist or to the woman who had offered me a place to stay, I indulged in *all* of my addictions.

In the small dining area, Johnny and I picked through the words we both knew, puzzling out communication while we drank the wine. He drew pictures of the islands, telling me about his family and the tiny island where they lived. Big, sexy man, he knew how attractive he was and exactly how to play this game. Like a predator with his cornered (though very willing) prey, he was not holding back. He turned off the lights, closed the little window to the kitchen, put on some music and took off his shirt. We danced, him in a sort of masculine hula style, arms up to the side making waves. When he worked out that yes, I did like to smoke, he took my hand and led me through the labyrinth of narrow passageways forward, avoiding the main dining, ballroom and front-desk areas. We went through a door that led to the front of the vessel, where the stacked-up cruise ship ended and the long, flat deck piled up with shipping containers stretched to the bow. We sat in a dark alley between these big steel boxes and smoked. By this point we were talking directly about what was going on between us, piecemeal, as it were. I was explaining how I wanted something serious, I wasn't a little girl anymore, plus I was celibate: no, no, no. But given that our shared language was stilted and my body spoke fluently, it's no surprise he took its meaning perfectly: yes, yes, yes.

He led me up to the bow, the only place on the whole boat that was dark enough to see the stars. The cockpit, from where the Captain and officers were navigating, was four stories up and way back. The partially full moon was closer than usual, windy clouds scuttling over her light, the churned up gush of the sea streaming out behind us. He turned me to face him, put both his hands under my armpits and lifted me up onto a huge, drum winch. Pressing his smooth

French Polynesia

chest between my thighs, he effectively parted them, and reached his face up to kiss me. Hot damn.

Once he knew his prey wasn't going anywhere, he knelt in front of me, peeled my panties down from underneath my skirt and burrowed his face into the, by now, wet, hot place between my legs. The night, stars, moon and sky, wind, sea and water swirled around me, and rushed through me, riding the waves up and down, him sucking and licking, until there was a deep ache inside my womb. Then he made his way up to my face, his soft, full lips and tongue melding into mine while his cock slid and pressed. Right then, the green, parrot-feather earring I'd made while in Panama—when I'd made my vow of celibacy—whipped out of my ear and took flight. He pushed his penis in and in and in, ohhhhhh. And all of a sudden I felt a gush. I pulled away mad, wiping the wetness across his smooth chest with my hand to make my point, but he assured me, *"C'était tout toi"* (That was all you).

"Condoms."

"Oui, condoms."

So he set me down on the deck and led me by the hand back through the maze of containers and then through narrow, dark passages till he was standing behind me, opening the door to his cabin. I stepped in and just about into the chest of Oscar, the other guy with whom I had been heavily flirting. Also a broad shouldered, young sailor with a ready smile, his few missing teeth not diminishing his good looks but emphasizing his sweet, child-like nature. My mind raced ahead…

Putting a hand on Oscar's chest, I turned back and kissed Johnny, meeting his eyes, sparkling and devious as I pulled away. Then I turned to Oscar, my eyebrows a question mark, as I leaned forward and pressed my lips to his, something I'd been wanting to do over our flirtations, which was all the more delicious with Johnny watching. Johnny stepped into the room and closed the door behind him. Oscar, with his big hands on my lower back, pulled me up against him and Johnny pressed up behind me, pulling off my shirt. Off came Oscar's, velvety skin all around. And then Johnny, on his way down, peeled off my skirt as he crouched behind me. My fantasies of sailing the South Pacific …ohhhh.

I jerked up, awake, bleary eyed, groggy and alone. The boat wasn't moving. The constant drone of the engines was suddenly missing. It was 6:30 am, I'd only just made it back to my own bed a few hours before. Swerving slightly, I rushed outside to see what was going on, and was shocked that we were already at the dock. Since I hadn't bothered to find out anything about the disembarking schedule, I assumed I'd better hurry up, and in a panic got my shit together. But after the chef offered to cook me up an omelet, I relaxed a little; clearly I had some time.

Though communicating with words wasn't easy, Matahi and I understood enough through laughter and good energy to know we were friends. When he passed me the scrumptious omelet and a desperately needed coffee, he asked me what I was going to do. I shrugged, blankly: I had no idea. My brain wasn't working: I just felt stunned. Later, while I cleaned and swept the D class accommodations, knowing that job would fall on Matahi's shoulders, he passed me a folded paper with his number on it and said I could stay at his house if I needed to.

There was no part of me that wanted to get off that boat. When I began my descent into the bustling parking lot—little girl lost with a big ass backpack—both Hiro and Michael told me to wait around and one of them would give me a ride. I sat in a little gazebo and bummed a smoke off someone, no thoughts in my head, just the oppressive heat and a burning cigarette, with indecipherable chatter all around me. An hour later a car pulled up. Michael was in the back with his 3-year-old daughter and his wife, who beckoned me to sit with her in the front. They offered to drive me to the marina where all the sailboats were, which was logical, but I seemed to be out of logic. I insisted, instead, that they drop me off on the waterfront by the bus stop. On the sidewalk, Michael, who'd come around to the front, gave me a hug and slipped something into my hand. As I watched them drive away I found a prepaid cell phone and the equivalent of $30 in my hand.

Hefting my monstrous bag in the heat, both of them weighing me down, I wandered the wrong way, winding around the bustling city streets aimlessly before finding a place to get on the internet. Then I gave in and bought a beer, as this was clearly no time to get on the wagon, and sat at the bus stop. A lady, apparently concerned about this wayward child, asked me where I was going. When I said the marina, she wagged her head no, and then insisted on walking me the four blocks and used exaggerated hand signals to make it excessively clear: *this* was the bus I needed. She looked a little worried about me as she walked away.

My Tahitian Family

Papeete, Tahiti
August 1, 2010

Away from the bustling city center on the waterfront, where the colorful vibrancy of the tropics was still apparent in the big, glass-fronted shops, open-air markets and tropical foliage, the bus took me through the generic cement, asphalt and graffiti of any concrete jungle before depositing me at the marina. From there, the lush green volcano that had formed the island of Tahiti way back when rose up behind the man-made gray blocks and held sway. Louie met me at the gate. It was good to see him, but he looked worn out, like life without a woman had been hard on him.

We went to happy hour at a bar that opened up onto a lawn overlooking the docks. Boats floated in water so crystalline you could see the underside of their hulls and colorful fish darting about. I duly sipped a beer, but the mostly middle-aged white male crowd and usual boatie conversation around me felt like the same ol', same ol'. I feigned interest, but I was really just bored.

That night, I stayed on a Kiwi man's yacht, someone I'd been in touch with since the Galapagos due to a potential crewing position. He was a nice guy, soft spoken, slightly unsure of himself, substantiated by a little stutter. He had a beautiful, sleek, 55-foot sailboat and needed help sailing it, plus he was willing to pay. I'd been upfront with him about my need to make some money. In the morning we went into Papeete (pronounced pa pe ay tee), and I would have followed him around trying to prove my worth as crew, but he wanted to leave the next day. I didn't want to leave at all, especially not that fast, and the thought of sailing alone with him onboard sounded dull. I knew I would end up drinking too much and sink into a let's-get-this-over-with attitude.

So instead, I found an internet café and focused on turning my CV into French, using an online translator. My plan was to get myself a job on the *Rakinui*. After such a good experience onboard, I figured it would be perfect—combining boats and the service industry. I could cruise French Polynesia, learn French, explore the islands and make money. My friend Tony, the guy who originally bent the rules and allowed me onboard, had suggested it. Apparently they often had guest speakers who did presentations for the tourists. When I was feeling up, especially just after getting high while onboard, I'd fantasized about doing theatrical readings of my Pirate Girl adventures in the islands. But given my depleted mental space, void of the audacity or confidence required for performing, I figured waitressing would be a better bet. Once I got as far as I could with my translating, no doubt creating a choppy testimony to my lack of fluency (but demonstrating initiative, I told myself), I wandered out and ran into a Swiss cruising family I had met in the Galapagos. They had two, preteen kids and were happy to help me smooth out and perfect my resumé over lunch at an outdoor café.

When I met back up with the Kiwi Captain, he was acting like we'd sealed the deal, so I let him know that I would take the job on *Rakinui* if they wanted me. Otherwise, we'd see. Knowing I'd need to find somewhere else to stay if I wanted to keep my options open, with my shoulders back (to show the confidence I didn't feel), I asked if he could keep my backpack for the night, said we'd catch up the next day and purposefully walked away.

I had a few possibilities of places to stay. Johnny, from my adventures onboard, had given me his number but, once on the phone, our communication was so patchy and our history so sordid, I got nervous and hung up. The only person I really felt comfortable calling in Papeete was Matahi, my personal chef from the *Rakinui*. It took a lot of back and forth, each of us trying to be clear about the plan. Eventually, he got me to understand that he'd meet me where I was, near the pay phones by the waterfront, in half an hour. And, just as it was getting dark and I was getting anxious, there he was. As soon as we were walking down the street away from the city center, me pushing his bike so he could roll a smoke, we became like two teenagers, good friends whose depths were understood. Each sentence constructed between us was a tower, and it was fun to see how high we could make it. He kept pulling out English words that he apparently hadn't realized he knew to add on. Once we were near his place, we lingered in the park and got stoned.

He lived with his sister, he explained. "The kids are still there," he said.

"Your sister's kids?"

French Polynesia

"No, my little sisters and brother. My dad will pick them up soon and I don't want to see him. There is electricity between us." So we loitered to avoid a confrontation. He told me about street fighting, about two guys who had called him out to box, which left me confused since he didn't seem upset about it. Later he showed me the video that he had set to music and I realized boxing was his hobby.

Matahi and his sister lived in a one-bedroom place in a suburb of Papeete. It was humble and clean, with tile floors, a little shower room as an afterthought squeezed in behind the couch in the living room, a small kitchen and a mini, tiled patio out back in the alley. His sister, who usually stayed at her boyfriend's house, had decorated with big posters of sleek, white women advertising perfume. There was a computer on a messy card table and a big central TV. We slept in the living room, Matahi on the couch and me on a mattress on the floor.

In the morning, his sister came in with a baguette and a singsong voice, "*Yur a na!*" (hello), not at all surprised to see me. Mimi was 24, small and curvy, with smooth, mahogany skin, long, reddish, sun-bleached hair and stylish clothes. She worked as a teacher, a well-paid and secure job in Tahiti. She and her brother giggled profusely about everything.

Matahi borrowed a bike from his cousin for me, and the following morning we rode to where the *Rakinui* was docked. I didn't have a change of clothes and was wearing slightly dirty board shorts, sweaty from the long ride. While Matahi stayed down the road to hide from his boss, I found Tony driving a forklift and he told me to look for Greg, the owner, onboard. I waited for an hour in the front lobby of the ship, which was covered in dropcloths as workers tromped in and out to prepare for their next voyage. Finally, after conferring with Tony again, I settled on talking to the owner's sister in the office building down the street. She explained that they weren't hiring; they already had enough people who spoke English, and a work visa was extremely hard to get. Deflated, I didn't persist.

I rode back to Matahi with a hanging head. My first impulse was to have a beer, but I resisted. I was *not* going to drink. So I had a cigarette instead, trading one addiction for another. Shit, now what was I going to do?

Matahi said I was welcome to stay with him and his sister while I figured it out. I didn't want to go with the Kiwi guy, but with less than $50 of spending money, I also didn't want to put any strain on my sweet-hearted hosts. I Skyped my mom because I was feeling so conflicted, but she didn't understand my dilemma since I obviously wanted to stay.

"Follow your heart," was her advice.

Mimi appreciated this sentiment and arranged to use her parents' truck to help me get my stuff from the marina.

The next morning, I found myself alone. I microwaved myself an instant coffee in a small glass bowl and sat out back in luxurious solitude to roll a cigarette. Matahi's mom came in, singing, *"Yur a na,"* and I quickly stamped out my smoke, ashamed to be caught in such a filthy practice. She came through the house and sat down on the step beside me, her face radiating love and kindness. We exchanged a few simple sentences before she got up and bustled around, complaining about lazy Matahi, still sleeping.

They were a close family. The parents came and went like they lived there, stuffing food in the fridge, having a casual meal and often leaving the younger kids for half the day or a few hours in the evening. The kids would play video games on the computer or pile on top of Matahi on the couch and stare at the ever-blaring TV.

I stayed separate, sweeping the floor or doing the dishes. Mostly I wanted to hide from the world; I wasn't feeling particularly social or outgoing. I didn't even learn the kids' names. That evening Matahi's mom returned and was disappointed in us for being so lethargic. She thought he should be showing me around, sightseeing. She offered to take me somewhere that night, but I got out of it, claiming I had plans with a friend.

"Tomorrow," she insisted. "Tomorrow we go to the mountains."

Matahi and I walked to the beach to escape, his prepaid phone playing the five-song loop that was our soundtrack. We walked through cement suburban sprawl to the beach, where there was a big wall dividing the black sand from the town. Not the sort of idyllic paradise you'd imagine as Tahiti.

"I worked on the computer almost all day," I defended myself to Matahi. His mom wasn't the only one disappointed with our sluggishness. We sat on the small, dismal beach and looked out over shallow, stagnant water.

"I'm realizing how lost I am when I'm in between boats." Trying to capture this thought in French—and then making it clear that I was just learning this

French Polynesia

about myself—took a half hour. I had practiced my French lessons faithfully in the Caribbean, but had slowly stopped since being in the Pacific where they would actually help. Though I did start writing down verb tenses and little useful words while loafing with Matahi—*almost, still, already, soon*—it was more a brainless pastime than engaged study. My French was lazy and half-hearted. He, on the other hand, seemed to have a magic bag: every time he reached into it he'd find more English words.

Our roaming reminded me of my high school years, hanging out with my brother, when smoking pot had been our main activity. Matahi's and my range was limited to the park on the corner, the convenience store, and the drainage ditch in his neighborhood—which would have been beautiful with its overgrown foliage, small babbling creek and banana trees, if it weren't for the fallen down, corrugated metal fencing and the trash strewn about. While I felt bored and guilty for wasting my time in Tahiti, Matahi was at peace with our lazy days. After all, he was still recouping from his few weeks of nonstop, heavy work onboard *Rakinui*. He listened to my conflicted feelings as a benign presence, insisted on paying for cold drinks and food, and was always checking to make sure I was okay. "Are you good? You want to walk?"

"Don't worry... (worry, how do you say *worry*?) I will let you know when I want to go. And you don't have to wait for me." But, of course, he did.

The next day we went to the mountains. I thought I was going alone with the family, which meant I wouldn't be able to stay in my teenage stupor. So I was relieved when it turned out that Matahi's dad had planned the trip for a visiting colleague, and Matahi and I were hitching along. We sat in the back seat of the clean, new pickup truck, and I wasn't expected to say anything; all I had to do was stare out the window.

Away from the city, Tahiti started to look more like what I'd expected: lush, green bush and blue sea peeling in perfect wave formations before crashing on the offshore reefs. Once we got to the dirt track that traversed the mountainous volcano that formed the island, Matahi and I got in the back and stood up, holding on to the cabin roof as the truck clawed over the treacherously steep, rocky road. The misty rain cloaked the mountains, and it was as if we'd driven into the Polynesian equivalent of Mount Olympus, our tiny vehicle making its way like an ant through the silhouettes of towering, green walls, lush Goddesses. Streaming cascades of water adorned the verdant deities with white ribbons. It was stunning.

When it got too wet and cold in the truck's bed, we got into the cab. Mostly I stayed quiet, but when Matahi's dad brought up God, I got excited, my voice growing in volume as I searched for the French words to express my ideas. I explained that my nature-based beliefs were probably closer to ancient Polynesian ones than their Protestant views were. But it didn't really matter what words we used, since God was bigger than words, and we spoke different languages anyway. We both believed in a higher power, as did people everywhere, and that was saying something of its existence. Though it wasn't clear how Matahi's dad felt about what I had to say, I think he liked how heated I got.

We stopped a bunch of times and took the same posed photo in front of different vistas, and, once we reached the sea and sun on the other side of the island, we had a picnic big enough for 10. Driving home, lulled by the huge meal and the long day, Matahi lay across the seat with his head on my lap, and I could feel something within me shift slightly.

Over the four days we had shared, I had been amazed at how comfortably platonic our relationship felt. He treated me like a preteen boyfriend would, content to hold hands and cuddle; sex never came up. I soaked up his sweetness, a balm for my inner turmoil. But after our day in the mountains, a slight craving surfaced in me, an awareness of his touch. That night I woke in the middle of the night to his gently pleading voice, asking me over and over again to stay with him, "S'il t'plait, restez avec moi."

One day, Mimi took me to a museum, where we wandered slowly through the display of intricately carved and decorated artifacts, costumes and weapons of the ancient Tahitians. Afterward we stood outside smoking the incessant cigarettes: Marlboro Lights was her brand. She shared her thoughts on the Tahitian culture: how it had been beaten down, trampled, but how little shoots were re-emerging. The kids she taught were learning their native tongue.

This got me thinking about Pirate Girl: She is not owned by government or state. She's a free agent, a citizen of the world. Part of the lure of the sea for me was to escape my country. I was not proud of my culture—at least not the white, invading, conquering one, the corporate sprawl of fast food and unsustainable consumerism, the military stronghold of war and political manipulation, the plastic or the greed—but I definitely appreciated and enjoyed the privileges it afforded me.

French Polynesia

I went to sea to separate myself from the brainwashing. I belonged to the earth, not the United States, and I refuse to carry the shame of that ancestral heritage, especially as a woman. Women never had a say in the colonization of the natural world and its tribal people; we have been colonized in much the same way. My ancient ancestors were pagans, people of the earth, and we are still here. The ancient knowledge of our Mother Earth, her healing powers and our connection with her have been trampled, but they are not extinct. There are thriving shoots of the tribe everywhere. The work is to connect those roots, to remember, to remind and uplift each other.

One night, Matahi's cousin, with his wife and new baby, came for a visit. They were all stoked to see each other and the house was lit up with a party vibe. I tried to put on a smiley face, took a turn holding and admiring the baby, but really I didn't want to talk or be social. I didn't have anything to contribute. I just wanted to hide, which was compounded by feeling bad about it. I excluded myself by going out back for a smoke and then slipped away unnoticed, down the street to the small park on the corner. I sat on a bench in the dark shadow, completely alone. I didn't know what I was going to do; I didn't have any money and everything felt so heavy and hard. When Matahi showed up, tears instantly began rolling down my cheeks. He didn't make me explain why I was crying or try to get me to stop. He didn't try to shuffle me back to the party or worry about making his cousin wait. He just wrapped his arms around me and I collapsed into his chest, sobbing. He just held me and in French, more as a soothing mantra than a yearning plea, said, "*Reste avec moi, reste avec moi,* I will buy you a ticket home in a few months. Just stay, *reste avec moi,* I will take care of you."

After that, we began sleeping together on the floor mattress, cuddling and sharing sprinkles of sugar kisses; he never pushed for more. He'd hold my hand and be affectionate, even in front of his family, but his declarations of love made me sure I couldn't stay. It felt so good to be with someone who seemed to genuinely care about me, but connecting over bad habits was no ground on which to build a relationship. Besides, Matahi was only 23. I didn't want to break his heart when I got over the funk I was in.

Plus I knew I didn't have the energy to find a job and a place to live, or to pull myself out of this downward loop without even the money to get started. I was on a destructive track. I remembered a comment someone had made way back in Sint Maarten when I'd first started this journey and was still so healthy and happy. He'd said, "We all drink and smoke to get to the good feeling place that you already radiate." And I did when I was healthy. But with all the smoking and drinking I'd lost my shine. I felt gray.

Then I got an email from *Mistress*, a boat I had met first in Grenada and again in Panama. They wanted me as crew and were willing to pay. I might not have enough oomph to get my act together in Tahiti, but I did have momentum to move and the Universe seemed to be prodding me west. It was the right thing at the right time. I also went ahead and signed up for a 10-day Vipassana meditation course at our destination: Australia.

That night, I connected with Matahi's mom and dad; they were deep and honest people. We had a long conversation about Tahiti, which, along with the rest of French Polynesia (the Society Islands, Tuamotos, and the Marquesas) had been colonized by the French in the late 1800s. We talked about how things were changing, how the Tahitian culture and language was still draining away, how the young people were being influenced more by the French culture. They told me about the movement for independence in which they were involved.

Matahi's mom asked me about myself; I showed them photos and told them my story. She said her life was so different from mine, but she was impressed with how strong I was to follow my own path.

"I hope you find a man to have a family with," she said, and I explained that it wasn't for lack of desire that I didn't have kids.

"You need Tarzan," commented the dad, rather astutely (or so I thought at the time).

So, after a week in Tahiti, I gave Matahi a big hug goodbye. He had to work preparing the *Rakanui* for another voyage, so his dad drove me to the airport. We had coffee, for which he, surprisingly, allowed me to pay. Though a little shy, he did what he had been instructed to do, encircling my neck with a lei of shells and handing me a little note in English, written in his wife's careful hand. When I cooed as if for an adorable baby, he asked me in a slightly embarrassed whisper what it said. I smiled up at him and translated, "Our family loves you."

I had been down while with them, my self-destructive and antisocial tendencies reminding me of the depression I had experienced as a young teenager. The Davina they knew was not the upbeat, outgoing one that I preferred to present

French Polynesia

to the world, but still they had welcomed and accepted me. Their generosity was amazing. If they could love the me that I usually tried to hide, it was about time I truly learned how to love and accept her too.

CHAPTER 10
Mistress

Making the Decision
Bora Bora westward
August 10, 2010

 I had crossed paths with *Mistress* several times, but I'd never felt they were a good match before. In Grenada, I hung out with their departing crew member, Itmar. He had described his duties as "co-captaining," though Ernest, the owner/Captain, wouldn't acknowledge him as such. At that time I wasn't interested in such a vague job description, especially if I'd have to pay my way. There can be only one captain on a boat. If he or she can't or won't take charge, there are going to be problems.

 I saw *Mistress* again in Panama. Mary had just sailed her across the Caribbean with another Captain because Ernest, her husband, was in a hospital in Australia. Again she was looking for crew. The Captain who'd gotten her that far wouldn't continue without being compensated. I was just joining *Cariño* and still wasn't interested in a boat that needed more help than they were willing to admit. Plus, they didn't drink.

 While in Nuku Hiva, I heard them on the radio, and curiosity prompted me to make contact. They got back to me by email and again were looking for crew. I still wasn't interested, though I gently suggested that they couldn't expect crew who are buying their passage to be too keen on working. I wished them luck.

 It surprised me when they persisted, and by the time I got to Papeete, everything had changed. What was once a minus was now a plus: they didn't drink. Partying was not making me happy, but quitting wasn't going to be easy surrounded by drunks. Also they were a couple and had one other crew, a change from the pseudo-partnership situations I had been in up until now. They described themselves as healthy and active. On the home stretch to Australia after such struggles to keep crew, they seemed desperate. They quickly came around to offering me $2000 (U.S.) for the two-month trip. Louie had given glowing praise of me, which set their expectations high. They offered to pay for a plane ticket from Papeete to where they were in Bora Bora and I jumped on it. You may not be able to run away from yourself, but sometimes a change of scenery can help when making a big change. When everything around you is new, it is easier to reinvent yourself.

The flight gave me an amazing bird's-eye view of green volcanic islands melting white into the deep indigo sea. The island of Bora Bora is an atoll with a ring of island and reef around a lagoon. The remnants of an extinct volcano rise up with two impressive peaks in the middle. The contrast between the rich cobalt ocean on the outside of the lagoon and the ridiculously luminous turquoise water on the inside was stunning. The plane landed on a sandy strip on the outer edge of the atoll. As we disembarked into the tiny airport, a few islanders stood playing a ukulele welcome and encircling people's necks with flower leis. I was still wearing my shell ones. The passengers funneled out onto a dock that stretched over this incredible water and we all piled into a ferry.

James, the other crew member on *Mistress*, met me at the dock. He was good looking, mid-50s, with olive skin and a firm handshake. Mary and Ernest had described him via email as a chameleon and weren't sure they liked him. Now, back at the boat, Mary whispered to me that he could come or go; now that they had me, they didn't care.

Less than an hour after I landed, we were pulling up anchor and heading for Nui, an eight-day voyage, where we were supposed to assist researchers in recording whale songs, a cool project that helped seal our deal. Watching James in action, I couldn't see their problem: He seemed like ideal crew to me. While Ernest (who was 70 and acted it) hemmed and hawed, James had the outboard motor mounted on the stern rail and was instructing me on the procedure to lift the dinghy on deck. Then he popped below to change into Speedos, top-sider shoes, and sail gloves for the muddy job of lifting and stowing the anchor in a locker (it wouldn't be needed for the eight days at sea).

Adventures of a Pirate Girl

Once we were underway, with nothing but silvery water out in front and Bora Bora fading behind, James, who was also doing all the navigating, declared it was time to jibe. Ernest asked me what heading I thought we should take once we completed the maneuver, as if testing me. "I don't know. I don't know the boat yet and what's the point of intellectualizing it? Why don't we just do it and see?" I said.

We settled into the routine of three hours on, nine hours off. The boat was a 65-foot MacGregor, long and skinny like a paper airplane, with a small bulb keel and an undersized rig. The interior was utilitarian sterile white plastic. Mary and Ernest had the stern cabin and James slept on the top bunk forward of the main living quarters. The bottom bunk was more like a coffin, so I decided to sleep on the settee where the dining table was. We always ate up in the cockpit anyway.

Being paid crew, I wanted to know what Ernest and Mary expected of me. Mary said not to worry about it; I should just see where I fit in. But from the get-go it didn't seem like there was an empty spot.

James, who was paying his own way and didn't know that I wasn't, was quick to jump up on deck for sail changes or to start hauling in a sheet when we tacked, even when I was already doing it. I let him know, nicely, that his well-intentioned help was not appreciated. Mary agreed. Though she'd sailed across the Caribbean alone with another Captain, she felt that the boys wouldn't allow her to participate. The way she wore her bikini and her hints of stylish flare always tickled me because they seemed incongruous with her highborn English-lady accent and the properly stuffy way she sipped her tea. I could imagine her in a tailored buttoned-up-to-her-neck blouse and long skirt. She had all of the traditionally female jobs covered: food organizing and cleaning. When I needed something from the freezer, she insisted on getting it so as not to upset her system. She also did the nightly radio contacts and the clearance paperwork whenever we reached a port.

Ernest was in his own little world. He was long and utilitarian like his boat, taut skin stretched over a muscle-and-bone frame. His communication skills were atrocious: He mumbled under his breath and refused to speak up as if the rest of the world was the problem. He spent his time tinkering slowly on little upkeep projects.

Cooking was one thing I could do. Except for Ernest, we all took turns, and I claimed the first afternoon as my day. Ernest was severely allergic to wheat and seemed to be morally against anything flavorful. I tried to enhance the lentils I made without my favorite spice, but it's hard to make food good without salt. I handed the bowls up into the large cockpit, which was walled in by chest-high coaming and a shade cover. Everyone got to the business of eating without a "thank you" or "this is good." Maybe I was spoiled after sailing with Louie, who appreciated every contribution I made, but I felt like James and I were being sucked into this tired old marriage in which the partners had no appreciation of each other. After that, I began to understand James's sickly sweet, elevator-music voice, asking if he could make me a tea or coffee.

"Oh, thank you darling, that is so nice of you," I joined in his rebellion.

Whoever didn't cook did dishes. Sailors usually conserve water, but Ernest took this to the extreme. Even though there was a water-maker onboard, he calculated how much each liter cost, which was 43 cents. Even seawater was used and reused to an absurd degree, due to the cost of the electricity to run the pump. Ernest would do dishes in greasy, gray salt water; licking them clean would have been more effective. I tried to abide by his rules and resigned myself to being dirty. But I began to notice Mary nonchalantly washing bits of clothing, and James decadently washing his face. My obedience relaxed.

About three days out, the clouds on the horizon looked like a fluffy gray duvet being pulled over the blue sky. Ernest got nervous. I'd never met a more cautious sailor, as if the sky was a field of landmines. He would use the radar to pick out the dark clouds and attempt to sail around them but there was no sailing around this. He tacked the boat as if we could outrun it; like trying to outrun a prairie storm on a hobby horse, he hemmed and hawed. When he asked me what I would do, I told him: "We already have the main reefed. I would roll up the furling, pull out the staysail and keep going. You can't tell what it's going to be until you're in it, and I doubt it's going to be that bad."

James concurred. Ernest paced below, while James and I waited for his direction in the cockpit. Eventually, James stuck his head down the companionway and pressed him: "What do you want us to do?"

Ernest dragged out the storm jib, which was folded as if it'd been ironed and obviously never used before. Then he began digging around looking for suitable sheets (the lines used to control the sail from side). James and I looked at each other and shook our heads. We would have to go up onto the foredeck while the boat bounced around into the wind, pull the roller furling down, then thread this crisp sail up the track and run new sheets. This all seemed extreme when weather was coming and there was an easier alternative.

"We can't avoid it, Ernest, but it's not going to be that bad," I assured him. He sulked and dropped the storm jib back inside. Within five minutes, James and I had the jib furled and the staysail out, and we tacked back to face the fury.

As we moved toward the dark clouds, Ernest and Mary huddled down below. Mary offered to fetch our foul-weather gear, but James turned to me and winked.

"Nah, we're okay." And to demonstrate how real sailors do it, we stripped down to our skivvies, both of us grinning from ear to ear. The sky darkened and we were struck with rain and buffeted by wind, but it never blew more than 30 knots. We stayed out in it, laughing together, howling at the storm… and rubbing it in.

Unexpected Gem

Palmerston Island, Cook Island Group
August 14, 2010

We were still a few days from our planned destination but, as the sun rose over the endless sea, we nestled in close to a tiny island that brought to mind the classic cartoon of a castaway leaning against a single coconut palm on a deserted sandspit. Palmerston, part of the Cook Island Group, was only slightly bigger than that. A few other islands in the near distance were part of the same atoll. The heavy weather had disabled our radar and Ernest had decided that we couldn't go on without it. The plan was to spend the morning doing chores, then get going. The humpbacks were migrating and we'd have to hurry if we wanted to get to Nui to help with the whale-song project.

I cranked James up the mast in the bosun's chair to reconnect the radar. We had done the same procedure three times already, so we knew the drill. Then I scrubbed the interior walls and floor with gusto, glad for a chance to earn the money I'd be making. When a round, brown local man named Bob and his daughter came by in an aluminum skiff, we explained that we were only going to be there for the morning. He smiled and nodded, letting us know that if we changed our minds he would be our host. It would cost $25 (U.S.) each to go to shore; the money would go to the locals. He discreetly mentioned that any boat gear we no longer needed would be put to good use on the island; the cargo ship only passed every six months with supplies and the donations of transient sailors were an invaluable resource to the island's economy. Mary immediately started rummaging and came up with a red plastic fuel canister half full and a propane tank that she gladly handed over. It seemed like an interesting place, but we all agreed that we'd rather get to Nui.

Of course, the work took longer than expected. Then James and I decided it would be a shame to miss snorkeling in such a remote spot. The water under the boat was a deep purple toward the depths and, when I dove down, I could hear the haunting lullaby of whales in the distance. As we swam into shallower water, the pastel colors of the intricate coral shimmered through the blue. Parrotfish and other preposterously colorful beauties swam by in groups to check us out. "Ahhhh," I sighed, "*this* is what it's all about."

We stayed the night and, in the morning, discussed our options. There was only a slim window of opportunity to help the whale researchers and we'd be pressed to get there on time. Or, we could stay and check out Palmerston, an opportunity that we may never get again. We decided to stay.

Bob came out in his skiff with the immigration official and we completed the paperwork and paid our money, making sure not to mention the gifts we had given him. Once we were cleared in, we piled into Bob's launch and he buzzed by two others of the six moored boats and picked up several passengers. The three families that lived on the island took turns hosting visitors.

An atoll is a coral ring that has grown around the ancient remnants of a sunken volcano. These little islands were the bits of the kidney-shaped ring that cleared the surface. Palmerston appeared so small and fragile, it was hard to imagine that humans lived there. The seven moorings were outside the atoll's calm inner waters. Bob drove us expertly through the reef, then jammed the flat-bottomed skiff up onto the sandy beach.

We walked across the "main street," white sand that led from the aquamarine inner lagoon to the crashing waves on the ocean side. The only traffic on main street was the hermit crabs and chickens. Lining the street were little buildings and houses, piecemeal but tidy. There was a church, a graveyard with tombstones of the original inhabitants, and a community water-catchment system; also a big diesel generator and a small white house with a phone and internet connection. It was all well organized and shattered my tribal palm-hut fantasies. The Marsters were more English than native.

Adventures of a Pirate Girl

Sixty-seven people lived on Palmerston Island and most were descendants of William Marsters. He was a ship's carpenter who, in 1863, was thinking outside the box; evidently fed up with both the rat race in England and life onboard, he had a ship drop him and his wives—three Polynesian sisters—off on this tiny, uninhabited atoll. They divided the island evenly, a piece for each wife, with main street slicing through them and, to this day, the three families still live there, all of them the progeny of William (the few exceptions being the school teacher, the immigration guy and a British grad student, who was doing research on remote communities for his thesis).

The outdoor dining area of Bob's family was a rickety wooden table shaded by a patched-together tin roof, encircled with sun-cracked white plastic chairs and benches. Here we sipped a sugary orange-powder drink before we began our tour. Bob and his eldest daughter, Taia (19), led the way. We walked down a tree-shaded path that was swept clean, along with the rest of the paths on the isle, every Friday. Palmerston was only a small sandspit, but in its center grew impressive tamanu (mahogany) trees, maybe four meters in diameter, which made the island seem less likely to be washed away by a hurricane. As we passed different dwellings with people peeking and waving, we showered our hosts with questions. I fell alongside Taia and we found a mutually interesting topic: the dating scene.

I was impressed with how open, intelligent and socially adjusted she seemed. She explained that, as a girl, the options were only two: you either marry a guy with whom you had grown up and remain on the island, or find someone off-island. She considered herself lucky that there were no available bachelors within her age range—10 years older to five years younger—so her family couldn't pressure her. If you found someone to marry from somewhere else and wanted to live on Palmerston with your husband, the whole community had to vote. I loved that Taia had no intention of dedicating her life to finding a guy. She'd already lived in New Zealand with relatives and made good use of the internet, keeping in touch with hundreds of well-wishing sailors from all over the world who had passed through. The girl was connected!

We visited the open-air schoolhouse with desks lining the walls, each partitioned with slats of wood on either side and individually decorated. The teacher was an Australian woman who was married to the immigration guy, both non-Marsters. They were proud of their school system, which had a religion-based curriculum, and the students worked at their own pace. We were impressed with the care, thought and effort that went into educating these kids.

Next on the tour was the island's main industry: fishing. We wandered past open dining areas, greeting families who were busy with other visiting sailors, and onto the beach where a small group of men and women stood around a table, filleting hundreds of parrotfish. The community worked together catching, preparing and freezing these reef fish, which they would then send with the cargo ship to sell to resorts on the other Cook Islands.

We wandered back along the beach to Bob's, where he smoked rolled cigarettes and his wife and daughters served us a meal of fish, chicken, rice, taro (a potato-like root vegetable), wheat-free coconut bread (Ernest was in heaven) with a banana mush, canned beets and fried bread. They waited while we ate until we insisted they join us, explaining that we'd feel awkward if they didn't. Then the adults sat around and talked. I had made friends with Bob's youngest daughter (10). She dared me to climb a coconut tree, saying I couldn't, so, of course, I had to prove her wrong. We took turns climbing up the tree's humped spine on steps of wood scraps fastened with jumbles of bent nails. Sitting on a bit of wood knotted onto a rope, I fell off sideways, swinging out and up, 20 feet into the air, screaming all the way.

The next day, we wanted to snorkel inside the atoll; Bob was our chauffeur. Ernest and Mary, both completely devoid of body fat, were busy donning all their lycra layers for warmth, while James and I kicked away in Speedo and bikini. By then James and I had covered the deeper topics of spirituality and energy and found that we had similar world views. We'd begun sticking together, providing refuge for each other in the sometimes crotchety environment on the boat. Now we snorkeled in water so clear you could drink it. We dove in among huge brain coral and bulbous outcroppings of reef decorated with lacy pink coral and purple fans. Once we'd had enough, we sauntered up the deserted beach. I suppose it was all too much for James. As if the lights had dimmed and slow '70s funk began to play in the background, I felt the mood change. Sure enough, James leaned in toward my face. I spun away from him to avoid it and sputtered, "Don't James. Don't. I've been on the boat four days; we have months of intimate living ahead of us. This is *not* a good idea." I shook my head and began to walk away. Granted, I *was* flattered. I may have nipped that in the bud, but I suspected the roots remained.

We wandered from the beach into a group of elders, who were sitting in the shade and invited us to pull up a chair. I was feeling scantily dressed in my wet bathing suit and, when I mentioned this, Bill, head of one of the three Marster families, reminded me that he had our clothes on the line. Before our snorkel he had offered to do our laundry in his machine. Bill's talkative energy contrasted with Bob's fat and happy, lazy personality. Now he insisted we take showers with assurances that he had plenty of water. Our clothes were just about dry in the sun and he set out tea, coffee, toast and corned beef, adamant that we stay.

Bill's land was the middle section of the island. He had built a "yacht club," complete with a bar, toilets, flags, signed tee shirts and penned notes from visitors from all over the globe. His house was an unending work in progress. He just couldn't stop, continuously adding whatever pieces he got his motivated and creative hands on. There was a big, enclosed room lined with old, yellowed family portraits; various bedrooms and tiled bathrooms and showers; a few different dishwashing stations outdoors; but no unifying plan. There was a raised cement patio with waist-high walls, a TV in the corner blaring Tina Turner videos, and tables. He had built it at a higher elevation as a place to socialize when hurricanes rushed water over the island.

Bill was industrious and hungry for company. He seemed disappointed in how lazy his fellow islanders were and told us how he had started buying rolling tobacco and beer to sell when the addicts in the community had run through their stash. According to Bill the three family heads took turns being policeman and mayor. There had been talk of putting in an airstrip on the tiny atoll, but they all had to vote on it so it would (hopefully) never be approved.

We had another huge lunch with Bob's family, and Taia showed us her two coconut-fed pigs, amazing us with the versatility and usefulness of the coconut tree. We visited the one lady who did crafts and then walked around the whole island on the beach, which only took half an hour.

After all of this, we understood that the $25 we'd each paid to come ashore—which at first seemed like a lot—was nothing. We were never asked for a penny more, and the kindness, the willingness to share and the genuine interest in connection was priceless. In a world obsessed with money, the islander's lack of financial scheming was a gift. Just to know that this place existed, unspoiled by greed, was a fragment of hope in a world of economic absurdity.

I lay in a makeshift hammock of fishing net, over-stuffed from our meal, and swung gently over the fine sand while dappled sunlight played through the coconut trees. The rhythmic wash of waves and clucks of chickens was overridden with happy shouts, as islanders of every age and shape played a game of volleyball. They seemed so amiable and content together. Though I could not imagine living in such a small and faraway place, it was good to know that people did, that they weren't backward or socially awkward, that it suited them just fine.

We got to the boat as the sun was setting. There were rain clouds growing like monstrous gray swirls of cotton candy in an otherwise clear sky, and the sinking sun set off luminous twin rainbows over the tiny islands in the atoll. It was a magical display to top off an amazing experience.

Fuck Ups

Tonga
August 24, 2010

Terra firma appeared as the late afternoon sun painted a masterpiece with pink, blue and purple clouds. By the time we were inching in toward the high, flat land that dropped perpendicularly into the sea, the clouds and sun had left, the full moon lit the magically calm waters, and the tall islands were dark and somber around us. We were on deck dropping the main sail when two, full-grown humpback whales and a baby broke the surface with a breathy rush, their huge, inky bodies glistening in the moonlight.

After four uneventful days at sea, in which I cleaned, waxed, and de-rusted the cockpit, we had arrived at the northern group of islands—Vava'u—in the Kingdom of Tonga. To get into the protected harbor of Neiafu, the second biggest city in Tonga (though a small town by American standards), we wound in through 40 little islands that, on a chart, seemed to hang from the larger main island like chopped-up tentacles from a jellyfish.

Though Christian missionaries had invaded Tonga with the word of God, the white armies weren't so successful. In 1875, *Taufa'ahau* (King George), declared Tonga a constitutional monarchy. It remains the only monarchy in the Pacific. The king owns all the land in Tonga and, perhaps because of this, the Tongans don't have the same sense of economics as the Europeans who settled there. So all the artsy little cafés and restaurants along the waterfront are owned by *palongies* (white people).

Adventures of a Pirate Girl

After clearing customs on the first morning, we began the ever-present boat chores. Ernest and I began with the backstay: the wires that run from the top of the mast to the stern. On *Mistress* these were hydraulic and one side had a leak. The plan was to replace the faulty one with a manual turnbuckle, though the hole on the stay and the hole on the turnbuckle were different sizes. Luckily, from his collection of stainless bits, Ernest fished out a clevis pin machined specifically for the job. This was entrusted to me, but somehow, while attempting to line up the stay with the turnbuckle, this one-of-a-kind pin jumped from my hand, making a clean break into the depths. This was the first of my many fuck-ups.

After Ernest's discourse on how hard this would be to fix—nearly insurmountable in such a faraway place—my logic was overcome with emotion. Luckily, James had an attitude of acceptance and "let's get this done," so I followed him to shore. He found a *palongie* who, for 20 bucks, machined a new part with efficient perfection.

We spent an afternoon folding and unfolding storm sails that had never been used, trying to figure out how to rig them. James was ideal crew; knowledgeable and industrious, he took the lead when Ernest didn't. If I had been paying my way as he was, I would have wanted to spend more time checking out the islands, but he didn't complain. The fact that I was the one getting paid weighed on me; I just wanted to do a good job and fulfill the agreement I'd made and get us to Australia where I would be free. I was relieved from guesswork when Ernest gave me a list of chores. While the others went to shore to explore, I wired a new plug in the anchor locker for the spotlight without incident.

Later that day, once they'd returned to the boat, I tackled another job that seemed straightforward enough: fix the light in the main salon. It was drizzling and we were all crowded inside. Ernest was into some project or another with his tools scattered around; James was working on his computer; Mary was sitting at the nav station, a raised desk across from the galley, above the refrigerator box and freezer.

I carefully pulled down the light and investigated the problem, which was obvious: the wires weren't connected and needed to be re-soldered. While I was groping below Mary's feet, dragging out the cooler marked "electrical gear," Ernest began inspecting the light. I quickly explained what I planned to do, assuring him that I knew how to use the solder iron and I didn't need his help. I cringed when James looked up to see.

"I can do it," I declared, and went to crank up the generator.

In this tight space with two guys watching my every move—ready to take over at my first hesitation—I felt like a medical student performing open heart surgery for the first time. I *had* rewired my whole boat—twice—and soldered every connection, damn it. I'd like to think I was confident enough in my skills to calmly do the job regardless of these guys breathing down my neck. But when James jumped up, I recognized the slight mania I was feeling and took a breath. "Davina," I thought, "You are confident enough to accept help," though I wasn't going to let him take over.

"Okay, James, you can hold this," I relented, and handed him the pliers to hold the pieces together. I plugged in the iron and stood on the cooler, waiting for it to get hot, which it quickly did. I held its tip to the piece and the solder to the wire, but the solder didn't suck up into the wire like it should. Then the iron cooled down. Huh? That was strange. James and Ernest were on it like I'd cut the aorta and the patient was bleeding out. Then there was a pop and Mary complained that the GPS had gone dead.

Suddenly I knew what I had done wrong: fuck-up number two. Though I knew enough to start the generator, I didn't think to ask where the plug that corresponded to the generator was. I had plugged the soldering iron into the inverter (where I was used to plugging things in), but the inverter didn't have enough juice. After Mary and Ernest made sure that all the expensive nav equipment was okay, I retreated to the bow to cry.

I allowed the wave of negativity and feelings of stupidity to pass through me, then gave myself a pep talk. "It's okay. That was stupid, but nothing's broken. You can buy another soldering iron. It's okay."

When I had recovered a bit, I made my way back to the cockpit, wiping away tears. I pushed past James, who was hurting to see me hurting. He had a daughter in her mid-20s, and his fatherly instinct was to coddle me. I couldn't stand that. I preferred Ernest's direct, "That was an airhead thing to do" comment, which was honest and much closer to my own sentiments.

I wanted to run to shore and buy a new soldering iron, so I gathered my stuff and made for the dinghy. But Mary wanted to go to shore, then so did James, and it took another hour before I could make my escape.

Finally I walked into the hardware store and found a large, airy room full of shelves but little else. It looked as if a swarm of people had just swept through and bought up everything, leaving only scant odds and ends in their wake. I asked the cute young girl (who looked like she should work in retail clothing) if they had a soldering iron. She assured me, decidedly, that they did not. But I spied what looked like one and asked to see it. It was almost exactly like the one I had ruined and cost only $40 Fijian, bringing my fuck-up bill to only $40 (U.S.)

"It's not so bad, Davina, it's not so bad."

Back at the boat I easily fixed the light. The satisfaction when I turned it on was only slightly dimmed when Ernest said, "Well, it may work now but it won't for long."

Again, James wanted to rescue me. After the near kissing experience on the beach at Palmerston, I felt my guard go up with him but, realizing that I needed his friendship, I decided to trust him and let it down. He tried to get me to go exploring or rent bicycles, but I needed punishing and redemption. I insisted on staying and scrubbing the water line, which took hours and wasn't even on Ernest's list.

He and I did get away sometimes during our stay in Tonga. We usually ended up at a little open-air restaurant on the waterfront, The Aquarium, to do internet on his computer. When the waitress came around, James ordered breakfast and invited me to do the same, "My shout." But I declined until the waitress walked away and we could talk.

"James, you are so sweet, and I would love to have breakfast, but I can't afford to return the favor and I don't want you to feel like you have to pay for me just because I'm here and I'm broke."

"Okay, let's make a deal. I will only offer when I feel like it and you will never expect me to."

"Deal!" I said, and ran to get the waitress.

All four of us went out one night to listen to a talk about how Tonga had changed. Afterward we went to a traditional dance performance at a bar/restaurant. It was crowded with cruisers and everyone was drinking. The musicians were seated on a blanket in the corner facing each other, a bowl of kava in front of them. The dancers were young: aged 4 to 18. The girls did their receptive, feminine hip-swirling dances, the boys, an aggressive, warrior display, all in palm frond splendor. James offered to buy me a glass of wine. I hadn't firmly declared I'd quit, but I was feeling very clear about it. In explaining it to James, I made my decision official: I was abstaining from alcohol and pot, at least until the end of October, after the meditation course in Australia.

Although Mary and Ernest were on an arbitrary time schedule, they were feeling a self-imposed pressure to get home. But James, wanting to enjoy some of the trip, made a spreadsheet to prove that we had a few unaccounted-for days that could be used spontaneously to relax and take pleasure in the beautiful locales we were passing.

One day, over breakfast in the cockpit, we were getting into one of the conversations James and Mary shrank from, but Ernest and I enjoyed. Like me, Ernest was opinionated, and I liked to engage him in what sometimes turned into heated but amicable discussions. He had a scientific, believe-it-when-it's-proven way of seeing the world, yet had experienced intuitions that he couldn't explain. I was pressing him on what exactly his beliefs were. Mary and Ernest both thought James's and my insistence on the law of attraction and the importance of positive thinking were absurd. Now Mary, who hadn't been paying attention, remarked that between the two of them, Ernest was the dreamer.

"Really? Ernest? I would have thought it was you, Mary," I said, surprised. She seemed to have a lighter-hearted take on things.

"For example," she confided, "I don't believe you can have a feeling about the future, like an intuition. Did you get any feelings about coming to Tonga? Because Ernest did. He had a bad feeling about coming here, like something bad was going to happen."

And—sure enough—Ernest's intuition proved prophetic. After being in Tonga for a few days, we were preparing to leave when Mary declared she was worried. Ernest had a bite. He swore it was from a water snake, though conventional wisdom would suggest that water snake mouths are too small to bite humans. It didn't seem like much to me but, given Ernest's medical history of toxemia, it was a concern, especially with four days of sea ahead of us. We moved the boat back to the main harbor and Mary escorted Ernest to the hospital for antibiotics. Then we waited over the weekend. The infection became an ugly black wound and they went back to the hospital for three more types of antibiotics.

The wind had been howling, which provided another reason to stay put, so we moved the boat to a picturesque bay where we anchored in more than 80 feet (25m) of water but could still see fish swimming on the sandy bottom. Ernest's bite hadn't changed and a weather window was approaching; we were all getting antsy to go. James and I pulled the dinghy and motor onboard, anticipating our departure the next day, which came and went; Ernest was feeling like hell. James suggested that if they were really worried, perhaps Ernest should fly home, which I secretly wished for. It would be clear cut and easier with James in charge.

James and I spent an afternoon with the hookah rig (a compressor that stays on the surface and allows you to breathe through a tube down below), searching the depths for another pin (which, this time, Mary had dropped), but without success. We flushed the outboard motor with "fresh water," which Ernest had been saving for the job. It was old dishwater that had been fermenting in plastic jugs. When we decanted it, it was rank with rotten bits of food. We were trying to devise a way to feed the water into the intake hole on the lower part of the outboard. I couldn't stand discussing the situation for hours, and so, as the boys discussed, I began whittling a plastic tube to fit. Ernest, like a proud father, made the comment that I could be an engineer. I pretended I hadn't heard, but inside my heart swelled disproportionately, as if he really was my father and I was a little girl starving for love.

The tube may have worked but, in the end, we opted to hold a bucket of the nasty sludge under the motor covering the intake valve, a job that went to James. I would have gladly done it but he chivalrously insisted. I couldn't help giggling as the toxic waste was sucked up through the engine and then sprayed all over him.

Finally, after two weeks in Tonga, we set sail. The seas were rough and Ernest was sick as death. He couldn't keep his watches, so Mary, James and I did four hours on, eight hours off. Fiji had better medical facilities than Tonga; Ernest just had to survive the four days it would take to get there.

One night at 4 am, it was the end of my watch and James was just coming on. I was explaining why I hadn't stuck exactly to his course because we were holding a better line than we had been (as if I needed to explain; as if I had

Mistress

done something wrong). I knew this was entirely my crap and was battling the feeling within myself. He was groggy with sleep and his only concern was that I help him jibe before I went to bed. I agreed. He was sitting by the winch and I assumed he would handle the main sheet. I pressed the jibe button on the autopilot, saying "here we go," thinking we were on the same page. I released the main brake. Expecting James to ease the sheet as the wind passed from one side of the boat to the other, I looked back at him, waiting, when SLAM! The boom cracked across the stern. James hadn't realized I had pressed the button. Though it was startling, no one was hurt and nothing was broken.

The next morning, when I emerged from a deep sleep into the bright sun of the cockpit, everyone was sitting there waiting for me, as if for an interrogation. Ernest asked, "What happened last night?"

"Uh," I rubbed the sleep from my eyes, "Oh, you mean the jibe? I guess James didn't hear me when I said I pressed the button."

Ernest's thoughts had obviously been churning all night because he had a lot to say about how serious and potentially deadly my mistake had been. In his mind the car with the main sheet block had slammed over on its metal track and I could have died. I began to explain that it hadn't, and that I had been fully aware of where the wind was. It had been a miscommunication, nothing more. I didn't want to be defensive; I wanted to listen and respond calmly. But his heavy words hit me hard, raining down on me like hammers, until I felt battered and bruised. My former logic and clarity about what had happened was buried in his words and all I could do was apologize, sincerely and profusely, and slink away. Though I was lying in my bunk alone, I carried on where he left off, adding every stupid thing I had done on this boat and in my life, until the abuse was a torrential downpour of negativity and self-loathing. I wasn't a good sailor. I wasn't an intelligent and conscious human being. I wasn't worth paying. I wasn't even worth having around.

I tried to be strong in the face of the truth about my pitiful self. The honorable thing to do, I decided, was have a heart-to-heart with Ernest. So later, when we were alone in the cockpit, trying to hold back sobs, with tears streaming down my face, I told him I was sorry; that I really was trying and I didn't know what was going on. Why suddenly on this boat I was being so stupid. I'd really done great on my own boat and on all the other boats I'd been on. I told him that I wished I could just say that he didn't have to pay me, but I was really counting on the money from this trip. Maybe I could do more work or be their indentured servant. Something. He listened somberly—which I took to be compassion—and said I just had to take more time with things.

Looking back, I realize that the difference between Ernest and every other captain I'd sailed with, was that Ernest was totally negative, he *never* mentioned any of the many things I'd done right or showed appreciation for my help in any way. And somehow this negativity and lack of acknowledgement peeled off the scab of an old wound. And all old wounds can be traced back to childhood, can't they?

But my father wasn't negative like Ernest. I took an IQ test in fifth grade and he boasted about my score and told me how smart I was. He introduced me to a friend as the "cool" one of his four kids. I always knew he liked me. Sometimes I even felt that he looked up to me. But he wasn't tuned into my life, he didn't interact with me on an emotional level, he didn't pay attention to specific things that I was going through and respond in a fatherly way. Maybe that was the source of this hurt place in me that enabled someone like Ernest to make me bleed. Or was it something more universal? Some ingrained lack that pervades our cut-off culture?

Later James reassured me that the miscommunication about the jibe could have happened to anyone. Ernest, who was sick and feeling shitty, had obviously driven himself crazy all night, turning it into a much bigger issue than it was and then, to James's disgust, had passive-aggressively taken it out on me.

I recovered emotionally and was feeling back to my able, confident and happy self. But apparently I hadn't fully learned the lesson, because there was still one more fuck-up yet to come.

Lučka

Tonga
August 28, 2010

One thing Ernest, Mary, James and I all agreed on was a Tongan feast. We saw them advertised at different *palongie* establishments, but we fancied something more traditional. I imagined a pit oven, a kava ceremony, food wrapped in banana leaves. Then a fellow cruiser told James and me about a small community on one of the islands that he had gotten to know and love. They were putting on a feast to raise money for a new wharf. Our ears perked up.

Mistress

We anchored at a nearby island and got soaked on the long dinghy ride across open water. Ernest slowed down to motor up to the tiny beach, angling the boat alongside the arm of crumbling rock where the community's old pier had been. We were the first cruisers to arrive. I scampered out into knee-deep water and handed the painter to the man who greeted us. He was dressed in a black shirt and a long, black polyester wrap skirt, topped by the traditional Tongan palm frond mat that encircled him like a stiff mini skirt tied with a belt. He immediately sent someone to fetch me a dry sarong. It was a white cloth, hand-dyed in blue and orange, which he insisted I keep as a gift.

A few curious children came down to check us out, and some shy women who busied themselves close by, but it was obvious this event was solely created for the *palongies,* not something in which the whole community would take part. There were palm fronds and banana leaves laid out on the ground to sit on. A large wooden bowl with legs stood at the head of this rectangular arrangement with a few men seated around it. I may have been off intoxicants, but kava wasn't one of them.

Kava is a root plant, and Tongans make a muddy-looking tea from it that has a relaxing, anti-anxiety, sedative affect. They have used it for centuries in ceremonies and while socializing. Traditionally, in Tongan society, it is only men who sit around for hours, drinking and talking. But being a *palongie*, I was exempt from this exclusion and was curious to take part in the experience. The few middle-aged men who were already partaking insisted that I serve, so I sat on the ground in front of the bowl and used the dipper to fill the half coconut-shell cup and pass it around. Each person polished off the contents before passing it back to me. The guy next to me—after establishing that we were both single—passed it back with a coquettish, albeit toothless, smile. Slowly the cruisers arrived and sat. I continued to fill and pass and drink. I had just begun to feel the effects: a tingling numbness in my throat and mouth, a peaceful sensation spreading through my chest.

Then the food was ready. There was a small, spit-roasted pig that had been cooked there on the beach, but everything else arrived in saran-wrapped dishes and was presented on a palm frond-decorated table. There was a surprising variety, mostly seafood. I tasted sea snails, which were mixed with enough mayonnaise to hide the fact. We all grabbed a seat where we could, on the pier or on the ground, with our plates in our laps, and watched the sun set. Then Lučka (pronounced Luch-ka) and crew arrived.

Lučka was from Slovenia, where my feminist, maternal great-grandmother had been born and we immediately connected. She was in her late 20s and tanned golden. She had sandy, shoulder-length hair, with a longer braided bit in front, dangling a shell. She wore a skirt, mismatched earrings, and the open-hearted smile of someone following her bliss. With her was a tall, thin Kiwi boy, maybe 20, with pale white skin and a cloud of light curls floating around his head. Their Captain, George, was a middle-aged American, compact, in a bright tropical print shirt and a buzz hair cut; his boat was named *Grateful*.

The next morning, a group of cruisers came for church, and we got a short tour of the tidy little island. Then the crew of *Grateful* stole me away. After my Vanna White-style assistance with George's balloon-animal entertainment for the kids the night before, and my quick friendship with Lučka, we were all stoked to hang out. They wanted to take me diving and, though I felt loyal to James, who was just as eager as I was to get a break from the slow, indecisive days on *Mistress*, I didn't argue when George told him there wasn't room in the dinghy.

I had already noticed the 48-foot motor yacht in the main harbor. It had Grateful Dead bears dancing around the tie-dyed name *Grateful*. This struck me as incongruous: a big, shiny, navy blue powerboat with a hippy motif. George was compact, cleancut and sober. I suspect he had learned a lesson from his wild hippy days following the Dead, but he still talked about them incessantly.

As soon as we had grabbed my stuff and made it back to *Grateful*, Lučka went into action. What a relief to be on a boat where people made quick decisions and promptly followed through! She demonstrated the electric boom and winch system to me and the Kiwi kid (who had just joined the boat) and lifted the hard-bottomed inflatable up onto the top deck. Then we lifted anchor and were underway. With the press of some buttons on a handheld steering remote, we basked in the sunshine on the top deck and watched paradise whizzing by. Soon we were re-anchored in yet another perfect spot: 90 feet of clear swimming-pool water, white beach and lush green vegetation.

Zooming over to the dive spot in the dinghy, George and Lučka sang songs, laughing and carrying on. I could tell it was exaggerated to entice me, but I welcomed the lift in energy. We tooled along the cliff face until we found a handful of snorkelers. This was Mariner's Cave, a well-known landmark with its entrance hidden below the surface. George and I donned scuba gear and went in through the deeper opening at the bottom of the cave. Suspended in the dark depths, we looked up toward the piercing rays of light dancing around the silhouettes of Lučka and Tom, who were just snorkeling. They had entered through another opening above us to emerge inside the cavern. I lay on my back and watched their legs kicking like frogs to keep their heads above the surface. There wasn't much, besides rock, to see so far down. George beckoned me to follow him and I did, but I would have preferred to be up in the air and light with the younger set.

Back on *Grateful*, Lučka stripped off her wet bikini and showered on the back deck, as if unaware that the boys hovered, basking in the sight of her naked, long limbed, sun-kissed body. George, hoping I'd be into it, was excited to tell me about their new sport, "skorkeling." Lučka piped in to say it was a combination of skinny-dipping and snorkeling. I love being bare-skinned in the sun but I would never frolic naked in front of such an eager man who I had no intention of having sex with. My previous Captain, Louie, had thanked me for not flaunting my nudity when we were alone on the boat. But no one held that against the beautiful Lučka.

That evening Lučka and I made our beds under the stars and talked long into the night. She had been traveling for 10 months, like I had, but was filled with wonder and magic. Some of that time she had been on boats and dreamed of owning her own boat in Hawaii with her partner, who was still in Slovenia. It sounded like they had an honest and deep relationship, which could withstand the test of long distance and time, even surviving a love affair she had had while traveling. She was full of inspiration and insight, talking about how we create our own lives and how the best way to do this was to follow our bliss. These were all things I believed, but I appreciated being reminded. Her name, Lučka, means light, and I pictured her—arms open, palms up—glowing with the loving luminescence of an angel.

What began as a single afternoon on *Grateful* stretched into three days of carefree fun, appreciation and smiles. Those three days were especially great because George and Lučka didn't drink or smoke. We moved the boat around to different anchorages each day, jumping in to snorkel every chance we got.

One day we spotted humpback whales and chased them around, willing them to come closer. In Neiafu Harbor, one night, the opaque water was filled with thousands of jellyfish that glowed in undulating sapphire brilliance when George flicked on blue underwater lights, creating an out-of-this-world visual display. We oohed and aahed and took pictures. Each meal was a celebration worthy of the highest thanks. We talked. Tom, the Kiwi, played his guitar. We watched movies and ate chocolate cake.

Our last night together, again sleeping on the top deck, Lučka showed me her *We Moon* calendar, a beautiful astrological date book that featured lunar cycles, natural rhythms and Goddess art and poetry. From the book, I jotted down my astrology reading:

"You're a perfect warrior, champion of a new world rising. You're most powerful weapon is desire, the enthusiasm for your unique role in the world. Hold firm to your optimism and hopefulness for the future. Get clear on an image of what you want, paint it, collage it, sing it, write it. Focus on simplifying. Don't fret about how anything will come about. Just dream big and don't dream alone. Life will compel you to get your act together, clear away blocks that drag you down or keep you stuck in the past. Your contagious passion and fearlessness will ignite in you incisive leadership in service to Mother Earth."

As I scribbled my eyes filled with tears and I felt a whoosh of uplifting Pirate Girl energy. "It's pretty simple," I declared. "We just need to change our prevailing story."

"Ha, yeah," Lučka laughed, tickled at how easy it would be.

"Okay, so you know," I said, "the current world view is based on a pyramid. Father, Son and Holy Spirit on top, of course. The rich on top of the poor. Men on top of women. And everybody on top of the children, the animals and the Earth."

"Yes, that's true," she nodded, following my rant.

"What we need, instead, is a story—a world view—based on the yin/yang symbol, where the polar energies of the world are in harmony and balance. For the past five to 10-thousand years, the feminine principle has been completely devalued, as if women and the caring, nurturing qualities of all humans aren't essential, or even important."

"So true. Our society definitely values the masculine over the feminine."

Yeah. Thinking over feeling; rational over intuitive; independence over interdependence; aggression and forcefulness over receptivity and vulnerability.

I think of it like a battery: Yin and yang are the negative and positive poles. The yin, or feminine, is the ground, the earth. If an electrical system isn't properly grounded, the appliances that are connected to it risk being fried. An overload of power that's not earthed can even cause a fire. We are all made of energy—everything is—but because our world society and its prevailing story are so focused on the yang, the masculine principle, and not grounded in the yin, the feminine principle, homo-sapiens' amazing, creative energy has been predominantly destructive to ourselves and our Earth.

"Men have totally suffered because of this imbalance too," I continued. "It's not *just* about raising women and Earth up in our collective story so that they actually hold the honor and respect they deserve. It's about honoring the feminine in all of us. Men have had to cut themselves off emotionally and, in doing so, have separated themselves from feeling love and connection on a deep level, which really is the best stuff in life. The yin and yang energy is in each of us and because of our prevailing story we are *all* out of whack. I think that's why it's so easy to feel alone—lonely—because the energy that we are made of has been affected. We are all one; the whole Universe is. At the most microscopic level, matter is vibration. We are all made out of energy. It's all there is. God. So why don't we sense that more consistently? Why is it not our default feeling? It should be. We just have to change our story, we need to change the pyramid into the yin/yang symbol, the feminine and masculine in harmony. When we do that on a worldwide scale, then everything will change. But it *is* changing. I have to believe it *is* changing." Lučka sat watching me as my volume steadily increased, her appreciative smile beaming me with love, while Pirate Girl danced in front of her, expressing my deeply held beliefs with passionate conviction.

Though I had had a great time, I finally told George, who'd been joking about stealing me, that I wouldn't join them because I was getting paid and needed the money. But that wasn't the whole truth. Lučka would be leaving soon, Kiwi Tom was temporary, so it would end up being just George and me. I was bored enough on fancy sailboats that had buttons instead of winches. A crossing without even sails to deal with sounded dull. And though George was a nice and interesting guy, I was sick of being the captive audience for a lonely man. George's longer-than-friendly hug goodnight made it uncomfortably clear that when he said he wanted to keep me, he had more in mind than as just a deck hand. So, after three days, we met *Mistress* underway and, when the two boats were alongside each other, I hugged everyone goodbye with hopes that we'd meet up in Fiji and jumped across.

My fire had been rekindled. Lučka had been an inspiration. Lying under the stars with her, sharing stories, theories and dreams… her light encouraged mine and I could feel its warm flame flickering up within me. And now I knew I could do it: I could set myself free.

The Final Fuck-Up

Lautoka, Fiji
September 9, 2010

It was after noon when we carefully entered the arm of small islands and reef that protected the northwest waters of Viti Levu, the main island of Fiji. It took us another few hours of sailing along the coast before we dropped our hook near the town of Lautoka. Mary had already informed immigration by VHF that we were approaching. She was now stressed out, rehearsing our excuse for being tardy. Fijian officials were, according to what she had heard, red-tape bureaucrats. Plus she had explained to us that her personal motto was: "Expect the worst." So, true to form, she was conjuring up all the horrible repercussions if we didn't follow the rules.

James and I dutifully inflated the dinghy and mounted the engine as twilight was descending, a speed record for the *Mistress* pit crew. We lowered the dinghy in the water and climbed in. Four of us in the small rubber ducky was a bouncy, wet experience. We slowly poked by another cruising boat and asked the couple on deck where to find the immigration office. They assured us that it would be better to wait for morning; the officials might be strict, but they wouldn't be happy if we made them return to work.

I had read in one of the cruising guides about the cannibalism of the Fijians of old: How they not only ate their enemies, but sometimes mutilated the dead

Mistress

bodies and flaunted the dismembered private parts during ceremonies. The last recorded act of cannibalism was well into the 20th century. It was no wonder Fijians had retained their language and culture! They have many connections with the ancient Polynesians, especially their Tongan and Samoan neighbors, but they are descendants of the Melanesians, with kinky hair and skin the color of chocolate milk.

In 1874, the British colonized Fiji. The new governor, apparently a humanitarian, had forbidden interfering with the native culture and way of life, an idea that was revolutionary at the time. But then the British brought laborers from India to work on the sugar plantations; along with the Indians came the measles, which killed over 40,000 Fijians. Today, the population is almost half and half, Fijians and Indians, both fully integrated into the society, with small populations of Chinese and Europeans. The Indians tended to concentrate on the bigger islands and towns and were more motivated as business people. The Fijians populated the small islands and stayed closer to their agricultural roots.

We went to immigration the next morning. I was happily surprised to find the feared officials, if not terribly efficient, were at least friendly. We learned the word for hello: *bula*. As we headed toward town from the guarded compound on the jetty where the immigration offices were, past tied-up cargo ships, past the smoke stacks and huge metal warehouses of the sugar processing plant, we were greeted by everyone, Indians and Fijians alike, with this word, sung in a happy refrain: "BU-LA!"

All of this positivity gleamed defiantly in contrast to the gloomy cloud hovering over Ernest and Mary.

The sun was hot and overly bright, and everything was covered in a fine layer of dust. The town felt flimsy and crowded, like two stories of glued-together, random cardboard cutouts. There were decrepit wooden storefronts, expansive fast-food chicken places, little second-hand shops with grimy windows, and modern department stores whose mannequins were clothed in jeweled saris and Australian surf clothes.

We ducked into the cool, dark shade of a high-ceilinged warehouse that turned out to be a market: a gigantic area with thousands of tables all piled high with a rainbow of every kind of fruit, vegetable and spice, along with eggs, grains and seafood. The floor was dirt-covered concrete; the tables were grubby slats of plywood or just a tarp on the ground. But each vendor's goods were artfully organized in neat piles: red peppers, oranges, yellow bananas, green lettuces, purple eggplants, all precariously balanced. I watched a woman creating her display. She was bent at the hips, doubled over a small mound of brown root vegetables on the ground, painstakingly attempting to balance one on the peak of a pyramid. She turned the yucca every which way before finally selecting another one to try.

Our plan was to do all our shopping, fix the radar (yet again) and get underway. We had spent too much time in Tonga and the pressure, though arbitrary, was on. But at the dock that morning we ran into the cruisers who had advised us about immigration the night before. Sam—the 13-year-old girl, with long, stringy blond hair, a freckly nose, and an American accent, despite her English mom and Danish father, (due to American movies, she explained)—loved my shell earrings. The friendship was sealed when we discovered we were both artists. They told us about a regatta at nearby Musket Cove. Sam had painted a mermaid on a sail for the decorated dinghy competition that I wanted to see. James and I were desperate to get off the boat, and Ernest and Mary agreed to sail to Musket Cover for at least one day of fun after our chores were done.

Since James was getting sick of doing it, we agreed that I would go up the mast to fix the radar. This was the fifth time it had failed since Panama; the movement of rough seas kept causing the plug to get yanked out. We came up with a plan to pull more wire through the mast, hoping to eliminate the problem once and for all.

Just as I was being hoisted up, friends of Ernest and Mary stopped by. Ernest seemed glad for the distraction. Once I was in place beside the radar, dangling high above the boat, James straining his neck up at me, and Ernest and Mary out of sight in the shaded cockpit, I felt above it all: my past stupid mistakes, my bad habit of beating myself up, and all the subtle tension building up like static electricity. I was my Pirate Girl self, purposeful and confident; ready to solve this annoying problem for good and show them how it's done.

According to James, while I was up there, Ernest's guest made the comment that he wouldn't have amateurs working on *his* radar; if he had ongoing radar problems he would hire a professional or do it himself. Well, Ernest didn't want to fork out the dough *or* go up the mast. Instead he sipped his tea and let me deal with it. And when I removed the shrink-wrap on what appeared to be a broken wire and found instead a complicated rainbow of tiny wires, I realized

Mistress

I was in over my head (leaving the radar thoroughly disabled), and he didn't want any part of the responsibility either.

But this time my emotions didn't overwhelm me. That abusive internal voice stood wordlessly in the corner, held at bay with the loud, empowering logic of my self-confidence: "Shit happens on boats and the radar was already a problem. Ernest knew that I wasn't a proper electrician when he had me do the work. Maybe this is for the best: Now he'll have to pay a professional, which he should have done back in Panama. They were already planning on taking the boat out of the water in Fiji anyway. It's okay, Davina, it's totally okay." At that, the voice in the corner no longer looked abusive, but meek and scared and in need of a hug.

There were no professionals available until Monday, so it was Musket Cove to join the cruisers' party for a few days! We lifted anchor and got the sails up, slicing through the protected water at a strong clip, aiming at an island in the distance. James tried to get me excited about taking the wheel for the cutting-edge sail, but I'd withdrawn energetically from the whole situation and was reluctant to make any nautical decisions.

Then George on *Grateful* called on the VHF and told us Lučka was flying out the next day. They'd just left Musket Cove so we'd miss each other. I ducked below to the nav station to say goodbye, and though the *Mistress* crew couldn't hear my side of the conversation, Lučka's radiant voice sang through the outdoor speakers. Her words of love and inspiration bolstered me, whatever negativity was still loitering was Ernest and Mary's problem, not mine.

As we approached the reef, Ernest was a nervous wreck and had James guide us slowly into the cove. And as soon as the anchor was set, James and I began getting ready—almost frantically—to depart. It was Friday night and we were on a mission: there was a regatta going on and we were going to revel in the lighthearted fun of it.

We parked our inflatable at the empty dinghy dock, walked past quiet, tied-up sailboats and the deserted yacht club bar, then onto the silky sand, past empty lounge chairs, shower and laundry facilities, a little café and a market, past hidden bungalows, a saltwater swimming pool, posh restaurants and tastefully hidden resorts in the manicured version of a white man's paradise. Apparently the sailors had partied all day on a disappearing sandbar and were having some downtime before the big Saturday night blowout.

James and I sat at a small table overlooking the pool that featured a decorative shipwreck and had a lovely meal. If James had his way we would have kissed but, despite that, it felt like we were honest friends. The interpersonal dynamics on the boat provided interesting subject matter; we talked about how much the negativity weighed on us. We were both dedicated to proving the superiority of *our* belief system over that of our dour shipmates and aligning to the positivity of the Universe. I had confided in James, after the last fuck-up, that I intended to get off the boat. Now I felt like everything was exactly as it should be.

"I'll stick it out," I declared. "I said I would and I stand by my word." I felt strongly that the lessons I was learning were extremely important and, overall, I was thankful for the whole experience on *Mistress*. Maybe I was learning to be kinder to myself. If I had attracted this scenario to learn a lesson, I'd also included James to support me through it and I was thankful to have him. It all felt cosmic and aligned.

"It was even good for Ernest, I reckon," I said, recalling an early email in which he had been complaining about James and the last crew constantly breaking things on his boat. "He was obviously creating this dynamic. Besides," I said, "I kinda like Ernest; he's alright."

"I don't," declared James. "He is an uneducated, close-minded bigot."

"True," I smiled and nodded thoughtfully.

The Cruisers Regatta

Musket Cove, Fiji
September 12, 2010

I felt great—alive and anticipating the day! I stretched awake in the sunny cockpit and surveyed the tropical scene. Musket Cove was full of cruising boats for the week-long regatta, an excuse to get together and party with other sailors. Even the Fijians who worked in the resorts and restaurants seemed genuinely happy to find themselves in this man-made land of leisure, even though it wasn't leisure for them.

We didn't tarry over breakfast: all four of us climbed into the dinghy to spend the day on shore. Both factions, owners and crew, were more than ready for time apart. James and I set up camp for the day, plopping the computer at a big table on the café/market's shady deck. We ordered flat white coffees in bowls and restfully sipped while our laundry washed in the facilities across the sandy path. When I sashayed over to check on our clothes, I had that tingly heart sensation that I get before doing something thrilling, like jumping off a bridge. It's a butterfly flutter I associate with new love potential, but this time no man came to mind. This was the pure stuff; I was totally stoked on my own life and buzzing with possibilities. After I'd had my turn with the internet, I left James to it and strolled across to the beach.

"*BU-LA*," sang a cute blond guy who had zoomed by earlier in a Zodiak full of surfboards.

"How were the waves?" I asked, passing him by a few steps.

"Good. Hey, where are you from? Do I detect an American accent?" he cast his bait, luring me back to him.

"California," I smiled.

"I spent some time in San Francisco. I'm from Milwaukee. I'm Steven."

In just board shorts and a wide-brimmed sombrero, he had the golden tan and muscular broad shoulders of a surfer. His eyes gleamed blue and his blond beard, braided to an elfin point, framed the grin of a fisherman who was used to catching.

"Are you on a boat?" I asked.

"Yeah, I have my own boat. But things have been crazy. There's this girl I've been seeing. It's been a whirlwind," he confided.

"You mean like a good, in-love, whirlwind?" I asked, curious.

"No, bad. It started just casual, but it turns out she's totally insane. She's a drunk. I feel like I've been falling down a well. It's funny how miserable you can be in paradise."

"Yeah, I can totally relate. I actually quit drinking and smoking like a month ago. It's so easy to fall into the daily habit and it can suck you down. I finally feel like I've clawed my way out. I feel so good finally. But I know it can be hard."

"It's bad to say, but I'm ashamed to be associated with her."

We chatted for another few minutes, remarkably open, as if old friends, before he had to run. He was signed up to be a judge for the sailing race that was going on. I was delighted to meet him, but knew our encounter was only a cherry on top of my already sweet mood.

I hitched a ride back to the boat and made Mary and Ernest a crunchy salad with apples and nuts. Though the beautiful atmosphere seemed to relax them a little, we all sat in different parts of the boat to eat. Steven zipped by in a dinghy and I did a little wiggle with my wave. Sound carries over water and I could hear him telling his friend about meeting me. Before heading back to shore, I donned my short, parrot-green skirt. And, for the first time since the Galapagos, I felt like sporting my pirate-girl tee shirt that I'd made at sea. Tonight was going to be a good night.

Onshore, I planned to meet up with my shipmates for the barbecue at the yacht club, which was providing a big fire pit so all the cruisers could bring their own food to grill. Just as the sun was setting, I started to make my way down the dock lined with boats. There was a young guy with dark, honey skin and fluffy sun-bleached brown hair on a boat that looked like a charter. It had "destinocanela.com" in big letters down the side and a pile of surfboards on deck. He greeted me in a Latin accent, asking, "Do you like a beer?"

"She doesn't drink," another voice chimed in from the center cockpit. It was Steven. "We just use that as an excuse anyway, just trying to get some female company. Why don't you come aboard?"

"I'd be happy to," I said, giving him my backpack and accepting a hand for the big step up onto the boat. "I know how it is. Feminine company can be hard to come by on boats."

"Are you chartering?" I asked, joining the four guys in the cockpit. I found out that Joao and three other Brazilian guys were being sponsored to sail around the world. It took me a few tries to get his name right.

"I'll just call you *Ja Wow*," I said coquettishly, finding it hard to pronounce the nasal O sound.

I made myself at home as Steven started playing a guitar.

"I'm serious," he sang, with Joao accompanying him on the bongos. The following lyrics were creative, intelligent, and funny, and I assumed it was someone else's song until he started ad libbing. The few times he stumbled, the rhyme magically came out of my mouth as if I was channeling the words from the same Source. It was an awesome song and we all laughed and sang together. I had just been writing in my journal that I wanted young, fun and artistic people in my life and here they were! I snapped a few photos and then handed

Mistress

the camera to one of the guys to take one with me in it. On a whim I splayed out across the two cuties for the shot, surprising and endearing myself to them with my spontaneity. I'm sure the handful of breast helped, too.

Steven's next offering was called "Cheese Dick Love Song." It painted such a clear picture of the game between guys and girls—how guys will say anything and how girls eat it up—that I had to laugh. It reminded me of how addicted to the idea of love I had been. And I marveled at how different I felt now: self-possessed and stoked on myself. I was enjoying flirting with these guys, but it didn't come with the fantasy of anything more. And the song prompted me to make a mental note to leave it at that.

I left the boys and walked across the dock to the yacht club, which was on its own little spit of sand at the end of the floating metal dock lined with sailboats. It had a small, circular bar with a palm-frond roof and picnic tables scattered around in the sand. I sat with the *Mistress* crew for a bit and chatted with the sailors from *WindBorne*, a classic wooden schooner that I had been admiring. They invited me to join them for the Pirate Regatta the following morning but, alas, *Mistress* would be leaving early and I would miss the best part of the festivities.

The Polish girl crewing on *WindBorne* had waved James and me down from the square-rigged antique the night before, and we'd given her and an older guy a lift to shore. This morning she shared her story with us. The guy was twice her age and not attractive in the least, but had wooed her with promises of love. Then she found out he was married and his wife had just arrived to vacation with him. Now he was attempting to play her on the side, buying her drinks when his wife went to the bathroom. She was love-struck and heartbroken and didn't know what to do. It completely baffled me why such a lovely girl would be interested in such a loser; but it was a great example of how pathetic we girls can be when it comes to the fantasy of love—how quickly we are willing to give up our power for the promise of a man.

Steven joined us at the small table and tried to help in my attempts at uplifting her, but we quickly tired of the effort and began talking boats. He told me the story of how he'd gotten his: It had belonged to an unmotivated friend and had been withering away in a boatyard. Steven helped the guy finish the work and pushed him to follow his dream to sail across the Pacific. They succeeded in getting the boat to Hawaii and spent many months there; but his friend finally bailed out and left the boat to Steven. He had sailed it to Fiji with his girlfriend as crew, but they had since broken up. After 10 months of hanging out in Fiji, he had been lying on his surfboard at what had become his home break, the world-class wave that most people only dream about, and was surprised to realize that he was bored. It was time to move on, but the thought of sailing to Australia alone, where he planned to sell the boat, intimidated him.

"It's really crazy how you dream of cruising your whole life and then when you're actually doing it, it can be so depressing. So many retired cruisers remind me how lucky I am to do this while I'm still young—and I know I am—but it doesn't make it any easier. I'm still stuck with myself."

"I know exactly what you mean," I laughed, glad to be talking about this truth so openly. I told him my story: How I had bought my boat at 22, how she had sunk and how I had rebuilt her. I could relate about not wanting to sail alone. I'd done it, though not across oceans, and it was damn hard work—and lonely.

"I always wanted a partner to do it with," I admitted.

"Yeah, it was great sailing with my girlfriend for a while there, though in the end it wasn't her thing. But I imagine if both people were really into it, it could be amazing," he said. By now we were sitting alone and had scooted in closer to each other.

"It's too bad you are already on a boat," he said, overly casual, as if we weren't both tuning in to what was happening.

"Yeah, and that I have no money. Otherwise…"

"Who needs money? I've got cans of tuna—we could make it to Australia."

My grin broadened. We spent the next few hours talking about a whole world of ideas. We both listened intently, as if we had known each other in a past life and were now catching up. He had studied product development in school, which he only completed for his father's sake, and we began to brainstorm inventions, tickling each other with our ideas. His, Virty Smokes, were make-believe cigarettes for people trying to quit. I nonchalantly mimed putting a Virty between my lips and began frisking myself for a light. Catching on, he produced a pretend lighter and shielded it from the wind while I leaned in and inhaled deeply. We came up with a whole marketing strategy—Virty: a satisfying, social breathing-awareness exercise—as I continued pulling drags on the non-existent smoke.

He told me about his group of friends in San Francisco. They were into costumes, traveling, and music, and called themselves moisies, a term meaning anyone with moisture. The people with no moisture—the dry, uncool, fearful people—just didn't get it.

"And as moisies, you know how it is: You always connect with cool people, the other moisies." Then he initiated me into the tribe with their ceremonial greeting: each of us placed one hand on the other's forehead and one on our own stomach, looking deep into each other's eyes and slowly, like a guttural OM chant, mouthed the word, "mmmoooooiiiissseee."

We told each other about our families and their patterns, of our dreams and philosophies. Each detail and all the ways it connected to the rest of our lives seemed important, as if we were painstakingly drawing maps of each other, so that each new bit could be sketched in, linked and referenced to the rest. The more we shared and laughed and explained, the more the world around us—the bar and the drunken patrons—became just a blur of color, as if we were grasping each other hard by the wrists, leaning way back against gravity, and spinning with abandon.

Eventually I got up to find the bathroom and, as I sauntered down the gangway, I did a systems check, making sure that any little tentacles of hope or expectation that had grown from our obvious connection were cleanly severed. Our conversation was exciting and fun—but it was only talk. Regardless of what happened, my happiness still lay centered within myself.

When I got back, he asked me to redo his beard in a French braid. We sat facing each other, straddling a bench, our knees overlapping. As I divided tufts of his blond facial hair, tugging and plaiting, I told him about a vivid dream I had recently had. It now seemed like a premonition of meeting him, especially since he had been an extreme skier. The dream featured a young guy whom I'd watched swoop dramatically down an impossibly steep incline on a skateboard. I saw him a few times and introduced him to friends with open admiration. Then the guy grabbed me and dipped me in an elegant salsa dance maneuver.

"Do you dance?" I interrupted myself to ask Steven, happy to hear he did.

I continued with my dream: "Then the guy had to go study, and I made sure not to cling to him, going happily on my way. But it turned out we were heading in the same direction. Then we were waltzing around this huge hall, flying up and around the corners. Then there was this colorful firework explosion thing, which was part of a performance piece that his friends had created, and I felt like I had found the community of artists I wanted in my life. Then I wondered if we were going to be a sexual match. He was young and I didn't know if he was man enough, so I lay on top of him and asked him what he thought."

"And what happened, what did he say?" asked Steven, intrigued.

"There was a black, molded plastic tool case, and he said…," I widened my eyes to punctuate the cryptic message, "… 'Open the box.'"

Just then someone cranked up the sound system and the song, "I'm on a boat, motherfucker!" thudded through the speakers, rousing a handful of us to jump up, hooting the anthem while bouncing around in a small circle.

Then Steven busted out a free-flow rap, keeping with the sex and boat theme: "She's got her hand on my tiller." That had us all howling with laughter and encouragement. Our little group had a good solid dance, cracking each other up with our most exaggerated, theatrically lewd moves. At some point someone asked Steven where his infamous other half was. He glanced at me before answering, "Oh, she's been demoted to 1/16."

The night was getting late, but I was sure I would be even later. After asking Steven if he would give me a ride back to *Mistress*, I went to let my shipmates know. I approached the table and was immediately stunned by the awkward silence. I informed them that I'd be getting another way back to the boat. Mary tried to respond, mumbling something about them sailing early for the Pirate Regatta.

"You mean we will be sailing in the race?" I asked excitedly.

"Ah,…" she stuttered and said something about sailing and the morning, but the words floated by separately without a meaning to hold them together. She looked across to James and Ernest for help, but it was as if a big fat elephant was sitting on their laps, squashing their lower bodies, making their faces blue and expanded like balloons. They all stared back at me as if hoping I would just understand. James finally broke free from the trance, jumped up, and took me aside.

"They are kicking you off the boat," he told me.

I had been vaguely aware that Ernest had been talking to several young men during the evening, but my focus had been elsewhere; besides, it seemed like they would have told me when we'd been alone over lunch that afternoon so that I could take advantage of the party to find another boat. But still, the news came as a relief. "Really?" I squealed, shocked with the pleasure of escape.

"Yeah, but before you get too excited, apparently Ernest took your little talk about how you wish you didn't have to accept any money to mean he doesn't owe you anything."

Then James, my dear friend and legal counsel, coached me through what I had to do.

So I took Ernest aside and laid it out: He owed me money. When he tried to argue and warned me, in his passive-aggressive way, that I had better not make a scene in front of immigration, I decided to stop the bullshit and bad feeling in preference for the good vibe I had had all evening with Steven. Obviously, everything was working out perfectly.

"Look, we can talk details later, Ernest. Bottom line, I know you are a man of honor and you'll do the right thing. I know we can work it out so that we're all happy."

Then I walked back to where Steven was sitting.

"I just got kicked off my boat," I declared. I felt in awe of how swiftly my situation had changed. I had finally released my craving for a man and the Universe had instantly responded by setting me down in the lap of what seemed like my perfect guy.

"Well," he said jokingly, throwing an arm around my shoulder and leading me down the dock, "let's go shag."

We bounced back to his boat in his red rubber dinghy, our feet sloshing in the few inches of standing water in the soft bottom. The night was dark, the stars brilliant, and I felt totally in the moment. We climbed into his trash-strewn cockpit and went below.

"I have barely come back to my boat this week except to sleep," he explained, grabbing an armful of stuff off the bed to make room for me to sit. The small interior was shabby and cluttered. His bed took up one side of the main salon, since his quiver of surfboards filled the v-berth. I made myself comfortable on the salt-encrusted mattress.

He cooked us grilled cheese sandwiches and we carried on with our comfortable and intimate conversation. I talked about Ernest and our dynamic, realizing my pattern of beating myself up had something to do with the old wounds I had from my father.

Then Steven told me, in full detail this time, about what had happened the previous night with the girl he'd been seeing. She had been so drunk by the time he took her back to the boat she crewed on that the Captain had started to rig up a halyard to hoist her limp body onboard. She had slipped from Steven's grasp into the water and sunk below the surface like a stone. Steven dove in to retrieve her, swimming blindly down into the black water with his arms stretched out, searching for her. He had come up without her, desperate for air himself, and dove down a few more times, thrashing around in the darkness frantically hunting for what he imagined would be her cold, dead body. When he finally resurfaced, he heard her sinister cackle from another boat. It had scared him so badly he was still filled with anger, disgust and confusion.

He told me how degrading and dramatic their relationship was. "It's seriously easier and more satisfying just to masturbate," he half-laughed, as if seeing this truth for the first time. "I'm definitely done with it," he pronounced. I listened intently to support him but felt entirely separate from the situation. The girl sadly had a major issue with self-love. And Steven had his own shit to deal with. He invited me to stay. "We'll just cuddle," he assured me, but there was a lot more to clean up than a messy boat before I would spend the night.

In the cockpit we hugged a long, slowly swaying embrace of support and caring, and then he took me back to *Mistress*.

"I tried to get you a place on the boat I'll be sailing in the regatta," he said, "but we're already way too many. We could try and take my boat," he started, obviously not stoked on the idea.

"No way! That's too much work," I cut him off. "I've got a boat to sail on tomorrow, so don't worry about it. I'll see you at the party." His face spread into an easy, relieved smile. He cut the engine and we drifted up alongside the hull of *Mistress*.

"Bye," I said, sharing his feeling of relaxed happiness. Spontaneously we leaned toward each other and, through big smiles and starlight, we kissed—soft warm lips—and then again. Both content to have found such effortless company in the midst of so much turmoil.

CHAPTER 11

Free in Fiji

Pirate Party

Beachcomber Island, Fiji
September 13, 2010

I jumped out of bed at the crack of dawn. It was Pirate Day, and I was free and ready to take this party by storm.

Sailors are into pirates. You'll often see the skull and crossbones waving among rigging, decorating someone's bandana, or printed across a tee shirt. Not to mention everybody else: I went to a pirate party in Colorado, far from the sea, and a few hundred people came in full costume. Pirates are a major theme in kids' books, films and parties, and it's not all because of Jack Sparrow. So what *is* this fascination with pirates? Why are these vicious and violent thieves so popular?

To understand the current fascination with the pirates of old, you first have to understand the context in which they lived. During the late 1700s, naval ships from various European countries (England, Spain, France) roamed the seas in constant, bloody battle. There were also privateers—essentially pirates sponsored by kings and queens—paid to loot the merchant ships of opposing countries to fill the royal coffers. Often, privateers would turn pirate and keep the booty for themselves. There were public hangings and beatings. The slave trade was in full swing. Indigenous people were being massacred. Women had no rights; they were owned by either their fathers or husbands. It was a dangerous time.

Adventures of a Pirate Girl

Instead of accepting a life of servitude, pirates took matters into their own hands. Just like sovereign powers of the day, pirates used violent means. They were the infamous and often respected entrepreneurs of the deep.

It was a time when naval and merchant ships operated as strict dictatorships. Captains had absolute power to administer brutal punishments and even execute a crew member who got out of line. Things were different on pirate ships—revolutionary, really. Predating any modern democratic government, pirates organized themselves in relatively liberal, egalitarian ways based on elected captains and officers. A pirate's code—an actual document clearly defining each person's percentage of the take—often also described an onboard culture based on mutual trust.

Because of their refusal to be enslaved in the system, pirates remain in the collective consciousness as symbols of freedom and self-reliance. A pirate is an archetype for someone who takes charge of their own destiny despite the odds.

No sailor has thrown herself more whole-heartedly than I into the pirate theme. I was stoked I'd been kicked off *Mistress* the night before, just in time for the festivities. After filling my pack with all my belongings while playing music louder than was considerate, I dressed in my skull-and-crossbones bikini top, cut-off jeans, thick leather belt with my knife in its sheath, and a three-strand line wrapped around me for extra affect. The rowdy, "I don't give a shit what you think," pirate spirit was upon me, and I felt ready to cut loose for the day and charge into my future without doubt or fear. Of course I was excited to see Steven again, but my happiness and power lay buried, like a treasure, deep within myself. And no matter how it panned out with him, I wasn't going to give it away or let anyone steal it.

The crew Ernest found the night before to replace me came around in an inflatable to see his new boat. His skin looked rubbery gray and sweaty with a hangover; a cigarette hung between his lips. He couldn't be a poorer choice for Ernest and Mary's "healthy lifestyle." They might eat clean and not drink, but their negativity and lack of appreciation was toxic. The new guy didn't know what he was getting himself into. He agreed to take me ashore so I threw my overstuffed backpack into the dinghy and hopped aboard.

We spotted *WindBorne* at the marina and headed her way. Allen, her Captain, had invited me to join them for the party, and we approached the beautiful old ship just as they were pulling away from the dock, all loaded up with pirate-

Free in Fiji

clad partiers. As we swept alongside, I stood in the prow with my arms up and screamed in my gravelly pirate voice, "Arghh! Let's get this fucking party started!!!"

We swooped around the stern and pulled up on the port side. I hoisted my pack into waiting arms and grabbed the proffered hand up over the hip-high bulwarks.

"No swearing—we have kids aboard," cracked the Captain, putting me in my place as soon as I was on deck.

"Aye sir, whatever ye say, Cap'n." I barked back. "You're the only man by whose word I'll abide." I bared my teeth, wrinkled my nose, and growled at the two kids who, like everyone else, welcomed my enthusiastic theatrics.

"Don't worry about the swearing," one of the moms (lasciviously dressed in a black bustier) assured me. "They're used to it."

There were several familiar faces aboard: sailors I'd met the night before, along with some landlubbers on vacation. I greeted everyone in my cocky manner and in the process I coaxed out some ruffian personas for my camera.

WindBorne was a magnificent and proper pirate ship. I had noticed her in the anchorage, the way her bow dropped straight into the sea with her long proud bowsprit; the way her stern swept back; her classic, wooden elegance tempered by her beamy hefty strength. She was a 62-foot gaff-rigged schooner built in 1928, and Allen, the Captain, had done a huge amount of restorative work to her, including replacing her keel stem (the backbone of her hull). Now that I had a chance to really check her out, I loved her even more. On deck she was simple, with no winches or electric conveniences, just the hundreds of lines it took to maneuver all her canvas. She was built in the day when mariners were tough and sailing was work. Down below she had a comfortable wooden interior with a big, open salon complete with a wood-burning oven, a relic Allen couldn't part with. She was homey and lived-in.

We were off to a slow start—all the other regatta boats were spread out before us. To get us through the reef, Allen perched in the rigging for a bird's-eye view, and shouted out directions to his beautiful partner, who was new to sailing and nervous about being at the helm. The sailors aboard, not trusting Allen's alternate and daring route, added to her anxiety with their conflicting directions. Allen screamed at them, "Shut the fuck up!" and I stood as a barrier between them and her, quietly cheering her on.

"You've got this, girl," I assured. "It means a lot that he's making you do this. It's not every man who will empower you like this. You've got it, girl." I whispered.

She got us through unscathed, and we motor-sailed the rest of the way. An hour later, we approached tiny Beach Comber Isle. Its sugary white beach barely broke the ocean's surface, and I imagined that, without the palm trees that covered it and the protective reefs around it, it would have dissolved into the sea like sugar in my coffee. The only thing on the island was a resort with a bar and restaurant. Boats of all sizes and models were anchored in the clear blue water off this tiny bit of land and a taxi service was ferrying people to shore.

Once on land, we funneled through a roped-off walkway, across fake hot coals toward the crowd, and were handed a shot of rum before entering the open-air bar. I was still not drinking and was probably the only sober adult there, but my brash, obnoxious manner didn't give me away. I elbowed through the throng in a swagger, knocking people out of my path. One guy, getting in the spirit, growled, "Watch out, wench. I'll throw you in the dungeon."

"Argh, ye wanna fight, do ya?" I growled back, leaning into him and spitting my words in his face, "I'll have yur balls." He loved it.

I didn't win the limbo contest, though I hammed it up and had everyone thinking I would. The kids didn't know whether to fear me or love me, but either way, they enjoyed the show. I caroused around, loud and engaging, got crazy on the dance floor with the couple who had come as charter guests on *WindBorne*, joked and played and felt completely free from all social restraints.

After a while of coolly ignoring Steven who was coolly ignoring me back, I burst out of the crowd, practically tackling him, my buccaneer persona overriding my protective layer of chill. He half-heartedly threatened me with his sword and I twisted it out of his grasp. "Oh," he murmured, when I forced it against his neck—his eyes lit up seductively.

Later, I advanced on the quiet table where he sat with a few people, all nursing their hangovers with more alcohol.

"Argh, cutie, who might you be?" I winked at the girl I knew was his girlfriend and offered her my hand. Even though he had told me all about her and their destructive relationship, I could see that Steven was enjoying getting attention from both of us. He whipped out his camera, and I indulged him by grabbing her and posing for the shot with my plastic knife at her throat, my tongue out and nose wrinkled in a Polynesian warrior grimace.

Free in Fiji

"That hurts," she whined meekly.

"Oh, sorry, honey," I smiled, biting into a piece of fish I'd grabbed off Steve's plate. "It'd mean a lot to me if you watch the performance I'm about to do," I winked at Steven and wandered away.

I had been rehearsing my pirate monologue on the sail over and now my window of opportunity opened: The band had quit and the DJ was setting up his gear. I jumped up, grabbed the mic, and bellowed:

"I am a pirate of a new age."

Instantly the crowd gathered around the stage to watch the impromptu show.

"I sail a pirate ship," I roared. "I am a free agent, a citizen of the world."

My prepared words flowed naturally and I finally felt like they were true.

"I am not owned by government or state! I am not controlled by corporate powers or influenced by public opinion!" I declared vehemently, "I navigate by an internal compass. I am a high-seas revolutionary!"

The crowd hollered their approval, which apparently annoyed the DJ because he unplugged the mic. This only raised my fervor and I passionately declared, "I do not rape, pillage and plunder! The power I possess, I do not count in gold," emphasizing my point by throwing a handful of plastic gold coins into the horde, who scurried like beggars to collect them.

"For I know the value of *true power*, Source Power," I divulged in a lower voice, "to which we *all* have access. I capture the imagination of women... and the hearts of men," I smiled, striking a pin-up pose.

"But not by force! For it is always... more powerful... to seduce than to conquer!"

When I paused to let that sink in, the DJ began trying to push me off stage. I stood my ground to finish. "I know where the treasure is buried. I have the map," I pushed back, un-crumpling a piece of paper from my pocket to prove it.

"Our fortune is universal," I poked the map at the DJ, then turned my attention to the crowd. "The same X marks the spot for us all!" Then I slipped into the swarm of people and escaped the DJ who was angry at my audacity and popularity.

By the afternoon, an onshore breeze kicked up; the captains began gathering their crew like ducklings, pulling us away from dancing and posing for exaggerated photos at the hangman's rope. Steven, who saw I was leaving, came to say he would catch me later that night at Musket Cove for the after-party.

Once back on *WindBorne*, Allen started barking orders in the forceful vernacular of a scoundrel Captain whose crew lagged from laziness and not just complete lack of experience.

"Haul the main sail! Make fast the sheets! Quick with it, ya scurvy dogs!" After sailing with such an indecisive Captain, I found myself loving Allen's vigorous commands. And, though I'd never sailed a square-rigged schooner before, I jumped to as first mate, translating his barked orders by visually tracing the lines and then divvying out duties to the green hands who wanted to take part but couldn't follow the lingo.

Allen, who remarkably could sail this beast of a ship by himself, fit the pirate role perfectly, and after an entertaining slur of vocal floggings, winked at me and confided under his breath, "I don't actually believe in yelling and insulting crew, but the charter guests love this shit!"

We flew all the sails: the main, the staysail, forestay and yankee, the fisherman, the course and the grandy. *WindBorne* eased over as all of her glorious canvas caught the wind. Her bulk sliced through the sea with grace and power, moving toward the horizon with a determination I wanted to emulate.

My future was a complete unknown; it could even be aboard this same ship to New Zealand. Whatever it was, I stood facing it at the prow, my feet firmly planted on the solid wooden decks, my knees soft and bending to the rhythm of *WindBorne*'s flight. We moved as one then, toward my destiny. I felt *WindBorne*'s raw strength through me, melting away any fear or doubt that remained.

Wings

Musket Cove, Fiji

After *WindBorne* was safely anchored back in Musket Cove, all the sails covered, and everything put away, a heavy exhaustion came over me. While the others were making a move to shore, the velocity of the past few days finally caught up. Like a wake overtaking a quickly decelerating speedboat, I felt swamped with fatigue. The thought of more partying on shore, the inevitability of craving Steven's attention, hanging out with people who were increasingly sloshed, all without a place to sleep, sounded like pure hell. I quietly asked Allen

Free in Fiji

for permission to stay aboard *WindBorne* for the night; I'd figure out what my next move was in the morning.

Once everyone had left and I was finally alone on the old wooden schooner, sleep didn't come as easily as I'd expected. My body coursed with energy and I was in a romantic mood. Not romantic like the fall-in-love, hello-Mr-Right, Hollywood way, but a more enduring, personal romance, one that had withstood 10 years of the harsh reality of owning my own boat and the past year of ups and downs traveling on other people's boats. I was feeling empowered and dreamy, sensations that characterized my romance with the sea. Here, on this old classic ship in Fiji, my future was like the endless ocean, touching all continents, all possibilities. I climbed out of bed, up the ladder to the foredeck, and stretched out on the massive bowsprit, like a languid cat over the inky black water, under a round, yellow moon.

Despite this self-possessed mood, thoughts of Steven were running like Tom and Jerry round and round my head. We had motored past his boat on the way back to *WindBorne* and I saw his drunken girlfriend in the cockpit. I had expected her at the party, but the fact that she was still with him afterward made it clear he wasn't as "over her" as he had declared to me the night before. But the mental cat and mouse chase was more out of habit than anything. I'd been fantasizing about love since I was a preteen. I remembered pleading in my journal at 12, "Please God, let him like me." Old habits die hard.

Then I realized this mental pattern conflicted with my beliefs. We create our reality, and creation starts with a thought. By picturing future scenarios between Steven and me over and over, always with the same theme—me wanting him to want me—I was only creating more wanting.

"If I believe so much in positivity," I wondered to myself, "why am I letting these dark thoughts about love run helter-skelter through my brain?" So I gave myself a pep talk.

"It is impossible to rehearse the future, Davina. When I see Steven again I will know what to do. And though things probably won't work out between us, it doesn't mean I can't think of him in a loving way. We had an amazing connection and that was a blessing in itself."

And because my brain wasn't going to drop the habit just like that, I began to imagine all those fears like insidious vines strangling my heart, and I began pulling them out as they sprang up. I weeded my heart until its soil was clean and fertile, abloom with vibrant flowers.

"I am amazing, I feel great. My future is exciting and wide open, and anything can happen." I told myself. "My heart is fresh and receptive and ready for love. And if it's not with Steven, then it's because he's not the one for me. Not every guy can fly like I can."

The next morning I felt wonderful, though quiet. Pirate Girl had used up her voice the day before. Allen, who was relieved that the loud, brash character was gone, made his partner and me a beautiful breakfast of yogurt, crunchy granola and fresh papaya, then dropped me ashore with my gear. I stashed it on Joao's boat at the dock and wandered across to the Sand Bar, the center of all activity. On my way I stopped to chat with someone. Out of the blue he brought up EFT (Emotional Freedom Technique) tapping: an energy technique my mom had taught me as a way to clear out emotions and worn-out thought patterns. Inspired by how the Universe seemed to be supporting me, I began tapping on my wrist to clear away Tom and Jerry who, though slower that morning, were still making their frenetic rounds in my mind. I settled at a picnic table under some palm trees, where a small crowd was gathered to watch and participate in dinghy sailing races. An attractive Australian woman with whom I'd danced the day before was at the same table. She immediately began talking about the power of positive thinking and how we create our own reality. With all of these like-minded people around and the way this adventure was playing out, her words rang through me with the high vibrational frequency of a bell.

Just then Steven walked up, hung over and hurting from the night before.

"Hey, you," I cheerfully greeted him.

He sat beside me and came right to the point, "Hey, I don't think I'm really ready to take on crew."

"I know," I said.

I entered the woman's kayak race, which turned out to have only two contestants. The other woman and I dashed down the beach and hurtled ourselves into the awaiting plastic boats, each held in a foot of water by an attending Fijian man. They each gave us a strong push and we paddled evenly out toward the buoy. But once there, she paddled wide and I cut it close around the floating mark. I won the race. Later, she admitted she hadn't wanted to be rude by bumping into me.

Free in Fiji

Then I had an inspiration. Steven had gone back to his boat, so I borrowed Joao's inflatable and motored out to see him. I found him in the middle of straightening up.

"I'm here to give you a massage," I informed him. He had been complaining about a chronic pain in his shoulder that had been getting worse. I sat patiently in the cockpit while he finished cleaning. When he offered me something to drink, I raised my water bottle and said, "I come complete." I meant it in the deepest sense.

After he had tidied up his space, smoked his bowl, and lay down on his belly, I hooked my iPod to his stereo and let the relaxingly intricate layers of B-Tribe unfold in the small cabin. I took a few deep, centering breaths, then laid my hands on his shoulders. I've never been particularly drawn to giving massage and I don't think I'm that good at it, but somehow, when I pictured my root chakra connecting to the Earth's center, I could feel Gaia's power flowing up through me and into my hands. And while I was working on his shoulder, an image—like a subliminal message on a TV ad—flashed behind my eyes. I shared it with him:

"The reason your shoulder is hurting," I informed him in the confident voice of a doctor, "is because your wings are trying to grow."

Steven murmured in a stoned and deeply relaxed voice, "I have been having this recurring dream. It's of me standing at a bar," his voice barely a whisper, "but I keep falling down because I have these huge, heavy wings and I can't handle them."

"You can, Steven. Nature knows what we can handle; she wouldn't give you wings that are too big. Let your wings grow, Steven," I whispered. "Let them grow."

I slipped off the boat. My wings, in their enormous, feathery glory, were completely intact.

Adventures of a Pirate Girl

Trusting the River
Musket Cove, Fiji

Normally when I found myself between ships, I felt aimless and lost. But now, after being kicked off *Mistress* so abruptly, somehow the precarious position of being stranded in Fiji without much money didn't feel so bad. In the Law of Attraction, Abraham—as channeled by Esther Hicks—describes life as going down a river in a canoe. Most people spend their lives paddling upstream, with the belief that they have to struggle to get what they want. But, according to Abraham, we are attracting what we want—and the trick is to surrender and let the current take you there. Well, I was in whitewater now. Like a river winding through a canyon, my future was around the next bend; I just couldn't see it yet. And there was nothing to do but let go and see where this river would lead.

While mingling at the pirate party and telling my story, I was offered a temporary bunk on a luxury catamaran tied at the dock. The following night, I took advantage of the invitation and slept in a private cabin, though the stifling heat and blaring music from the bar made it hard to sleep.

In the morning, I tried to be as quiet as possible; the guys were still asleep and I didn't want to deal with the intimacy of an encounter so early in the morning. I just wanted a cup of coffee or tea and, though I felt slightly naughty searching the cabinets of the unfamiliar kitchen, I told myself repeatedly this was a legitimate thing to do. Surely their offer of a place to crash for the night extended to a cup of tea.

I opened the sliding glass door, mug in hand, and stepped out into the cockpit (more like a back patio) of the swank catamaran. Nestling into a seat around the table I sipped my tea, opened my journal and let a feeling of gratitude flow over me. The sky was blue and sunny. The slow rise and fall of the boat, the creak of dock lines and the tinny tap of halyards on metal masts were as familiar to me as the whir and buzz of electricity is to landlubbers stuck indoors.

People on nearby boats began to emerge into their cockpits like groundhogs: stretching in the bright morning sun and rubbing their eyes. Writing in my journal, I looked up occasionally to greet a fellow sailor meandering down the dock. I'd only been there a few days but, because of the regatta, I felt like most of the people wandering about were acquaintances if not friends.

Free in Fiji

I took a long walk away from the marina and bay where all the boats were anchored; past the bathhouse and café, the rental place with its kayaks, Hobie cats and other toys; past the restaurants and the bungalows. The calm, turquoise water was at high tide, leaving only a thin strip of sand. Finally I arrived at the end of this busy bay and around a rocky outcropping to where the beach was untouched and raw.

On my way back, I stopped at an office to buy a ticket for the ferry to the mainland, where I still had to sort out matters with *Mistress*. Ernest owed me money and still had my passport. After that I didn't know what I would do and, since I had a few hours to kill, I began looking for an empty lounge chair to sit and ponder. I was just wandering past the restaurants when I heard, "Hey, Davina!" The voice was someone up by the saltwater pool.

"Oh, hey girl, how's it going?" I had met Inger and her family two days before while sailing on *WindBorne* to the pirate party. They were on *WindBorne* as well. I had bonded with her 10-year-old son, had gotten funky on the dance floor with her husband Paul, and had a good conversation with her during our sail back.

"Hey, we were talking, and Paul wanted to ask if you wanted a job. You were so great on the boat the other day, the way you got everyone involved. That's just what he needs, someone with good leadership skills. If you just wait here, Paul will be back in a minute to tell you more."

It turned out that Paul ran a kiddy swimming pool franchise in Auckland, New Zealand, and needed someone to run a staff of Brazilian lifeguards. He assured me that a work permit wouldn't be a problem.

Though for the past few months I had believed my future was leading me to Australia, I had much more interest in New Zealand. Plus it was a lot closer.

"That sounds awesome," I told them, a huge smile slowly growing across my face. Not only did I have a job, but a job where I could hang out by a pool, be with kids and be the manager of Brazilian lifeguards, ha!

And, just like that, without having to struggle against the current or stress out about what I was going to do, my vista suddenly opened as if from the top of a canyon giving me a glimpse of the river ahead. Now that I knew New Zealand was where I was heading, all I had to do was figure out how to get there.

CHAPTER 12
Hakura

Fiji to New Zealand

September 21, 2010

    The race was on. Doug, the Captain, had the motor running at 22 rpm—as hard as he wanted to push it. *Hakura*, his 36-foot sloop, was gliding over glassy calm water toward a white line of waves smashing against the reef that protected the island of Viti Levu, Fiji, from the churned-up sea. Somewhere in that tumult was a channel, the illusive eye of the needle that would take us through a wall of coral; we had to thread the needle before the light was gone completely.

    Dark purple was spreading like spilled ink from the eastern horizon, washing out the brilliant orange and red light. We looked back at the hillside and searched through binoculars for the two markers that—once in alignment—would tell us we were in the channel that cut through the reef. But we could find only one. The calm water between heavy breakers was the obvious choice and we took it.

    There had been a gigantic storm in New Zealand that was pushing massive swells our way. I was at the helm in the small, open cockpit, my legs braced in a wide stance, my hands firmly gripping the wheel. *Hakura* didn't have an autopilot or any other fancy equiptment (no refrigeration, water maker, radar, SSB), so it would be hand steering, three hours on, six hours off, for the approximately 10 days it would take us to reach *Aotearoa*, the Maori name for New Zealand.

    Just as the purple sky was deepening into black, we cleared the last of the submerged dangers and left the safe waters. A monster wave nailed us, stalling the boat for a split second with a loud thud. My feet slid to the low side and a wall of cold, green water drenched all three of us. Fuck. What an ominous way to start a voyage. These were the worst conditions I'd been in—and I couldn't even see them. And *Hakura* was the smallest boat yet. For the first time in 10 months of sailing, my stomach began to churn. At least puking was easy, a slight lean over the lifeline and the ocean was nearly in my face. Nevertheless, I was confident with my choice: Doug and John were competent sailors and good, solid people.

After getting the job offer in New Zealand, I spent two days searching for a boat, but my energy and the feeling of endless possibilities drained. The bubbly, "Maybe I'll just hang out in Fiji for a while" was reduced to, "Just get me to New Zealand, quick." Lounging in paradise gets old, especially without much money and a heavy bag to lug around. Everyone I talked to at the modern marina at Port Denerau pointed to the small sloop tied up directly in front of the office, *Hakura*. They needed crew, but no one had been aboard all day. I kept chatting with sailors on the docks, looking for more leads.

I ran into a couple with whom I'd crossed paths a few times during my travels in the Pacific. After a pep talk from them, I confronted my previous Captain, Ernest. His boat was hauled out in the tiny boatyard beside the marina. We attempted to negotiate, but I was sick of his incessant negativity and his passive-aggressive refusal to take any responsibility for the situation. When he told me to calm down, I turned up the volume for the entire boatyard to hear, and then stomped off dramatically.

Later that night I had dinner with George from *Grateful*. Lučka had gone home. He wanted me as a mate, but not merely the nautical kind. I made it clear that I was only interested in a platonic relationship and left the possibility open as a last resort. He wasn't leaving for another month and he was going to Australia by way of Vanuatu. After 10 months of crewing on other people's boats, I was *so* ready to be autonomous, to live in one place, and have my own engaging life. The thought of hanging around Fiji and then slowly cruising yet another tropical paradise sounded like a twisted version of hell. All I wanted was to get to New Zealand.

Stupidly, I had made the assumption that after our dinner I could crash on his boat for the night, but a friend of his was flying in at 4 am. It was too late to go knocking on the few boats that had offered a bunk and I didn't want to blow a bunch of money on a hotel. George was taking his usual taxi back to *Vuda* Marina (pronounced Vunda) and his Indian driver told me to get in, he'd help me figure something out. I was too exhausted to think, so I shoved my pack in the back seat and slumped in beside it. After we dropped off George, the sympathetic driver made me an offer: I could stay at his house free of charge, but I'd have to cook for him. Or I could stay alone, also free, at his vacant house next door.

"That's very kind of you," I responded, thinking he seemed harmless enough. "I'll take the empty place."

Slightly surprised he asked, "Why don't you want to stay with me?" with a little Indian head bobble. I shrugged off answering but did answer his other questions, "I am American and yes, I am single."

He then giggled to himself, "I am a lucky man."

I quickly responded, "*That* is why I want to stay alone." When he showed me to the house, I made sure to lock the door behind me.

It was the next morning that I found Doug on *Hakura*. He popped his head out the companionway: a hefty, round man with a bushy, gray beard and long, fading brown hair tied back under a bandana. He invited me aboard for a cup of tea. His bare torso was decorated with various tattoos, including a parrot on his shoulder, and he immediately struck me as a down-to-earth person, a pirate type that I could relate to. His boat was obviously his home and he wasn't a wealthy yachtsman, but a Kiwi on his first sail abroad. In its size and simplicity, *Hakura* reminded me of my boat, *Azurlite*, and as a Captain I could appreciate the enormity of the feat he had accomplished, making the 10-day sail from New Zealand to Fiji.

I hefted my pack into the cockpit and ducked below out of the sun, settling into the cozy salon. I offhandedly rattled out my sailing experience. Doug busied himself with the ritual of preparing a proper pot of loose-leaf tea and then explained his situation. He and his best friend John, whom he had known since college, had enjoyed a few months cruising Tonga and Fiji. Their respective partners had joined them for a few weeks and other crew had helped with the passages. Now it was time for the big trip home and John refused to go without help, since they didn't have an autopilot. Doug figured $30 NZ a day as each person's share of the expenses.

"I know how sailing is," I said, "and I can't afford to pay by the day if we have bad weather or are becalmed. How about I pay you $200 NZ all up? A flat fee."

Hakura

Doug agreed to this. "But there's one rule," he added solemnly. "There are no put-downs, and that includes the one we put down the most: ourselves." I nodded knowingly.

"Okay," I consented with a smile. "That's a rule I can definitely agree to."

There were still a few prospects I wanted to check out, and Doug magnanimously offered me a bunk for a few nights and the use of *Hakura* as home base, whether I sailed with them or not. He even said I could use his computer. I hesitated, not wanting to take advantage of his generosity by using his laptop to check on other crewing options, but he read my mind and assured me, "Use it, even to find another boat," before leaving me in his floating sanctuary in blessed solitude.

With the knowledge that such a genuinely kind person had me covered for a few days, my whole body relaxed. Doug's offer not only released me from the burden of lugging my oversized bag around in the tropical heat, wondering where I would sleep, but also from the considerable weight of the single-woman-traveling-alone guard I'd been holding up.

When Doug returned, he invited me to join him on what had become his daily afternoon outing. We walked through the Westernized complex that made up the posh outdoor shopping mall and marina, and through the surrounding high-end suburb to the Hilton Hotel, with its luxurious, oversized swimming pool. Our white skin was the only ticket we needed to enter this opulent resort and we swam and sunbathed on cushioned lounge chairs. Since I didn't have to hold up my tough, independent guard anymore, my feelings from the past week of unresolved drama welled up. Doug listened sympathetically and coached me through it. He was thoughtful and easygoing, and treated me like a niece. By the time we made it back to *Hakura* I felt totally at ease.

We met John at their usual picnic bench in front of a café on the mall, on a wide cement quay overlooking the water and all the vessels. Doug and John didn't drink, and I smiled to myself in recognition that, since I'd stopped drinking, I'd attracted all of these non-drinkers into my experience. We all ordered fruit smoothies. John was good-looking, tall and broad-chested, with the unbreakable confidence and happy-go-lucky nature I associated with boys. I was not up to proving myself as good crew or good company, but they didn't make me feel like I had to. Their relaxed, unassuming vibe made it clear they were old friends with no power trips or ulterior motives.

Adventures of a Pirate Girl

When I returned from a trip to the toilet, Doug announced that I had passed the test; they both agreed they'd love to have me as crew for the passage to New Zealand.

"Cool," I nodded, relieved to be signed-on and moving forward. "Let's do it!"

While we sat there, my previous, stingy old Captain and his wife wandered by and stopped to exchange superficial pleasantries. These two big, fatherly men sat, one on either side of me, like sentries, and I felt protected from the miasma of negativity and bad communication that plagued *Mistress*. Doug and John were a much better match.

It was good that we came to our agreement that evening, because the next morning a cute young surfer boy, Rob, came by looking for a boat. Doug told him he already had me, but invited him aboard anyway. He wasn't experienced, just a Kiwi kid in Fiji on a solo surfing trip who thought sailing home would be a cool adventure to end on. He was positive and energetic; we all found his laid-back persistence endearing. But there wasn't room for one more. Once we were at sea, our sleeping arrangements would be "hot bunks": when someone came off their three-hour watch, they would take the vacated bunk of the person leaving it for a turn at the helm. We had a few days to wait out the weather, though, so Doug invited him to hang out till then.

I made one last visit to my previous Captain, Ernest, to make a deal. The fact that I had found another boat was a huge relief for him, since he was legally responsible for me while I was still signed onto his boat. Our original agreement was $2000 U.S. for the two-month trip to Australia, plus airfare to Bora Bora. He was adamant I pay for the radar, since my attempt to fix it had made it worse, finally forcing him to pay a professional. I reminded him that it had been broken *long* before I came into the picture, and maybe he should be thanking me. However, to avoid full-on battle, I offered to pay $100 out of what he owed me. He would pay me $1000 for the one month I'd crewed for them, minus the $100 for the radar. $900 and be free and clear of any further responsibility.

"Nine hundred?"

"Nine hundred." We both repeated it a few times and shook hands, planning to meet at immigration to do the final exchange.

The next morning, the three guys and I moved *Hakura* the few hours to Lautoka, with its big ship dock and paper mill spewing smoke. Doug accompanied me to the dusty and eclectic city to sign me off *Mistress* and onto *Hakura* and get my money and passport. I cordially shook Ernest's hand and his wife's, saying goodbye and wishing them luck, and they handed me an envelope. As we walked away I realized it contained only $720—they had subtracted my original airfare to Bora Bora. Ridiculous. But at least it was over and done with—they were the ones stuck with their own stingy reality. I was free of it, finally.

We spent the rest of the day provisioning and then pulled anchor. The murky, green water around the city port cleared slowly to blue as we left the dry, brown hillside of Viti Levu, the main island, in the distance. Rob, the Kiwi kid, and I perched up in the spreaders high up the mast and guided Doug between *bommies* (the Kiwi term for coral heads) to anchor in translucent water. We snorkeled around colorful coral outcroppings, and challenged ourselves to swim the distance to a tiny uninhabited island. We took turns cooking and enjoyed meals together in the cockpit. Though most of our two days of exploring was under motor power, we even got a little sail in for Robby's sake, since he had never sailed before. With all the drama Fiji had been for me, it was a blessing to end it with these few days of laid-back fun and mellow camaraderie.

We were all looking forward to getting underway. Doug was of a mind to just tough out whatever conditions we encountered, so I was glad John was adamant about making sure the weather was auspicious for our 10-day sail. He subscribed to the site of a New Zealander who made detailed weather predictions and even charted the optimum course for sailors through the changing weather patterns. According to the meteorologist, this was our window. We spent the morning doing our final clearance from Customs back at Lautoka and fueled up one last time, before barely making it through the reef as the light faded. While being seasick and puking wasn't fun, at least I liked and trusted Doug and John…and we were on our way to New Zealand!

Underway

Without a sunshade tent obscuring the sky, a center console blazing circus lights in my face or the autopilot running the show (as on the other yachts I'd sailed with), I was forced into a more active sailing role. I became fully aware of the more subtle, timeless performance taking place all around me. At first it was hard to stand and steer for three hours straight, without even the distraction of my iPod (for fear of a wet slap). But soon I was riveted by the way the elusive air conformed perfectly to the undulating body of the ocean and I wondered who was leading whom in this endless and intimate dance of sea and sky.

Actually working while on duty made my six hours off feel like I'd earned them and, since I was paying my way, I was relieved of the nagging obligation to be more useful. I loved that the rules, timetables and expectations of normal life were thrown out the window and the only remaining rhythm would be created as we went. Here we were, finally, Doug, John and me, with nothing left to do but sail this little ship to New Zealand: eat, sleep and steer. And the nine days it took us to accomplish this goal were exactly what every sailor would want them to be: uneventful.

The first three or four days were cold and, after 10 months in the tropics, I was glad I had purchased one of the few existing sweatshirts in Fiji. Doug's girlfriend had left boots aboard that fit me. To demonstrate how little land-based hygiene applied on a 36-foot boat at sea: After I was all suited up for my watch but still barefoot, I'd perch in the companionway. John, while still at the wheel, would remove his boots and strip off his one pair of slightly moist, overly ripe—but warm—socks for me to put on before I crawled out into the chilly night.

One day, unbeknownst to us, a big, bull mahi-mahi took the bait we were trolling. We weren't very attentive or enthusiastic fishermen and, by the time we realized we'd caught something, he had been dragged to death; otherwise we would have let him go. He was nearly four feet long—enough to feed us for a week—but without refrigeration there was no way the meat would last. We all lamented this beautiful, shimmering loss and Doug chopped off a sizable chunk before letting the rest slip overboard to feed the scavengers. We skinned only enough for that night's dinner, leaving the end bit with the impressive tail wrapped in a burlap sack in the cockpit for breakfast the following morning.

The weather was heating up. Being from the northern hemisphere I was used to equating south with sun so I took this for granted. But it was an anomaly here in the southern hemisphere. We were heading away from the tropics, ultimately toward Antartica, the freezing south. But each day dawned warmer and required fewer layers.

Hakura

At about the halfway point to New Zealand, Doug had a birthday and, to celebrate, we all put on clean clothes. We set up the table in the cockpit and laid out one of our cherished rounds of cheese, a packet of crackers, sliced tomato, fresh mango, and a packet of peanut cookies. But the real treat: It was time to decant the ginger beer.

In Tonga a great couple from Tasmania had given me a small amount of ginger beer starter and instructions on how to brew it. I'd been feeding it with fresh ginger and sugar, had bottled it with water and lemon juice, had carried it in between boats and, after weeks of fermentation, it was finally ready to try. Doug and John, who informed me of ginger beer's popularity in New Zealand, claimed their authority as connoisseurs. Not the best they had tried, they informed me, noses up in mock snobbery, but pretty damn good nonetheless!

Since *Hakura* didn't have a water maker, fresh water showers weren't an option. By the end of a week, we were all a bit smelly and salt encrusted. John instigated a seawater wash-down for the crew. I was at the wheel when he appeared in his Speedo with the soap. After catching a bucketful of water off the side and yanking it up quick before it dragged under with the weight, he squatted in front of the wheel and began slowly scooping it over himself. I sped up the process by dowsing him with the whole icy bucket, which made him squeal with shocked delight. This inspired me, and soon I was in my skivvies, screaming with laughter as we soaked each other with pails of the bracingly cold South Pacific.

After nine days, Aotearoa, which means "land of the long white cloud" in Maori, appeared as a long, dark smudge. That day, as we approached New Zealand, the sun was so warm we sunbathed in nothing but togs (Kiwi for swimsuits) as if we had magically carried the tropics with us. We passed a few seals that had the same idea: they lay on the surface, each with a fin extended skyward.

"Whadda you looking at?" they seemed to be saying, as we circled them, gawking.

The sun went down in a fiery glow and, in the remaining purple twilight, the silhouette of a dragonhead stood guard over the Bay of Whangarei (pronounced fung-ga-ray), on the northeast coast of the North Island. As we passed this sentry, the mystical bubble of our sunshine voyage popped—and we were enveloped in the heavy clouds and rain of a typical early spring in New Zealand.

That night we tied up to a cement floating dock at a deserted marina within what looked like a brand-new housing complex and slept the deep, watch-less sleep of the safely landed sailor. The next morning, the immigration guy came aboard like an old friend, "Hey, Doug! How was your trip?" and stamped my passport—even though I had no ticket to leave or money to stay, as is usually required.

It was one day's motor up the bay to where Doug's slip was. The rolling green hills, quaint-looking villages, and colorful boats bobbing at anchor charmed me. Doug pointed out the terraced hills and explained that these were called *pa*, where the fierce Maori warriors defended themselves from the British. The waterway narrowed and filled with boats until it finally ended near a low bridge. His slip was a tight squeeze among neighboring boats and surrounded by touristy cafés and nautical restaurants. The first thing we did—once securely tied up—was walk across the street (where the cars came from the wrong direction!) to the dairy (Kiwi for convenience store) where Doug shouted us an ice-cream cone dipped in chocolate. I had hokey pokey (vanilla with crunchy little bits of teeth-aching toffee) because, according to Doug, it was the Kiwi favorite.

While wandering around the small downtown, we came across an opening at an art gallery, and I got my first experience of the native culture. The three Maori artists greeted each other with the *hongi*—mindfully touching foreheads and noses and taking in a deep breath—then welcomed the crowd with a small ceremony in English and Maori. There were food and drink, beautiful pieces of tribal art in carved stone, flax and feathers, and an eclectic crowd. I was impressed with the seemingly peaceful co-existence of these two cultures.

Lorraine and Sharron (Doug's and John's partners respectively) joined us, and Doug treated us, as is custom, to a nice dinner. Afterward they went off in pairs, leaving me the luxury of the boat all to myself for the night.

I fell asleep thinking of this beautiful, green land. Though the native people had had to fight for their rights, and there was still plenty of injustice and struggle, they had retained much more of their culture than the natives had in the States. In New Zealand, nuclear power was nonexistent, the government supported single moms, and medical care was everyone's birthright.

After 10 months my head was spinning from all the traveling I'd done. Crewing on other people's boats was the opposite of what sailing had always represented for me: freedom. I didn't know what my future held, but I didn't think it was more sailing. I felt like lying facedown, arms spread, to hug and kiss the spacious mass of solid Earth on which I stood. This might be a tiny island nation, but it was a lot bigger than all the other islands I had visited and it had all the luxuries of the U.S. I didn't have to jump on another boat or leave anytime soon. The people spoke my language and couldn't tell I was a stranger just by looking at me. Doug thought my destiny was in New Zealand. So far it seemed like a storybook place. Whether I could feel a whispered premonition or I just wanted to stop moving, I could imagine my story weaving itself somewhere within its pages.

CHAPTER 13

No More Boats

Queen Street Backpackers, Auckland
October 2, 2010

Snicker-faced. Ha! Though I was slunk low and quiet in the back row, I couldn't stop the hiccup of laughter bubbling out of my chocolate-smeared mouth. After 10 months of foreign countries and being at sea, it was good to be doing something as familiar as watching *The Simpsons*. Lisa had a new boyfriend, a Sid Vicious look-alike, who got her hooked on his insatiable addiction.

"Let's get snicker-faced!" They crammed candy into their mouths until they were reeling with the buzz, then Sid beat his head against the wall.

"Ha!" I snorted out loud. This episode seemed aimed directly at me: I'd bought enough chocolate to make myself sick.

I was sitting in a corner near a ceiling-high window on the dirty couch of a Backpackers in Auckland, New Zealand. Three rows of sofas radiated out in a semicircle around the big black box suspended from the ceiling. It was mid-afternoon. Lounging on the grubby sofas was an international assembly of mostly under-30s: rosy-faced blond girls from Germany using the hostel as a stop-over while they organized their trip; various dark-haired, single guys from Chile, here to work and learn English; an enthusiastic Japanese kid who had just landed a job despite his lack of English. And a few rougher looking English regulars drinking beer who'd made this seedy hostel their home.

After accompanying Doug, my last Captain, a few hours north along the east coast to the Bay of Islands to drop off the life raft he'd rented, he had driven me south to Auckland, giving me a sight-seeing tour on the way. After promising to stay in touch, he dropped me off at the Queen Street Backpackers in the downtown area. I immediately contacted Inger and Paul, the people I'd met in Fiji who'd offered me the job in Auckland. To my relief they were excited to hear from me. They wanted to come right away and pick me up, but I was tired and so we agreed on the next morning.

"It's supposed to be a beautiful day tomorrow and it's Saturday," Inger informed me, "so we're going out on the boat. It'll be super fun. We'll swing by in the morning at about 9:00. Bring all your stuff. You can stay at our place for a bit."

New Zealand is a solid body of land split in the middle to make up two islands. At the top of the North Island, it's as if the land has broken up and been washed away by the tide. Auckland sits on the bits that are left. It is a city surrounded by sea, practically an island itself. To the east, the Coromandel Peninsula juts up, creating a protected body of water around Auckland called the Hauraki Gulf, which is dotted with islands.

Paul came in the morning, helped carry my pack down to his waiting car, and we drove to where the family kept their vessel. I helped Paul ready the 20-foot Bayliner, a tidy motorboat with a small forward cabin, while Inger, her niece and boyfriend (who were in their early 20s) wrangled the two kids (10 and 18 mos.) and gear. It was comfortably familiar to be back onboard a boat.

We motored out under the Auckland Harbor Bridge and took photos, the city skyline in the background with its Sky Tower pointing up above the high rise buildings. We cruised past Rangitoto Island (a volcanic island that rose up in a symmetrical green peak), then tucked into a quiet bay off Waiheke Island, one of the bigger and populated islands around Auckland. We stopped and took turns jumping into the still, cold water, screaming in delight.

Then we motored around to another secluded bay to do some fishing. While everyone else was busy casting their lines, I sat with the blond 18-month-old in my arms as he drifted off, lulled by the long day, the sparkling sun and the gently rocking boat. I drifted off, too. My sailing dream had carried me this far, but now, within the safe waters of this island in the protected Hauraki Gulf, a peaceful sleeping babe in my arms, the constantly moving life no longer held any interest. The sound of that biological clock that constantly ticked in the background of my consciousness now filled my awareness, reminding me of that other dream: the one that involved having one of these little people of my own to love and care for.

They were a lovely family and welcomed me into their home, but after some research the next day, it turned out the work permit for me that Paul had been so confident about in Fiji, wasn't so easy to acquire. It's common for young travelers to get a one-year work permit in New Zealand for a working holiday but apparently the cut-off age at that time was 30. I was 35. They were kind and offered to hire me to do some work around their house, but the fast-paced, busy life of a young family with two working parents was at odds with my travelers more relaxed pace. We were running at totally different rpms.

I returned to the Backpackers, dejected, with a week to kill until the meditation course I'd signed up for began. I'd done the same Vipassana course five times in the States and in Europe and knew it was just what I needed to cleanse myself of the emotional, physical and mental muck I'd accumulated while traveling. Hopefully I could hold out until it began.

Wearing the only set of warm clothes I owned—and shoes for the first time in 10 months—I wandered aimlessly around the city, through hordes of nameless people who all seemed to have somewhere to go. All I really wanted to do was hole up on my own and write. But my computer wasn't working and I couldn't afford to write by the hour on a desktop at the hostel. I felt uprooted, displaced and disconnected—and oh, so sick of traveling.

Unlike the States, all the addictive luxury items here were expensive: chocolate and coffee (cigarettes and alcohol were too, though I wasn't using those). But I still indulged in plenty of Subway sandwiches, flat whites (Kiwi for lattés) and biscuits (cookies), numbing my bad feelings with food and wishing I was back in Boulder—in my old, happy, active, friend-filled life. I was feeling sorry for myself and made the decision: fuck it—I would give up and use my safety-net money for exactly what I had it for: to buy a ticket home.

I followed a sign advertising free coffee with two hours of internet usage, down a dimly lit staircase into a flimsy basement. I planned to Skype my mom and buy the ticket. The coffee was cold, stained water in a mini styrofoam cup; the computer screen was invaded by dancing pop-up ads in Chinese. I was having a very bad day. Maybe it was cosmic, because my mom apparently was also having a bad day. When I told her I just wanted to come home, instead of the love and encouragement I was hoping for—the open arms of welcome—my mom worried about upsetting her roommate. Fighting back tears of rejection, I hung up on her and stomped out.

No More Boats

Totally dispirited, I wandered through the city in a blur of tears. I came upon Albert Park: a grassy expanse lined with huge trees that had twisted, knobby roots and massive reaching branches. I sat myself down on a bench and gave myself a stiff talking to: "You are going to have to buck up and tough this out, girl; you can't just go crying home to your mom."

I brought my awareness into my body: I was okay. I was here, on this bench. I focused on the sunshine on my face, the warmth. I took a deep breath and noticed a familiar, sweet smell: the same clusters of tiny white flowers I loved from California.

"You're okay, Davina. It's going to work out. You can go home, that's fine, but you gotta make some money first." Who knew? Maybe I could get a job on a big super-yacht or a cruise ship. Something would work out—but I had to pull myself together first, change the direction of my thoughts. This was as far down as I was going to allow myself to sink, and so, as if I was deep underwater, I turned myself upward and gave a good solid push off the bottom, kicking toward the light. And slowly but surely, the Universe responded to my attitude adjustment.

First of all I needed my computer: I needed to keep writing. All of the experiences I'd been through were churning around in my head, coalescing into lumps, and I craved the quiet catharsis of finding words for each mound, kneading and shaping them into stories. I paid for a computer by the hour and wrote a blog to the small but faithful group who had been following my adventures, asking them for financial support to fix my computer. And in the meantime, I decided to break into my safety-net money—the $1000 I'd been keeping separate in case of emergency—and took my laptop to a computer shop.

There was a couch surfing get-together at a downtown bar that I went to. I still had an account on the website but hadn't managed to put it to use while traveling. After mingling for a few hours with hopes of finding a free couch to sleep on, I realized that the logistics of living in someone else's space wasn't worth the money it saved. I wasn't in the right frame of mind for the give-and-take of couch surfing; I was feeling quiet and internal and just wanted to be autonomous. So I paid for a week at the hostel and bought some groceries.

One evening while crawling into my bunk in the shared room, I started chatting with a Kiwi girl, mentioning how unsure I was about my plans and my tight budget. In about two months, she told me, there would be heaps of jobs picking fruit down south. Not having a work permit was no problem and though it didn't pay much, she'd been able to work as many hours as she wanted while living on almost nothing in a tent onsite. Just the knowledge of this possibility lifted my spirits.

Staying active would help, so I took a ferry to Rangitoto, the youngest volcano in the region, and hiked to the top. When rain blew in, I found an old bunker and ducked into it. Also seeking refuge was an American woman, Tracy, who was my age; turned out she was a corporate workaholic whose company had sent her to New Zealand for a year. Her time was up and she was dreading leaving. We finished the hike together and later she took me to her favorite beach and to dinner at a great little Mexican joint (my ultimate comfort food), infecting me with her love for the place.

Back at the hostel I met a guy named Peter. He was probably the only person there over 40. Having just gone through a divorce, he'd decided to follow his lifelong dream of moving to New Zealand and had just arrived. He was energetic and eager to see some of the city. He invited me along for a 14-kilometer walk across Auckland from the east coast to the west coast and over two inactive volcanoes. After such an enjoyable day, he told me about the deluxe van he'd just bought, totally equipped to live in. He planned to cruise the country and invited me to join him. Though living in such a tight space with a man I wasn't romantically interested in sounded a lot like sailing, having a plan in place, especially one that felt familiar, was tempting.

One evening, while waiting my turn for a shower, I got into a conversation with Mathew. He was an American physician about my age, who'd been traveling the world doctoring in different countries. He was a pragmatic, believe-it-when-I-see-it kind of guy and we had a fiery debate about energetic medicine, and our spiritual nature. Though our views were very different, the intensity was fun. He was heading to Waiheke Island to spend a few months working, and told me to look him up if I ever made it over to the island.

Like this, the days passed. The activity and inspirational company helped buoy me, and I moved steadily up through the thick water, toward the sunshiney surface of my life.

Vipassana

Kaukapakapa, New Zealand
October 14, 2010

I believe that each of us has a light shining within: our spirit, a little piece of God, our Higher Power (HP as my dad likes to say), the Universe—there are many ways to express it. This light, our spirit, connects us with each other, with our Source and with everything that is. But as we travel through this life, with its pain and suffering that we can't or don't want to let go of, we collect emotional wounds. They're like mud and plaster over our shining light. Some people get so bogged down with the weight of the world that their light is completely smothered. I believe it's still under there, but because they can't access it, they seem dark, disconnected, evil even.

Or another analogy: a radio dial. God (or whichever title you prefer), is broadcast through all of us; each of us is an individual expression of the Divine. But as life knocks and jostles us, we get out of tune, losing the clear channel of what we really are.

Sitting a Vipassana course is, for me, like being washed clean of all the accumulated muck of life so my spirit can shine bright again; or it's like tuning in on that cosmic radio dial and receiving a clear transmission of my higher self.

Most people are shocked by the nine days of silence required at a Vipassana course. You, Davina? Not speaking for nine days?! But in Auckland, after 10 months of constant negotiations with the world and little chance to hide, I was ready to begin the not-speaking part right away: while waiting for the small chartered bus that would transport about 15 of us who'd gathered at the Auckland Bus Depot. I silently boarded and stared out the window as we drove for a few hours north through the city until the buildings petered out and became rolling green hills and we arrived at Kaukapakapa.

The first time I did a Vipassana course was at 18. I had heard of meditation as a teenager and had tried a few times to sit and let my mind become calm. But in my final year of school, a girl named Alicia came to talk to our class. She'd graduated the year before from the same Middle College program I attended and had then spent 10 months in India. At 18, my plan was to move to Santa Cruz with my best friend, Jessica, and attend a junior college, even though I hadn't ever liked school. But after hearing these fantastical stories about Alicia's adventures traveling through India, I knew that was the life for me. After graduating I befriended her, and we came up with the idea to go to England to work and save money before heading to the east. This was our plan for the next few months, but at the last minute, Alicia decided to go back to school instead.

I already had my heart set on the trip and had told everybody about it. So after working all summer, I bought a one-way ticket to London and left in the fall. Not only did Alicia spark my inspiration to travel but, before I left, she introduced me to Vipassana. She and I went to a meditation course in Northern California, surrounded by breathtaking nature, and sat—10 hours a day for 10 days—in silence.

I was brought up with an alternative spirituality. My parents taught me that there is a God, but left it up to me to figure out what that meant. I'd always felt a personal connection to a higher power and never needed a middle man. Sitting for those 10 days gave me a practical way to access that connection at an impressionable age.

Watching the landscape roll by on the bus to Kaukapakapa, I remembered that first Vipassana course. After three days of doing little else besides concentrating on the triangle between my nose and upper lip, training my brain to settle down, my monkey mind was still having a hard time sitting still. It was angry and wanted to propagate that anger. But without being able to talk or complain—to share it outside of myself—I was stuck with it. I poured myself a cup of coffee, even though I was trying to quit, and then had a realization: it was only *me* suffering from this anger, and it was within my power to change my attitude. I had committed to the 10 days and so could either carry around this seething sensation the whole time or I could just let it go. It was a life-changing lesson.

Doing that course at 18—before I went off to travel the world—had shaped and guided my life. The experience gave me a more solid idea about how connected I and all humans are and about how our minds influence our perceptions. It gave me an effective tool to ground and center myself through all the turmoil of my life.

Because there are Vipassana centers all over the world and they are run entirely by donation and volunteers, I was able to attend a few more courses in Europe and California while I was young and on the move. But by the time I'd sold my boat and landed in Colorado in 2007, I'd mostly forgotten about Vipassana.

No More Boats

After moving to Colorado I had a hard time finding my balance on dry land. In the first six months I was fired from two consecutive jobs and was about to be fired from a third. This felt cosmic, like some big energetic shift was going on within me.

It was the last day at my coffee-shop job. The pressure had been building because the woman who owned the place knew nothing about customer service and her business was floundering. Instead of being warm and inviting to attract more customers, she focused on profit: "That guy only bought one cup of tea! Davina, go tell him he has to buy a whole pot of tea to use the internet!"

Right before I reached my breaking point and refused to do her rude bidding, (getting fired yet again), a middle-aged woman came in asking if she could use the phone. Her car was having problems and she needed it to drive to a course the next day.

"What course?" I asked offhandedly, while handing her the phone.

"Vipassana." It turned out she lived a short walk from my mom's condo in the same complex. For the next two years, I sat with her for an hour nearly every day, went to several 10-day courses and got involved with the Vipassana community in Boulder. This was what I needed. Soon after I settled into a great job and a fulfilling life. Meditating daily oiled my feathers like a duck; all of life's challenges and frustrations rolled off my back.

The driver pulled our small bus off the main country road we'd been on for awhile and bumped along a dirt track that led us further away from civilization until we arrived at a lush, green valley in the embrace of hills covered in primeval forest: a natural sanctuary.

We unloaded our gear at the main house and checked in. A lot of the centers where I'd sat before had incarnated as a camp or recreation center and been converted to accommodate the meditation program. This center at Kaukapakapa had been virgin land before it was purchased from a Maori tribe and the buildings were designed specifically for this altruistic purpose. The top floor had a commercial-sized kitchen and the women's dining area.

Men and women lived and ate in completely different areas to lessen distraction. We came together only in the meditation hall, where the men filed in from a different doorway. Our assigned square cushions were ordered in neat rows, the men on one side and the women's on the other with a walkway down the middle and the teachers, a man and a women, facing the students. The women's living area had a grassy lawn nestled by forested hills on one side and a slope on the other with two levels of individual apartments built into it, each with a bed, a window and a heater. Nearby was a bathroom block with showers, and there was a short trail that participants could follow through the woods around the site.

It was heaven to have my own little room, to not have to talk to or negotiate with anyone, to have each day rigidly scheduled and, though people were around, to go about my time completely on my own.

Through the several Vipassana courses I had attended, I had found that the only tolerable way to deal with hours of sitting and meditating each day was to be completely in the moment. To not allow myself to think about anything beyond the next hour because all there was were hours and hours and hours of more sitting. If I was in the moment, there was no worry about what I would do when the course was over. For 10 days I was safe, comfortable and well cared for: eating healthy, vegetarian meals lovingly prepared by volunteers and sleeping in a private, cozy room, keeping busy from sunup to sundown meditating.

After a few days of such intense concentration—without the outer clutter of conversations, daily issues and media—my mind slowly tuned in to Source. My slow, mindful walks through the bush became touched with the awe and wonder of the natural world: the green, iridescent craftsmanship of a beetle's shell; the soft, moist touch of the forest floor; the fuzzy, brown, baby fists of the iconic New Zealand fern unrolling into nuanced fractal patterns of green. Someone had woven little organic shrines along the path and I took to adding a vibrant bloom or a particularly delicate leaf and other small treasures to these miniature temples. While sitting in the hall—which was permeated with a deep sense of peace in the still hours of dawn—the otherworldly song of some formless bird sang in an ethereal voice and echoed back in another, as if existing in different dimensions.

Through the whole experience, it was inevitable that I'd count the days until I could talk with others. It was a point of time to look forward to: When the actual day came, the last hour of sitting was over and I could finally get up, go outside and talk with these people whom I'd been living with so intimately, sharing meals and holding doors, eyes discreetly directed toward the floor.

You might think that everyone would begin chatting the moment they were set free from their commitment. But I found it hard to face coming back into life after delving so deeply into my own psyche. When the moment arrived, I sat for what felt like ages with my eyes closed, thinking that I heard people discreetly getting up all around me, almost scared to leave the quiet peace of the meditation hall. It seemed I was the only one remaining. I finally let my eyes slowly open, but, in fact, only a few cushions sat empty. The tranquil forms of my fellow meditators still surrounded me in their straight rows bolstered by cushions and blankets. I slowly crept out of the room.

There was one woman on the porch. We stood together, savoring the last moments of silence and taking in the lovely views, before slowly, slowly, with tentative giggles just to warm our voices, shared some words. Of Maori descent, she was the mother of a young boy and came to sit because she found herself yelling too often and wanted to be a calmer parent.

She invited me to see the glowworms later that evening. The moon was full and lit our way until we crept into the cover of the bush toward the crotch of the valley where the steep inclines met. There, in a clearing, stood two other women. One I'd been drawn to: a blond English woman who exuded confidence and vitality and, it turned out, had sailed the Pacific on a traditional Polynesian *waka* with a crew of people. The other was a young American girl who reminded me of an old friend with her dark, short-cropped hair and big child-like eyes.

Up the rocky wall beside us trickled a waterfall, and the eerie light of glowworms played in the wet darkness. After each of us shared our story in a reverent whisper, we took turns to *hongi*, which was my first experiencing sharing this traditional Maori greeting—leaning in to press our foreheads together two by two, and inhaling a shared breath. After nine days of no communication, and without all that muck that covered (but also, in a way, guarded) my spirit, the experience was intimate and intense. This organic and impromptu ritual shared with these beautiful women… what a powerful way to end such a profound 10 days and start whatever would come next.

Adventures of a Pirate Girl

Waiheke Island

Auckland, New Zealand
October 24, 2010

Somehow there was beauty now. Beauty I couldn't see before the meditation course. Auckland had been dreary and cold to me then, impersonal and lonely. But now, with my awareness so keenly tuned into myself, my mind at peace, there was something wonderful in the thriving pulse of people and cars, like a beehive buzzing with life.

I climbed the wide, worn, red-carpeted stairs to the main floor of the Queen Street Backpackers where I'd been staying before the course. I noticed the slight smell of stale beer as I joined the queue of young people at the long counter, plopping my pack down with the other various baggage.

"*Bula! Bula Vinaka!*" the big Fijian guy behind the counter sang with gusto, seeing my familiar face.

"*Bula*, Tom! How are you?!"

"How are you, my friend? How are you! You must tell me, how was the meditation?"

"Oh, Tom, it was amazing. You have to try it, it's such a beautiful place and so close. You get your own little room and delicious vegetarian meals and it just costs a donation, so anyone can do it. You have to go. It will change your life!"

"Are you talking about Vipassana?" asked a bronzed Spanish surfer, his board in its bag propped against a table. "That's so cool, I've done like 10 courses. Is there one around here?"

"Awesome! Yeah there is, in Kaukapakapa. It's beautiful."

After chatting more about Vipassana with the surfer dude and Tom, Tom turned his attention to the computer in front of him and began typing.

"Oh my dear, we have no more beds. It's a holiday weekend. All the Backpackers in the city will be filled up. You should get out of the city anyway; there are so many beautiful places in New Zealand!"

"Oh no! I would, but my computer's getting fixed. I don't go want to go too far away."

"Well, they won't be open until Tuesday anyway. You know where you need to go? I can just imagine you meditating on a cliff over the sea—you need to go to Waiheke Island! It's close by, you just take a ferry. You will love it!" He was already picking up the phone and dialing. The first hostel on Waiheke was full, but that led to another and they had one bed left. Tom reserved it for me.

The half-hour ferry ride was beautiful: past the stretch of city and various uninhabited islands—sailboats everywhere—until we finally motored in between impressive rocky cliffs topped with grassy, green slopes, into the protected bay of Matiatia on Waiheke Island. I flowed off the boat with the gush of other visitors and locals returning home, past the buses and pick up zone where cars were waiting, doors ajar. I stuck my thumb out and within a minute a car swung over and I ran to peer in.

"I'm going to the Backpackers on Pacific Parade," I informed the lady.

"Sweet, I can take you there," she said. So I hefted my pack into the backseat and got in.

Assa had an impressive halo of puffy afro hair, caramel skin and oversized red glasses on her flat nose.

"I'm going to a cabaret party, that's why I'm dressed like this," she said. Which brought my attention to the strappy peach lingerie top she was wearing, the mismatched slip and her fishnet stockings.

"How fun! My kind of island!"

"Do you want to come?"

"Normally I would, but I've been up since 4:30 this morning. I don't think I'm up for it. Thanks, though."

We drove up a hill from the ferry, through the main street of a cute little town called Oneroa, with shops and restaurants overlooking the ocean, and then descended again.

"I'm just going to stop real quick to get something to eat. This is Little Oneroa." She pulled into a busy parking lot shaded by huge cypress trees that I recognized from Monterey, California, where I had lived as a kid, with impressive twining trunks that reached out in all directions. There was a playground, a bridge over a small creek, and lots of grass—all overlooking the beach and sparkling sea. Rocky cliffs on both sides created this intimate cove in the corner of the larger Oneroa Bay. In the parking lot right in front of the beach was a food truck called Dragon Fired.

"They make the best food," my host informed me. I ordered a Mexican pocket made in a wood-fired pizza oven to keep for later. While we waited, I took in the scene: the squeal of kids running around, picnicking families spread out on the lawn, gulls begging, people sunbathing and swimming. The whole area buzzed with a celebratory, summertime vibe.

"You can stay at my place," Assa offered, once back in her car. This perked up my ears until she added, "$15 a night," only slightly less than the hostel. Seeing me hesitate she said, "We can go by to see it. Then, if you don't want to, I'll take you to the Backpackers."

We wound up and down hills on small curvy roads with overgrown foliage and lots of trees. Occasionally a gap would reveal stunning vistas of little bays filled with sailboats. We soon arrived at her place. It only took a second for me to see that it wouldn't be ideal—it was strewn messy with clutter and clothing—so I politely declined.

"I think I'll be happier where there are other travelers." So she drove me to the hostel.

The road it was on ran along a high ridge, but the Backpackers was tucked down off the road, obscured by trees with only a small mosaic sign, The Bio-Shelter. I said farewell to Assa, thanking her for the ride and wishing her a fun cabaret party. When I walked down the drive, the structure appeared like a magical castle. Made of stucco, it was organically sculpted with a tall, round tower, plants sprouting out of planters built into its walls, and a few artistically placed circular windows. The whole thing looked like a mushrooming fairy house.

The hostel's front door was around the side; I knocked and tentatively pushed it open, stepping in. There was a cozy kitchen to my right and a large, round dining table surrounded by glass doors and windows to my left. I could hear Spanish being spoken and peered in further to see a group of young people sitting around a wood-burning stove in a sunken glassed-in patio that overlooked the garden. They all looked up, smiling, and a guy with sparkling eyes jumped up to greet me.

"I called and booked a bed."

"Wait right here," he said as he headed up a staircase.

An attractive older guy, with streaks of gray in his shoulder-length dark hair, wearing a chunky wool sweater, came down the stairs, "Hi, I'm Ivan," he said,

No More Boats

"Come on, I'll show you around." I followed him up the stairs past little nooks at different levels tucked here and there, private little spaces with beds, yet all of them opened to the main interior of the tower. He showed me where I could sleep and I marveled out loud about what a cool place it was.

"It's been an ongoing project for the past 20 years," Ivan expounded. He had a calm presence and our conversation unfolded naturally. He told me about how he'd raised his son in the house while continually building. His master bedroom was at the top and he walked me through it, showing me the entrance to the roof, which he said I was welcome to hang out on. This was his home but he didn't separate himself. There were composting toilets and various built-in sitting areas. The whole thing was so creative, comfortable and homey. I expressed how much I loved it, engaging him about his building techniques and process. He went on to explain about his other, more beloved project: a nursery where he grew native trees. A handful of the travelers staying in the hostel exchanged rent for work at the nursery, though he didn't need anyone else at the time. Bummer.

Left alone on the roof patio I could see a green valley with houses tucked in under the abundant trees and a jewel-sized piece of the dazzling, blue sea in the distance. I sat and mindfully ate my delicious pita pocket. There was a slight, jarring buzz within me from my first day away from the sanctuary of meditation, so I sat in silence for an hour before retiring early. Tomorrow would be a good day.

The Party

Waiheke Island, New Zealand
October 25, 2010

The next day, I met Natalia from Chile. She'd been on the island for a few months, working for Ivan and living at the Bio-shelter. She invited me to a party. Five of us from the Backpackers—a Japanese couple, two girls from Chile (including Natalia) and I—spanned the small street as we walked down from the ridge. Like our mood, the island appeared festive with the roads curved and humped over small, green hills decorated with colorful cottages and flowers, all leading to the sparkling sea. Once on the main road featuring sidewalks, a few shops and a café, a jeep pulled over to the left. "*Oi! Amigas!*"

An Argentinean couple waved us over, inviting us to pile into the back with their adorable Australian Shepherd pup. They were on their way to the same party!

Five minutes later, we turned down a road on another ridge lined with houses, overlooking bays on either side of the street. Converging with other guests we trooped down steep steps cut into the hill and onto a flat grassy area, the same level as the water would be when the tide came back in. All the anchored boats were left sitting on mud flats, upright on twin keels or leaning awkwardly on single keels, accustomed to the big ebb and flow.

The salty smell of silt and marsh mixed with the wafting marijuana smoke and warm, spring sunshine. There were maybe 60 people there—some long-time residents, some visitors. Spanish and French could be heard as often as English, and the vibe was one of welcoming celebration. A DJ with a full sound system pumped out reggaeton, with a definite emphasis on ganja, "Legalize it, ye-a, ye-a." Nobody was shy to dance. I was in the perfect place at the perfect time.

I'd been on a cleanse for the past three months and so tried to avoid the weed, but the music and atmosphere was too compelling, and I ended up partaking in a single toke. After 10 days of deep meditation, I was already feeling at one with the Universe—and that little hit blasted me into enlightenment. I had boundless energy: dancing and laughing and mingling with everyone, having the time of my life.

After the DJ finished, a full salsa band started up. I couldn't believe how much this party resembled a personal fantasy. I could seriously be dreaming, though dreams are never that good. After making a scene on the dance floor with the few guys who really knew how to salsa, I wandered around behind a ramshackle boat shed near the water's edge to concentrate on my breathing for a minute and ground myself. There, tied up between four poles, was a little sailboat. Her wooden trim was painted the same deep red I had painted the trim on my boat and, though weathered, she was a darling. She was in need of some major TLC and, though it's taboo to get on someone's boat uninvited, I figured she must belong to the guy whose party this was and he wouldn't mind. I gingerly climbed aboard and gently slid open the hatch above the companionway.

Now I was really dreaming! She was small but perfectly organized with a miniature galley, camp stove stowed beneath a little counter top and a bowl sink; a tiny head with a place to put a bucket under a varnished teak lid; even a little wood-burning stove to cook on and bake in. *Lady Rebecca*: like a dollhouse with every cabinet panel painted with a flowery flourish, satiny varnish on the entire teak interior and matching blue covers and pillows for the bunks. During the years that I had worked on rebuilding my boat, this was the interior that I would fantasize about, though I never got that far. It tickled the dormant princess in me and I, in that moment, fell in love.

Owning another boat that clearly needed work—a boat that would never cross an ocean—was not part of any of my plans. But it was love—what could I do? My mind was spinning full speed: I would get this boat; I would start my Live Your Dream charters again, write my books, create the whole Pirate Girl shebang—there on Waiheke Island. I got so excited that, when I heard two Colombian women poking around outside, I popped out and invited them aboard as if Lady Rebecca was already mine. My tongue going a mile a minute in Spanglish, I laid out my whole vision for them as they sat, seemingly entranced, listening happily. They were either astonished with my energy or stunned by my mania, I'm not sure which, but either way, they gave off a supportive vibe.

"All I need now is a place to live," I declared and didn't think much of it when one of them nodded knowingly and said, *"Deja mi ver."*

Later on, when the evening was creeping in, those of us remaining gathered around a warm fire. I was chatting with a fellow meditator, a Chilean guy in a poncho, when a shy, dark lady snuck up behind me and said, "My sister tell to me you need place to live."

"Si, senorita," my face stretching into the biggest smile. *"Es verdad."*

CHAPTER 14
Finally, Home

Waiheke Island, New Zealand
November 1, 2010

The next day I went to Auckland to retrieve my computer and buy a phone. From there I called Cristina, the woman who'd invited me to stay with her family on Waiheke Island, and confirmed her invitation.

This time I bought a one-way ticket on the ferry and returned to the island, again sticking out my thumb. Within minutes a car pulled over. The woman turned out to be a local librarian. When I told her I was there to stay for awhile and planned to write a book, she dropped me right at Cristina's house and told me to come see her at the library. Now that she knew where I lived, she wouldn't need proof of my address for my library card.

The driveway was steep. I walked up, past a grassy hill covered in fruit trees. At the top was a small horse paddock with two mini ponies. Beyond that, the big glass doors were open to the house, so I stepped up the different levels of deck and went in. The interior was all wood with a long dining table to seat 12, couches and seats lining the walls, a wood-burning stove, and no TV in sight. Shelves along the ceiling were draped with vined plants and there were cases filled with books, various art and clutter. A counter demarcated the kitchen, with an organically shaped slab of wood suspended above the sink and filled with plants, food items and bric-a-brac. Woven baskets overflowing with fruit and vegetables hung down, framing the open plan. It was a well-loved, functional, artistic, and lived-in home.

Suddenly a hen squawked and I looked up to see Cristina, bent over, clapping and shouting, herding the chicken through the house. A black dog padded behind her, disinterested in the hen but half-heartedly following along, going through the motions of his job. Once the chook was out, Cristina turned her boisterous energy to me, "*Bienvenido, nena!*" she squealed, rocking me in an exuberant hug as if I were her long-lost daughter. Then she hurried me through the living room—a big open space with a cluttered desk, a drum set in the corner and covered keyboard along the wall, which she waved at, "*Jerome, mi esposo*, plays saxophone in a ska band, they practice here," she informed me, before escorting me out the back door.

Cristina was Colombian, small in stature, with black, shoulder-length hair that hung in ringlets. She had the air of a busy mother hen and treated me like one of her brood, but her smooth coffee-colored skin and work-taut body was ageless. She definitely wasn't old enough to be my mother.

Flowing out from behind the main house was a deck built around a trampoline and, in a semicircle around that, was a small art studio to the left, a few caravans, and another tiny house to the right. I poked my head into the studio and found it overflowing with large, colorful paintings that Cristina had done. Which clued me in to the fact that the other canvases displayed throughout the house and the hand-crafted elements of the home itself, all came from her creative flair and hard work.

Jerome popped down to make a coffee and say hello. He was French and informed me that he was usually tucked away upstairs in his office, working as a journalist for a French Caledonian newspaper to support his family. Also in his early fifties, he looked more his age, with balding salt and pepper hair, a goatee and an expanding belly. I found him to be easygoing and friendly. He also spoke perfect English, which was a relief because during my tour of the property, Cristina spoke Spanish to me, and after that, once she found out I was learning, she spoke almost exclusively French. Her English, it turned out, was still broken despite having lived in New Zealand for years. I suspected she had a bit of a block.

Their younger two (13- and 18-year-old) daughters still lived at home and were both trilingual and gorgeous with perfect, golden honey skin, almond eyes and big hair. Cristina's niece, whom I'd met at the party, didn't live there, but she, her husband and 5-year-old son often visited and stayed for meals, as did Cristina's sister, Claudia, Claudia's preteen daughter and husband.

Adventures of a Pirate Girl

Part of the lovely chaos were animals: two dogs, Tango and Samba, aging black lab mixes, and their newest litter of pups; two mini ponies; chickens; and a family of ducks whose babies would swim in the dogs' large water bowls. Cristina was frenetically busy, always welcoming and friendly but then off to do some chore: feeding animals or painting the floor or building a deck.

When I asked how much she wanted for rent, Cristina dismissed my question, saying I could just do chores and help out. So I settled into a caravan out back—a rounded trailer with a bed, built in couch, counter and a dresser on wheels—usually eating dinner with the family but often tucking away, luxuriating in my own private space. She insisted I relax the first week and never did specify how much time she expected me to work in exchange for rent. I soon figured out what chores I could do without triggering her need to control things. I took over doing the dishes and mowing the lawns, but when I tried to clean the bathroom or vacuum, Cristina would grab whatever implement I was using, give me a lesson on how to do it correctly, then ultimately take over the job. After awhile, I stopped trying so hard and just stuck to what I knew was safe.

"Why do you think I never do chores?" her youngest daughter laughed while we jumped on the trampoline one day. "She never lets me. She just takes over. And then complains that she has to do everything."

Cristina and Jerome had met a lifetime ago in the Caribbean. Cristina—a single mother of a small boy—had left Colombia and was living on Martinique, a French-speaking island, painting portraits to make a living. On the beach one day she noticed an attractive young man on a catamaran anchored out a ways. She left her son in the care of someone on the beach and swam out to make his acquaintance. Jerome was cruising and already had crew but she convinced him to take her and her son on, at least until the next island. Long story short: They ended up having two kids together and raised the three while slowly cruising the Caribbean and the Pacific for over 12 years. They had lived my dream!

Cristina and Jerome had an open-door policy: everyone was welcome. There were always people swinging by or hanging out, mostly speaking Spanish or French. I don't think I met a single Kiwi while staying with them. There were always various parties and impromptu dinners, a few friends hanging out on the porch sharing a roll-your-own smoke or strumming a guitar.

Cristina would walk the ponies to a market right across the street every Saturday. I helped a few times leading kids around on horsey rides. Then she

Finally, Home

arranged a table for me and I started setting up my own little stand to sell my jewelry. It was a great way to get to know the wider community, which so far felt inclusive, creative and supportive. The weekly event was part flea market—with used clothing and household stuff for sale—but also featured lots of regular artisans: a woman who made intricately crocheted hippy tops and a man who made glassware out of beer and soda bottles. Another woman with hennaed red hair created amazing feather and leather jewelry fit for rock stars, and someone else made natural tinctures and remedies. There were plenty of food vendors and people hanging out. Often someone would play music—and, of course, there were always kids running around.

I'd made a few close friends: I spent time with the two Chilean girls I'd met at the hostel. And there was a Mexican guy, Gustavo, whom I'd met at that first party. He was a regular at the house. Though he'd lived all over the world, he'd boycotted the United States due to how he knew he'd be treated: as a second-class citizen. New Zealanders thought of Mexico as the exotic, culturally rich place that it was. Gustavo was a filmmaker and we became quick friends while collaborating on a short film for Pirate Girl. I even let him into my bed a few times, since crossing that barrier made for a more intimate friendship, which I craved.

During the few months I lived at Cristina's, I wrote and hung out, went off island to do another meditation course and catch up with Doug and John, the guys I'd sailed with from Fiji. I worked for bits of time in a local café and a fancy vineyard restaurant, but I didn't have the right papers to keep a steady job for long. I was happy to celebrate Christmas with Cristina and Jerome's family and their community that year. In Latino style, they threw a big party on Christmas Eve. Everyone brought food to share, and there was dancing and drinking and carrying on until the wee hours.

Right after Christmas, Cristina and Jerome started getting ready to sell the house. They had a plan to buy a big plot of land on the rural part of the island where they could have more of a homestead with room for their animals. Cristina told me someone was coming to take photos at 11 am the following day, and she asked me to help clean up. I'd already made plans to work on my pirate film with Gustavo that afternoon. so I promised her I'd get up early the next day and go hard at it.

I got up at 6 am and started tidying, but it soon became clear that I hadn't understood to what degree she wanted the house to be de-cluttered. I had been piling every knick-knack and extraneous object on a sheet on the floor, figuring we could shove it all in a closet out of the way for the photos. When Cristina came down the stairs, bleary-eyed from cleaning late into the night, she flew into a rage aimed at me.

This wasn't totally new: I'd seen her go off on Jerome before in the same kind of verbal barrage, screaming about how stupid he was. Jerome would stay calm and let the torrent wash past him. Everyone in the household seemed to accept this as just her natural, fiery Latin temper. But I wasn't used to her verbal abuse: I had just been trying to help and I would have done whatever was needed to make it right. Yet the yelling kept on.

Jerome came down the stairs behind Cristina and tried to smooth things over, but I knew my time there was up. They had been so generous and would always feel like family, but I'd already been feeling it might be time to move on. I grabbed my backpack, shrugged my shoulders at Jerome, and with Cristina still yelling obscenities, I walked away.

Meeting Layla

With the rain camouflaging my tears, I stuck out my thumb. With nowhere else to go I decided to head to the Backpackers to see who was around. A German girl I'd met before was busy in the kitchen. She greeted me, declaring, "My mission for the day is to bake brownies!" But then, noticing my face, she put her arms on my shoulders, looked deep into my eyes (which teared up again with her concern) and said, "Aw, honey, you need some nurturing."

Sitting me down, she wrapped me with a blanket and made me a hot cup of honey-sweetened tea. After she'd listened to my woes, I felt lighter from her care, so we hitched together to a shop to buy ingredients and spent the day making and eating brownies. By the time I snuck back to my caravan that night, I was warm with gratitude.

The next morning I left early to avoid Cristina. I needed to find a place to live and steady work. With a misty, silver rain floating down, I walked out to the main road near the causeway, where houseboats lined the shore and a few sailboats were up on stilts at a small boatyard. I stuck out my thumb and instantly a car peeled over. There was a kid in the passenger seat so I got in the back.

Finally, Home

The lady, reaching back between the seats to shove things over, said, "I just have to drop him at school, then I'm going to Surfdale."

We swung through a roundabout and down a road in front of the school that was lined with cars dropping off kids. Layla breezed past them all, chatting with me the whole time and at the end did a sudden U-turn at speed before squealing to stop at the curb. She gave her boy a kiss, told me to get in the front, and off we went, without missing a beat.

"So how long have you been on the island?" she asked.

"Just a few months. I'm writing a book." This prompted her to tell me about her best friend's death, and how she'd always wanted to write a book about the experience. We passed the turn-off to Surfdale but by then we were deep in conversation. She told me she'd take me the entire way to Oneroa, where I planned to check with some of the cafés to see if anyone was hiring. When we got there she pulled over and we kept right on chatting. At some point I brought up the fact that I needed a place to stay, and she lit up.

"I have a caravan! It'll be available on the first of January. I think you'd be perfect. Do you want to rent it?"

"Yes! Awesome!"

With a place to live sorted, I bounced through the bustling little town of Oneroa, stopped in a few of the many restaurants and cafés to drop off my resume, and then got a lift back to Surfdale to hit up a pizza joint, the one place where a manager happened to be on duty. We chatted for a second, but she was rushing out for a staff party, so I left my CV. By then the sun had come out and I decided it was time to soak up some rays. I called Gustavo. He picked me up and we headed to Palm Beach, where massive palm trees stood in a row along the top edge of a long beach. There were public bathrooms and a barbecue where anyone could just press a button, heat it up and grill away. I saw Cristina's sister at a picnic table with a group of people. Claudia called out and waved, so I walked over. In the group was the woman I'd chatted with earlier from the pizza place.

"You know Claudia?" She asked. "Can you start Saturday night? We need someone full-time!"

This island was magic!

267

By New Year's Eve I'd reconnected with Cristina and was able to leave with her blessing. That night, there was a party at a café right across from her house and after work I walked over. The place was called Planet, and it had a Middle Eastern vibe with small rounded doorways, the doors ornately painted. The party was in the walled-in yard behind the café. There were a few lavish Turkish tents set up in the corners, one with pillows, padding and blankets, a designated chill zone for the many kids running around playing. An older Maori man with white dreadlocks down his back passed me a joint. World dance music throbbed and pulsated and, as the sun went down, fire spinners lit up the night. Everywhere on the different levels of the lawn, along the stucco tops of the planter boxes and up on stage, people danced. There were so many beautiful women of all ages, dressed in earthy, funky authentic style, dancing with full courageous abandon. Behind a screen, from where a laser-light show was being projected, ladies were taking turns playing and laughing with each other, creating a spontaneous erotic shadow show, radiating lighthearted Goddess energy and encouraging everyone to just be themselves and let loose. The scene cemented my love for this place.

The following morning, January first, I settled into the caravan in the overgrown front yard of Layla's house, which was just down the road from Cristina's. Layla was welcoming, making me feel right at home to share the kitchen, bathroom and living room with her and her 5-year-old son. With red hair, a youthful figure in stylish op-shop finds, ready to celebrate at the drop of a hat with wine and endless cigarettes, her energy seemed light and fun. But the longer I stayed, the more I caught glimpses of the precipice that lay beneath her gaiety.

Manifesting Men

I settled into a satisfying routine, spending mornings in the camper, writing in my sunshine-saturated bed. Then I'd borrow a forgotten bicycle, doubtless belonging to one of Layla's older sons, and ride the 15 minutes to the beach, my knees lifting to my chest on the rusty dirt bike. There I'd climb over the rocks that separated Nudie Bay from the main beach and bask topless until the heat drove me into the clear, lapping waves. A quick change back at home and I'd hitchhike to work—still salty—and wait tables for the evening, then go out with girlfriends afterward, either to dance or catch up with them on the beach.

I was happy in this daily pattern. And I also started to notice that, with all my self-contained contentment, to-ing and fro-ing on this miraculous isle, a charge was starting to build.

Finally, Home

I met Steven while dancing at the Sandbar. The floor was tiny, everyone's hot bodies bumped and rubbed. The smiles were infectious. He was broad-shouldered, with a bronzed tan, high cheekbones and a blond beard. We got to moving together, pressed close because of the crowd. Impulsively, I flung my leg up around his waist—and he dipped me back as if pouring me from a pitcher. Later, along with his roommate, we went back to their place for drinks and discovered he was French and had traveled extensively. After that I saw him everywhere. I ran into him at Nudie Bay, and we chatted about the dilemma of traveling and wanting to have a family. I happened across him in front of Malone's and he invited me in for a drink. And, though I found him extremely attractive, my energy when I was with him swirled within my own orbit; I wasn't shooting out lassos to rein him in.

And the power grew.

There was Sebastian. Though I'd been introduced to this tall, good-looking Argentinian numerous times within the Latin crowd I often hung out with, somehow I always forgot his name. He must have found my indifference alluring because, on about the third time, he leaned in to kiss my cheek—a South American custom—and whispered seductively, "Ah, la Divina! Of course I know who *you* are." I still didn't give him the time of day, until I saw him at a party where they were playing salsa music. The South Americans who flocked to New Zealand on working holiday were into dancing, but they didn't grow up with salsa. So when I saw him expertly spinning a girl around while looking directly at me, I held his gaze and nodded, with an amused smirk on my face. And suddenly it was me he was whirling around, attempting to dazzle with his smooth moves. Which worked: After a few turns, held close within his hungry arms, he loomed temptingly appealing. But he called the play too fast, grabbing my hand and pulling me out front of the café. I followed coquettishly and even indulged in some kissing, which was as polished as his salsa moves. He wanted to go to the beach, but then I remembered my sandals and ran back into the venue. When he returned to find me, I was busy dancing in the arms of someone else, and I winked at him, giggling at his fumble. My charge kept building.

I met Willem in the city the day before officially moving to Waiheke. He was a tall, lanky Dutchman. Courting me earnestly and without guile, we swapped stories of our experiences with relationships and he sweetly confessed his relative inexperience, though later that night he sulked like a child when I chose to sleep on the couch and not in his bed. A few weeks later while he was working a delivery job that brought him to the island, he accompanied me to Nudie Bay, my favorite beach, for his lunch break. I lay languid in the sun while he ate his sandwich, then gave me a hug and headed back to work. Once I was sufficiently sun-drenched, I ambled with loose limbs to the water. Sliding into the cool crystalline bath, the granular sand in perfect focus through the water between my toes, I sensuously breast stroked out and peered back, absorbing this paradise that was my new home.

Nudie Bay was a small bay at the end of Palm Beach. A barricade of rocky sentries separated it from the more public beach next door. At high tide the rock sentries were foreboding, allowing only the intrepid to cross. At low tide they presented a maze of rocky pathways that led unsuspecting visitors into the private world of the unabashed Waihekeans. Here, familiar faces with bodies of all shapes, ages and sizes, in every state of dress, but mostly completely naked, cavorted free of their local context in our community Eden.

I'd only been in the water for a few minutes after Willem left and was lazily floating with just my eyes above the water, when a man slowly drifted into my vicinity. We started talking and comfortably continued our conversation while lying side by side on the beach. His body was chiseled from obsidian; his smile and laughing eyes gleamed like a beckoning light from his face. From Nigeria, he'd made Waiheke his home and in order to prolong our flirtatious ease, he offered to drive me around to do a few errands before dropping me at work. I was delighted when we stopped by Cristina's and she greeted him by name with a big hug.

"Look what I found at the beach," I laughed with her in Spanish. He was charming, had two kids who lived in Japan with their mother, but was a bit too eager to make more babies. Showing up at my work uninvited and constantly interrupting my attempts at conversation to kiss me, he was too intense.

Maybe I was mastering this law of attraction, learning to be the lure instead of the huntress. I was feeling like a man magnet and it sure was fun.

The Barbecue

January 12, 2011

"Let's have a barbecue to celebrate your living here!" Layla exclaimed. "I want you to meet my friends, and you can invite whoever you want."

"That sounds fun," I replied, though her cheeky grin told me there was more to it.

"What's that smile about?" I asked.

"One friend in particular," she wagged her eyebrows. "He's your age and just sailed his boat back from Great Barrier Island. I think you two would get along—you're both sailors. I want you to meet him."

The afternoon of the party, I came out of the shower in a towel, heading to my caravan to get ready. But Layla's honored guest had arrived early; they were sitting out back on the patio where she had a few chairs set up around an overturned cable spool with an enormous overflowing ashtray on it. I tried to hurry by, waving with one hand and holding up my towel with the other, but Layla stopped me, "Davina, this is Robert."

I held my hand out for him to shake and he popped up enthusiastically. I was glad to see he was close to my age, mid-30s. The majority of men who own boats are past 50. He was a big guy, tall and solid with honey-brown skin and long, stringy light brown hair bleached blond by the sun.

"Aw, come on, give him a cuddle," Layla insisted. But I hurried away to put on clothes. When I returned, dressed in a short, fluttery skirt and satiny yellow tank top, I flung my arms wide in an exaggerated gesture, as if we'd been looking forward to this reunion for months. Playing along, he swooped me up in a big bear hug and then, carried away with the silliness, grabbed my ass on impulse. Normally I would've slapped a man for that—I didn't suffer from weak boundaries—but it was as much a surprise to him as it was to me, and we laughed about it.

We had plenty to talk about, both being sailors and both having rebuilt sunken boats. I could tell from his thick, rough fingers, dirty nails and the sincere way he interacted that he was more of a man's man than a ladies'.

I'd invited a bunch of people, but the only one of my new friends who showed up was Julanne, a woman I'd met out dancing, then again while she had pizza where I worked. She was my age exactly and, with her youthful energy and funky style, I found it hard to believe she had four kids—and one of them was 18! She showed up with her 10-year-old daughter who joined the other few kids in the living room.

Layla's handful of friends showed up and made themselves at home, setting the dishes they'd brought in the kitchen, cracking open beers and rolling smokes. One of the guys got to work heating up the barbecue. But after a few drinks and a toke, I got bored with the dull conversation and incessant cigarettes. These were Layla's best mates but the vibe was heavy, with unhealed wounds festering under the thin veneer of intoxicated laughter.

Robert had gone off to buy alcohol, so I wandered into the dark living room where the kids were all huddled, their faces illuminated by the fluorescent glow of the TV screen.

I'd already met one of them, a 3-year-old punk with a cast on his arm. I liked his miniature bad-ass attitude. When he'd kicked me earlier, I grabbed him by the feet and hung him upside down for a minute, pirate style, cementing our mutual respect. It was a shame they were watching TV on such a sunny day—so I said, "Come on, Jack, let's go on an adventure," knowing the other kids would follow.

We traipsed up the hill in the backyard and went through some bushes into someone else's property, the kids following behind me. There, like an oasis appearing in a desert, was a trampoline. With wide eyes and an open mouth, I sucked in my breath and turned to the kids with a dramatic show of excitement.

"Watch this!" I climbed up and started bouncing exuberantly, intending to show off the move I'd perfected at Cristina's: a single back flip. Once I'd gained enough momentum, I flung myself backward —but must have gone around more than once because I landed on my head with a clang. Dazed for a minute, I waited until my vision cleared, then gingerly unhinged my head from between the springs, just inches away from the metal frame that would have cracked my skull. Layla had followed us up and luckily had the wherewithal to block me from flinging myself completely off. But I must have clocked her, because when my vision cleared she was still reeling with a big purple eye that was swelling by the second.

Finally, Home

"Stay here," I commanded, sitting her down in the grass and running down the hill to get ice. Halfway down, I noticed that my leg hurt, and looked down to discover a huge lump—like an egg—sitting right on the front of my shin.

Later, after I'd gotten Layla sorted with some ice, I sat on the grass with Julanne to contemplate the significance of my trampoline accident. I was not prone to accidents, yet three times since I'd arrived on Waiheke I'd hurt myself in the exact same spot on my left shin: once while falling off my chair at the market. The next when I tripped at the Christmas Eve party, and now this. Julanne declared with confidence, "Your legs: that's to do with your direction in life, the path you're walking. I'd say your path is definitely about to drastically change."

When Robert returned, we sat comfortably, my wounded leg propped on his lap while he held an ice pack on the goose egg. Suddenly, a large bird landed noisily in a nearby tree and was joined by another, flapping and rustling the branch as it settled.

"Do you see those birds?" someone remarked. "Those are kereru."

They looked like extra-large pigeons with white bellies. Their wings and heads shimmered iridescent green, purple and blue, with hints of pink.

"They mate for life."

When Robert said that, somehow the whole scene altered slightly, as if I was seeing it through a new lens—and I knew deep down it was another sign that my life was about to change.

Robert

It all happened at lightning speed.

Everyone at the party seemed to be taking their intoxication to the next level and I had no interest in joining them. Then a shady character showed up and Layla's 17-year-old son, who was home visiting, took offense to this guy's lewd behavior. A drunken brawl broke out. Robert, who still had his wits about him, took charge and got the situation under control, splitting the boys up and calming everyone down. That's when I slipped away to my caravan.

A while later, when I was in my jammies in bed, there was a knock on my door. It was Layla, not wanting her match-making job to go unfinished. She practically fell into the caravan when I opened the door.

Slurring her words, she was loud and insistent when she said, "Robert just wanted to say good night. You'll take care of him, right, Davina?" Behind her was a mortified looking Robert.

To get rid of her, I pulled him in and pushed her out. "Yeah, Layla. Goodnight."

Though he and I both laughed at how smashed she was, he still looked extremely uncomfortable, so I put him to work assembling a fan I'd just gotten to ward off the mosquitoes. We ended up talking all night; in the morning I went with him to water his horses.

In his rustic white ute (short for utility, Kiwi for pickup truck), we drove through the last few little towns on the one main road and then around a bend where the island suddenly spread out in rolling green hills, pastures and valleys, most with sheep scattered like popcorn. I was surprised by how much land there was. Apparently Waiheke has almost 36 square miles of land mass, 12 miles from the west to the east, with the five little towns and 8000 permanent residents predominantly concentrated on the west side of the island. Robert drove up and down and around, through bush and grazing land, as I caught occasional views of the sea in the distance.

We visited his two horses. One had been given to him and the other he'd adopted to save it from being put down with a damaged leg. He paid all her vet bills while knowing full well he'd never be able to ride her. We spent the rest of the day touring the island in easy and flirtatious companionship, messing around and dreaming up adventures to do together.

That night at work, I was kept busier than usual serving families and young children ordering pizza, but I was having a hard time concentrating through the internal swirl of excitement and the rush of hormones. A little girl came up to me while I was typing her family's order in the computer. She wanted to clarify what type of ice cream she'd ordered. I kept nodding and repeating back to her, "You want vanilla," which she reiterated several times. She must have been well aware of the trance I was in—hypnotized by her cute little nose and ringlet curls—because somehow, even though she'd communicated more than clearly, I still brought out chocolate.

Julanne was having a party before she moved into a new place, so I brought Robert to meet my people. I was impressed with how social and fun he was, dancing and interacting with the young, vibrant, international crowd. Another

Finally, Home

girlfriend was DJing and played some salsa music, so I took the opportunity to show off my moves with the one person there who knew the steps. Robert watched in appreciation and later admitted that in the past he would've been jealous. He had matured beyond that, he assured me, and was keen to learn. It takes a strong man to be with a strong woman, and someone with less confidence might have felt intimidated by my outgoing, flirtatious ways but, on the walk home that night, they only seemed to enliven him. He said he used to be a boxing star and could relate to that feeling of grandeur, of enjoying the limelight. Julanne informed me later that he'd shown up at her house unprompted with his tools the next morning and fixed her porch rails.

The next party we went to was with his friends: an older, rougher, rocking crowd. A band was playing heavy rock 'n' roll at a sports club. Robert knew everyone and I loved that he danced all night—completely driven by the music— in his own unique style.

After that, we went sailing around the island on his boat for a few days. He told me about how he'd worked for and traveled with some Gypsies in Europe, and was keen to see more of the world. One morning I woke up and peered out of the companionway; the wind was slightly rippling the otherwise still water. Robert was already on the bow hauling in the anchor. I got up on the cabin top and pulled up the mainsail, then we slid out of the empty bay without having to exchange a word, as if we'd been sailing together for years.

Another time, a friend of mine was organizing a sweat lodge, and we took Robert's boat to the tiny outcrop of an island nearby to collect the volcanic rocks needed for the ritual. He didn't laugh at me when I sprinkled a little tobacco, as my friend had instructed, and gave thanks to the grandmothers as we heaved the porous black rocks into the dinghy. In fact, even though this Native American ceremony was totally new to him, just like most of my alternative views were, he not only put his resources and skills into making it happen, he participated with reverence and an open mind. That was how he treated my beliefs in general.

Robert rented a two-bedroom house from a mate; it was surrounded by a moat of miscellaneous boat gear: tools, coiled line, electrical cords, timber and all manner of useful stuff stacked, piled and strewn around the property. All of this belonged to his friend, the landlord, who didn't charge Robert the going rate for rent. He would pop by at all hours, welcoming himself to whatever meal was being cooked or beer was being drunk. Robert was a great cook and an avid fisherman, so he usually had fresh seafood, and we both enjoyed preparing and eating delicious meals together. When he'd been a boxer in his early twenties, he'd been all about a clean diet and exercise, and assured me that he was as keen as I was to aspire toward a healthy lifestyle again.

The dark room came into focus around me: the bed I was lying in, rumpled and too soft; the wooden walls and window hazy with dust and cobwebs. I lay on my side and, for the first time in my life was struck with a strong sense of what it might be like to have a baby in my belly: the warm protective feeling of my body curling around a growing life; the sweet, all-encompassing love. My attention was drawn to the ceiling, where I could feel as surely as if I could see and hear, a presence—like the light of Tinker Bell flitting around a stage production of Peter Pan. There was something there. A spirit. A baby.

Later that morning, Robert and I had sex for the first time. In that dreamy, barely-awake place, where the realities of life hadn't yet come into focus, twisted up together in the sheets, he slipped inside me. I didn't argue. The naughtiness of a quick dip in that delicious half-sleep state was too tempting. But then I felt a warm gush.

"What the fuck!?" I was immediately fully awake. "What did you do that for?! Do you want to make a baby?!"

Stunned, he didn't say a word. But I knew from other conversations that yes, he did want to make a baby. It was clear to me at that moment: if I wanted to avoid getting pregnant—which I had successfully done for the entire 20 years I'd been having sex—I would have to be extremely vigilant with Robert. But, for the first time in my life it occurred to me… I could also choose not to be.

The first part of my original dream, to sail around the world, felt complete. I hadn't fully accomplished it, but I had spent a significant amount of my life in its pursuit—and I was ready to let it go. With that out of the way, the other part of my dream had taken priority, loud and clear.

And that's how, one month after we met, Robert and I started to deliberately try for a baby. Two weeks later I was pregnant.

Epilogue

And they all lived happily ever after. . .

Just kidding!

You must know by now that "happily ever after" is a lie. After getting pregnant with someone I hardly knew in a foreign country, there were stormy seas as far as the eye could see. But luckily I'm a good navigator; I just kept steering toward the light. And after some years, the seas calmed. My son and I still live on Waiheke Island, New Zealand, close to his dad but far from the craziness of the rest of the world.

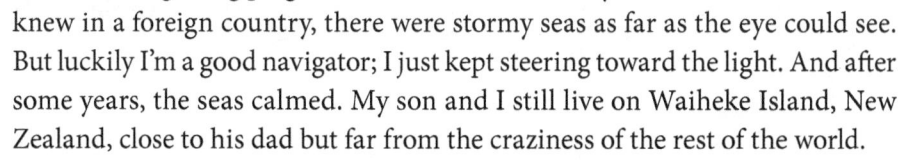

You might be wondering what happened to that lovely little boat—*Lady Rebecca*—that I fell in love with. Shortly after settling on Waiheke, I tracked down the guy who was keeping an eye on her. He explained that the lesbian couple who owned her lived in a different country. "But they'll never sell her to you. They have more money than God."

"Perfect," I'd replied, without missing a beat. "I don't want them to sell her to me, I want them to give her to me!"

I wrote numerous letters to make that happen but, being caught up as I was in new motherhood and stormy seas, none of my missives ever left my journal.

Five years later I met Frida, a fellow single mom at the Steiner Kindy Harvest Fayre. She and I had an instant connection that made me think we must have known each other in a past life. A year down the line, our kids were playing happily on the trampoline as Frida elaborated on the ongoing saga of her mother, who was just ending a long-term relationship with a woman: "Yeah, so my mom has this boat. Can you help me move it?"

And all of a sudden, the floating bits of information clicked together in my mind like a puzzle and I knew. Hurriedly I opened my computer and found the file from my first days on the island, seven years before.

"Is this the boat? *Lady Rebecca*?" I asked, while clicking through the photos I'd taken of the pirate princess interior.

"How do you have pictures of my mom's boat!?"

I helped Frida move *Lady Rebecca* and did some work on her. A year later, after attempts to sell her had come to naught, Frida got fed up and said to me, "Davina, you have her. I think *Lady Rebecca* should belong to you."

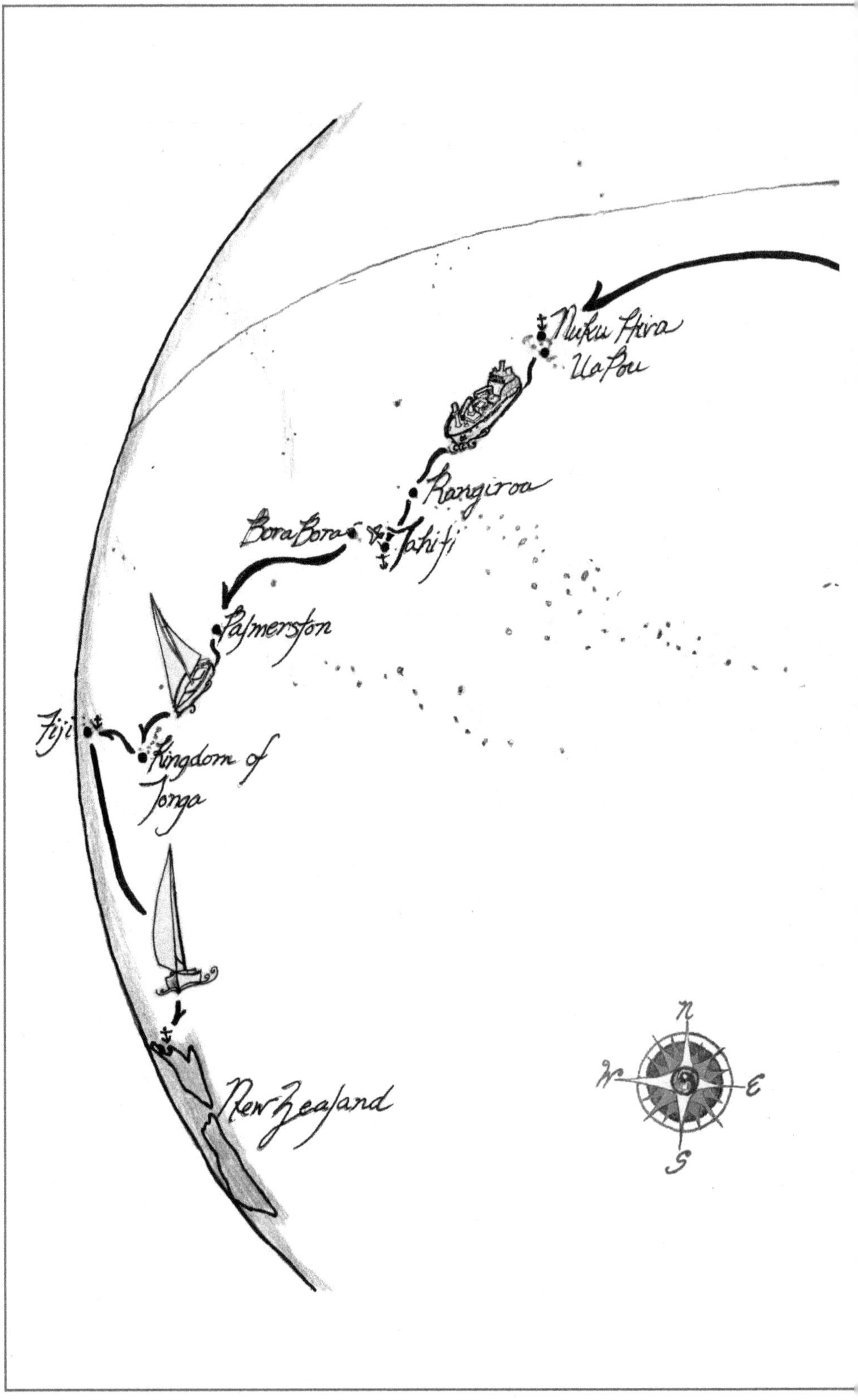
Nuku Hiva
Ua Pou
Rangiroa
Bora Bora
Tahiti
Palmerston
Fiji
Kingdom of
Tonga
New Zealand
N
W
E
S

the Equator

Panama

Galapagos

South America

Pacific Ocean

Second Leg
Panama to New Zealand

Acknowledgements

Deep breath in through the nose…

…letting it out slowly through the mouth…

…feeling my body as it relaxes…

…allowing a feeling of gratitude to suffuse my body

I have so much to be grateful for.

First, I thank you, reader, for reading my book. And, if you like it, I would be so grateful if you tell people about it: post about it on social media or maybe buy your girlfriend a copy for her birthday. There's no big publishing company behind me, so it's up to us to get it out there. Join the effort if you feel so moved!

Next, I thank all the people who lived this story with me and have landed as characters in this book: all the captains who took me sailing, all the people who supported me and all the friends I met along the way, I am so grateful. Thank you for being part of my journey. I hope your journeys have continued to unfurl in uplifting ways and that you have had support and connection through the hard bits. I've changed many of your names in this book to protect your privacy, but I hope you will recognize yourselves and accept my love and gratitude.

I am grateful to everyone at the Adult Literacy Center and the Library here on Waiheke Island, especially Lynn Jude, who nailed it by matching me up with Pauline Francis.

Pauline: I think every writer should be blessed to have someone like you, with your killer combo of editorial and life coaching skills. Our regular meet-ups while I wrote this book were invaluable. I am grateful for your encouragement and belief in me and this work, especially when I faltered.

Dee Austring: Thank you for your time and effort doing the original copy editing.

Margaret Pevec (my mom): every step of the way, not only on the journey of writing, editing, layout and figuring out how to get it out there—but through my entire life. You have been my main (and often-times only) support system. I can never express how grateful I am. I hope one of these go-rounds I can be your mama and give you all the support and love you have given me. Everyone should be so lucky.

Ann Erwin: I've really enjoyed nutting out the cover art and the maps with you. You offered the perfect blend of expertise and trust in my vision, and so generously helped me bring it into physical form. I haven't had much community for my art and creativity. Working with you has given me the feeling that I am talented and that I know what I'm doing. Thank you for that. Thank-you for all the hours you spent going over the copy with a fine-tooth comb. You are a gem!

Jordan Fox (my sister): Thank you for being the official first reader and pointing out bits that needed work. Invaluable. You're next!

Wendy Kendall (my employer): Your belief in me, your collaboration on the pirate parties and taking me sailing made an enormous difference. You are such an inspiration and I'm glad to have a regular dose of you at Waiheke Herbs. You're a star.

To the Universe: Just when the years we'd been working on this project seemed too long, when the shimmer of the sea in the distance was but a glimmer, and peeling myself off the desert floor to get there a true struggle, the Universe stepped in with some magic to put me on my feet again. I love when that happens!

Tessa Mascelle (marketing maven): Meeting you at Waiheke Herbs was a gift from the Universe. All of the previous people I've mentioned helped create the book, but promoting it has been another story. You breathed life into that effort, and with you by my side, I know we'll be able to find the tribe who will love it. Thank you so much!

The other bit of magic happened when Jessica Brooks, aka Ms. Boox (my best friend): When you called and said, "I couldn't stop thinking about you the whole time I read this book! You need to read it!" I immediately bought a copy of Amanda Palmer's *The Art of Asking*. The whole time I was reading, I felt like Amanda was talking directly to me. Turns out she lives on Waiheke Island!

Amanda: You bad-ass pirate rock star mama, thank you for agreeing to read my book and write a brief review for the back cover.

And, finally, again, I thank the Universe for continually reminding me how magical you/we all are. How the law of attraction is real. How we can create our reality, *and for giving me hope that we are, right now, as we speak, actively creating an amazingly colorful, peaceful, thriving, healthy future for all of us on this planet.*

Breathe out.

About the Author

Davina lives with the love of her life, Andrew, on idyllic Waiheke Island, New Zealand. He spends weekends with his dad.

Although her adventures have become smaller in size, they have increased in meaning and wonder. Davina spends her time parenting, connecting with friends, walking the beach with their dog Badger, swimming at Nudie Bay, reading, writing, meditating, dancing and dreaming about *The More Beautiful World Our Hearts Know Is Possible.**

She envisions a pirate take-over of our future, and is calling all captains and crew; together we can change our story. Sign on at: DavinaMenduno.com. You can also see photos from *Adventures of a Pirate Girl* and cruise along via Google Earth. Follow her on Instagram at Adventures_of_a_Pirate_Girl. And look out for the next Pirate Girl book.

*One of my all-time favorite books by Charles Eisenstein.

CPSIA information can be obtained
at www.ICGtesting.com
Printed in the USA
FSHW021645020621
81978FS